MW01284110

# NORTH: THE JOURNEY

## HIGH SCHOOL FRIENDSHIPS THAT LASTED A LIFETIME

## RAYMOND PHILIP HERON II

Raymond Philip Heron II
**NORTH: THE JOURNEY**

All rights reserved
Copyright © 2024 by **Raymond Philip Heron II**

Editor: Keith Heron

No part of this publication may be reproduced, distributed, or transmitted in
any form or by any means, including photocopying, recording, or other
electronic or mechanical methods, without the prior written permission of the
publisher, except in the case of brief quotations embodied in critical reviews
and certain other noncommercial uses permitted by copyright law.

Published by Spines
ISBN: 978-965-578-741-2

# CONTENTS

# DEDICATION

This book is dedicated to the many classmates, students, teachers, teammates, coaches, and other school staff who were part of my Valley Stream North High School experience during the wonderful 1950s. Because of them all, my high school years were filled with education, joy, and friendship. My classmates have especially been such a great blessing to me, so this book is a gift of thanksgiving to them all. Without them, the rest of my life's voyage would not have been nearly as rewarding and fulfilling, so without them, I would have never authored this book. My hope is that they will travel back in time to their youthful high school years where their memories will awaken them to smiles, laughs, and perhaps even occasional tears as they re-experience a life of so long ago. My aspirations are for my story to also reach their children and grandchildren, and for them to understand how the lives of their parents and grandparents were shaped by the very special era known as "the happy days" of the 1950s. And I extend my apologies to the North High class of 1961 for taking thirteen years to keep the promise of this gift that I made at our 50-year reunion way back in 2011.

This isn't just an autobiography about my life, but a story about the people who helped shape the person I grew up to become. While reading this adventure, you will find the names of over 100 individuals interwoven within my journey. This book is also dedicated to them all. I was so excited to bring their stories back to life for themselves, their children, and their grandchildren to enjoy. I knew many of the people characterized in this book very well, like my classmates and life-long friends who supported me and motivated me to write our story. I only knew some others mentioned in the book for just a few brief moments in time along the joyous ride through high school. Nonetheless, I want everyone to know that you have all made a positive difference in my life and I thank you all for your enthusiasm, caring, and friendship. In return, I have always tried to pass along those same gifts by striving to make a positive impact in the lives of others after the good old days of North High came to an end.

I would also like to dedicate this book to my late Mom and Dad who raised me to trust in God and my religion. My parents encouraged me to never give up, to always think for myself, and to never be afraid to think outside the box. At an early age, they taught me that asking questions was always more valuable than remaining silent. My mom always told me to shoot for the moon and if I were to fall short, I could still look back to see how high I had come. I owe much of this success to them and thank them both for making me a leader and not a follower. If my mom and dad were still living, I think they would agree that setting out to write this book was certainly shooting for the moon. And they would be so proud of the finished product that they might think I overshot the moon and landed on Mars with this project!

Most importantly, this book is also dedicated to my family. My wife Lois, and my children John, Nicole, and Keith were all incredibly encouraging, lending the invaluable support I needed to make this idea I have had for so long become a reality. And last but certainly not least, I dedicate this book to my grandchildren. I hope that they will learn some valuable life lessons from this book, cherish their copies of it, and look back on it sometimes as a special way to remember me, their Pop-Pop, for the rest of their lives after I am gone.

# FOREWORD

"Memories, even in their silent wait have an immortality. Our inner lives have their own palettes to color the fragments of our past recognitions. Seen again, as in a passing screen before our eyes, our loves and passions, our successes, and the shadows of our failures.

All was a 'muddle stew' of schoolwork, sports, dating, and the ice cream gluttony of the Kitchen Sink at Jahn's. New friends and old friends were found and lost and found again, seated at our "special" table at the North High cafeteria, where we giggled about the morning's events. There was the clamor of the hallways and the passing conversations that birthed the beginning of enduring relationships.

Ray Heron's book, "North, The Journey", celebrates

a time we all shared at Valley Stream North High, a time inherited by remembered words, images, and experiences. These are the songs of ourselves."

*- Classmate, friend, and published author: George Robert Minkoff*

# AUTHOR'S NOTE

I have always loved to think differently, and I have also always enjoyed my own unique point of view. As a youngster, I was not concerned with fitting in, so I was never afraid to test limits and step outside the lines of the proverbial box that confined what others considered to be normal. Of course, my unconventional approach to life often led me down roads that were difficult to travel, but in my later years, I became thankful for all the lessons I had learned along the way. For it was the insights I gained from my youthful experiences that equipped me with the skills necessary to raise three children who grew up to be successful, intelligent, and happy in their lives.

# INTRODUCTION

This is a true story about my life, mainly told through the
eyes of a teenage boy who traveled to the beat of his own
drum during the 1950s on my journey through Valley Stream
North High School located in Long Island, NY. Most stories
told in this book are funny, warm, and make the case that the
world was much better off in the '50s than it is today. I want
readers to get a glimpse of how simple life was over 60 years
ago when we didn't have modern technology or most of the
comforts available in present-day society. We didn't have any
electronics and we had a lot less money, both of which create
a lot of distractions and problems in today's day and age. Back
then, the only alternatives to the most common communication method of talking with others face-to-face was writing
letters by hand, or the very rare, occasional phone call.
Important non-verbal cues like facial expressions, body

movements, hand gestures, handshakes, hugs, or kisses made talking to other human beings in person priceless and complete. Feelings, views, and beliefs were all understood so easily back then without any of the ambiguities, misunderstandings, and unnecessary disagreements that occur so frequently when trying to communicate electronically nowadays.

As years went by, the personal experience and friendship of the '50s just seemed to have gotten lost in today's age of virtual contact and instant gratification. Nowadays most people would have difficulty imagining what life would be like without electronic devices. Many today probably wouldn't know what to do with all the extra time or peace they would have without the constant bombardment of information they receive from news and social media platforms almost every minute of the day. So, I am hoping this book will provide some useful life lessons to today's generation. I am hoping this book opens minds to the advantages of a simpler, more rewarding, more fulfilling life focused primarily on relationships with family and friends like it was way back in the very special time known as the '50s.

During my school-age years having a good time, making lasting friendships, playing sports, going to parties, and dancing were all more important to me than getting good grades. As a result, my final GPA was 73, just above the minimum passing grade of 65, but I wouldn't change a thing. I learned so many invaluable lessons from all the friends I made and got so much more out of life from all the fun we had along the way than I would have if I focused more on studying and less on socializing.

As it would turn out, I also learned so much more than just academics from my dedicated teachers and coaches, many of whom were only a few years older than we were. They were friendly, caring, enthusiastic, and eager to teach us all about what was truly important in life outside the classroom. Growing up, I had no idea what a leader was, nor did I ever think about it until the fourth grade. I was only ten years old, but I'll never forget the day that my teacher Mrs. Colletti stopped what she was doing and said to me, "You're going to be a good leader." I hope that during my life I have exhibited some of the leadership qualities that she saw in me at an early age. I thank God that I had teachers like her who made such a tremendous impact that after all these years I can still remember their words and can still appreciate how they helped shape me into the person I am today.

Playing three varsity sports also taught me many invaluable first-hand life lessons including patience, discipline, endurance, perseverance, teamwork, hard work, the thrill of victory, and the disappointment of defeat. I was part of championship football and baseball teams, and my participation on the basketball team was a tremendous learning experience thanks to my coach, Joe Shannon.

The story of the experiences I shared with family, friends, teachers, teammates, and coaches opens at my 50-year high school reunion and then flashes back to my beginnings before returning to my high school days. Most of the story details the big North / South ABC Television High School Football Game of the Week and the series of homecoming festivities leading up to the game including a float parade and bonfire. Finally, the story concludes with my more recent years and what my high school years and friendships meant to me later in life. To end the book, I share some of my life lessons, regrets, yearbook quotes, and updates from some classmates, my lifelong friends. I am blessed and thankful to the good Lord for allowing me to be born and raised during the 1950s and for surrounding me with friends with whom I have shared a wonderful life.

I was either involved in or knew about the stories and pranks included in this book, which took place during my six years at North. Though many of the stories took place at different points throughout our high school journey, I decided to portray many of the stories as if they took place during senior year, particularly during homecoming week leading up to the big North / South football game. Believe it or not, all the stories are true as best as I can remember them except for a few times when I took creative license for effect like the nametag swap story that appears at the end of my welcome speech. That story was purely fictional. The trickster still living inside me since high school always wanted to try the nametag swap, but I never got the chance to pull it off. However, I decided to add that one fictional anecdote for humorous effect. I think you will enjoy it and who knows, maybe you will try the nametag swap yourself one day!

My attendance record may also appear misleading. In my

senior year, I was absent 21 times and late 30 times for a total of 51 times that I missed all or some of my classes. I didn't miss every Monday nor was I late all 180 days of school. As you will find out in the story, my dad pushed me to succeed in school and didn't accept my lazy attitude towards academics. Thanks to him and his persistence, I failed the junior year advanced Math class he insisted I be placed into, so I had to repeat that class over the summer between my junior and senior years. In my second attempt, I managed to earn a 93 and stay on pace to graduate with the class of 1961 after finally deciding to open a book, study, and attend every class.

Now that I look back, I can again say thanks to my dad for making me prove to myself that I had the potential to succeed in school if I applied myself. That was nice to know, but I still went into senior year preferring to focus my energy towards other, more interesting pursuits instead. I think you will agree that my choices led to a life full of fun and many entertaining stories to tell. I hope that you will enjoy a few laughs while reading about my adventures, learn something interesting while reading about times past, and gain some wisdom from the messages I share in my story. Come, enjoy this journey back in time with me.

# PROLOGUE: A SPECIAL CLASS

Over the years, the Valley Stream North High School Class of 1961 has had many reunions, both formal and informal, which have always been well attended. You may wonder why classmates still come from near and far, sometimes at great expense to gather, celebrate, and reminisce. Why is this class so special? To answer these questions, you will need to understand a little bit of the history of how things were on Long Island, NY in the good old days. 1955-1961 was a very special time and has affectionately been referred to as "the happy days" of the '50s. As the latest conflict in Korea had ended in July 1953, it was the first time in many years that our country was not at war, and the area around the quaint Long Island village of Malverne, NY was growing and prospering.

There were only two high schools in our area in 1954,

Valley Stream Central High School in the south and Sewan-haka High School in the north. Many families began to move to Long Island from the city and the population was growing. New grade schools were being built and new high schools had to be constructed to keep pace with the rate at which the area was developing. Valley Stream had a very large school district, so two new high schools were needed to accommodate the growing numbers of students, one on the north side of town and the other on the south. Their locations would determine their names; they simply became Valley Stream North High School and Valley Stream South High School. The schools were not finished on time, so the "North" students had to begin the seventh grade by attending classes for a half-day at Memorial Junior High while the "South" students did the same at Central. Both schools were completed during that year, so in the late fall of 1955, my seventh-grade class entered the brand-new North High. We were proud to have graduated as the first class who spent the entirety of seventh through twelfth grade together in that new and special building.

Many of us had been classmates since grade school, our families knew each other and most of us were being raised in similar financial situations. We had blue-collar, hard-working parents raising us with the hope that we would have a better life than they did. Our parents were part of what was considered "the greatest generation," that lived through World War I which lasted from 1914-18. The war claimed twenty million lives with an additional 23 million more being injured. Then there was the great influenza pandemic of 1918 which wiped out 25% of the world's population. The remaining survivors of the generation would then have to endure the stock market crash of 1929 that crushed the economy and put approximately 25% of Americans out of work. This event started the great depression of the 1930s causing many people to wait in long lines to receive bread, or if they were lucky soup, which was being handed out by charities in the streets to help people survive. December 7, 1941, brought in World War II which lasted until 1945 and brought about the death of 75 million people worldwide.

My grandparents were both born in 1895. My dad was born in 1918 and my mom in 1921, so it was a difficult time for them and their families. By no fault of their own, many of my class-mates' parents had similar upbringings as children being raised through the dark days of so much war, disease, and financial burden. Then growing up most of our parents had some part in the Second World War. My father-in-law, while serving as a soldier in the US Army was stationed in Italy where he met my mother-in-law when she was only eighteen years old. After the war, he returned to Italy to marry my mother-in-law and bring her back to the USA by boat to start a family here. This and so many other similar stories make it easy to understand why "the greatest generation" worked so hard and was so determined to give children of my generation a better life by all means necessary.

The students in my class were of primarily European back-grounds with most students coming from either Italian, German, Irish, and/or English descent. The class was split down the middle between Christianity and Judaism. Due to the diversity of the people in our class and our teachers' experiences, we learned a lot about what our parents went through. Some of our younger teachers were born in the 30's during the depression and some of the older teachers fought in Korea so we got different perspectives on our parents' generation based on the stories our teachers would tell us.

Some of the teachers came to work at North just after finishing college, so the youngest among them was just a few years older than most of us students. Filled with the passion and excitement of starting their careers in a brand-new school building, our young teachers were eager to teach us everything they could. It made our parents so happy to see their sacrifices pay off as they watched us, their children, go to school in a much better situation than they experienced during their school-age years. Our parents always supported the teachers in their efforts in and outside of the classroom. If one of us had an issue with a teacher, we could count on our parents to always take the teacher's side. We knew this well, so we never tried to blame the teacher for any of our marks or our actions. Personally, I had no problem standing up for myself and taking punishment, so I had a lot of firsthand experience learning these lessons. It was the same for all of us. But the teachers were good to us, and we learned so much more than just what was in the books. They were much more than just classroom teachers; they were life teachers who cared so much about us and about their profession. Looking back now, thinking about how young our teachers were and the conditions in which they grew up, makes it easy to understand why they were so dedicated and cared so much for us.

Those six years from seventh through twelfth grade at North High encompassed tremendous changes in the lives of our class. We grew together from awkward twelve-year-old seventh graders riding bicycles to school to invincible seventeen-year-old high school seniors driving cars to class. Everything in life changed drastically as we all grew up from youth to teens to young men and women. We had our teachers to thank for molding our future, supporting us through those formative years, and helping lay the foundation for our successful futures, most of the time in ways we never realized back then.

The following is a testimony from some of my classmates reflecting on the profound impact our teachers had on our lives, 50 years after graduation:

"I think North High was an amazing place, way ahead of its time in terms of the extracurricular opportunities we were given. In particular, I think it was a remarkably non-sexist environment; no one ever told me I couldn't do something because I was a girl! As a result, I was able to take advantage of many leadership opportunities that provided me with an excellent foundation for my career in city planning. Political activities like student elections, student council, and the 1960 mock political convention were real training grounds for me when I had to compete in the political world of city government. I also think we had some outstanding teachers. Ms. Smith, (M.G. of course), Ms. Green, Ms. Dowdeswell, Ms. Cascio, and Mr. Gamerman especially come to mind. And of course, I have to mention the wonderful music department. Mr. Mital had the patience of a saint when it came to encouraging "non-musicians" and convincing us that we could play in an orchestra. And who could forget Mr. Kubach? I think he yelled at me more than anyone else at this point in my life!"

   *- Barbara Benson Kaplan*

"We had a wonderful education at North High. I learned how important it is to respect other people and myself. Our teachers were not only educators, they were friends and people we could count on. I only hope my grandchildren have the same happy memories about school that I have!"

   *- Christine Beuttenmueller Russo*

"How neat it was walking home in the seventh grade from Memorial Junior High and Mr. Lawn, my favorite art teacher, giving me a ride home in his 1955 MGA with the top down!"

   *- Steven Dorso*

"Mr. Gamerman taught us to think for ourselves. He was a true role model for me and an inspirational teacher. I have fond memories of Valley Stream North, particularly the Yorker club trips with friends, Hi-Y activities and dances, varsity cross country, and acting in various plays. I have remained best of friends with some of my classmates throughout my life."

- *Ronald Gordon*

"We had great teachers and coaches who cared about our education and our future. Mixing with students from different backgrounds and religions was a good life preparation with solid middle-class values."

- *Michael Griffith*

"Most teachers at North made learning fun. Since we had small classes, we got to know them and they knew us. When I taught income tax preparation, I tried to incorporate the way my teachers taught me into how I taught my class. Socially, we "kids" didn't know whether we were rich or poor. It didn't matter. We enjoyed each other without distractions like the newest iPod or the latest big-screen TV. I tried to teach my children that simple was better. I often wish they had known the way we grew up in the 'old days'."

- *Marilyn Grispin Perez*

"How wonderful it was to have all those great teachers who are friends as well as mentors. We were all intro-duced to the sciences, and this formed a foundation of interest that carried me through and into my many successful career endeavors. Sharing learning and intellectual stimulation with a bunch of bright, funny, and close friends also made those days of school a laughter-filled, enjoyable experience. We had the benefit of teachers who cared about each one of us. People like Mrs. Lehman took us to the Spanish opera and great restaurants... Who knew what paella was at age sixteen? Al Snow who sprayed me with the $CO^2$ extinguisher for talking in chemistry class, and then lent us his car on weekends... That was a sweet Austin Healey! Mr. Popper made science a fun game. Mr. Shannon created special clubs with activities to stimulate and enhance our lives, and many others. Some exceptional coaches loved the sports they taught and carried principles of fair play and good sportsmanship into our lives. Playing soccer provided time for teaching us to be a team that shared a common goal. These team activities were an enjoyable and valuable addition to my education. Those many afterschool hours spent practicing, sweating, and running the track in the winter it was all a foundation of motivational training they continued throughout our lives."

- *Steve Hachtman*


"Coming to North High was a new experience for me as a product of New York City schools. All I knew beforehand were very old, dilapidated school buildings. We moved to Valley Stream when I was in the ninth grade and North High was a palace. It was new and not over-crowded as city schools were. Home economics... Never heard of it in the city, shop classes, the same. North was a whole new world where I met wonderful people who became lifelong friends. I did my student teaching under Mrs. Welch and Mrs. Katz. It was wonderful learning from them. My education at North allowed me to go to NYU for both my Bachelor's and Master's Degrees."

*- Emily Hayos Grossman*

"The teachers trusted us as demonstrated by Mr. Pohl letting me watch (babysit) his young children for some extra money."

*- Bernie Havern*

"I was fortunate to have had amazing teachers. They have had enormous effects on my continuing love of learning."

*- Ruth Klein Gach*

"I consider myself fortunate to have been part of such an incredibly caring community at North. Teachers were outstanding as they nurtured us through those impressionable years. They inspired an amazing close-ness among the students and while learning academi-cally, we learned how to be involved in school activities and to care about each other. The school spirit at North was terrific and most importantly the friendships I made have been life-long."

- *Evelyn Evie Meyerson Adler*

"We were very blessed to have young energetic teachers to guide us through our formative years. My classmates and teammates encourage me to compete academically and athletically. I never forget my high school friends who remain my friends to this day. Their friendships are always something I will treasure."

- *Salvatore Pepitone*

"My business teacher Mrs. Welch always made me feel like I was special. She took me under her wing and we had a close relationship. Upon graduation, she gave me a little red book that secretaries use. It was the one she received from a shorthand teacher when she graduated. It was very old and slightly falling apart. I cherish that book to this day. She gave me the confidence to go into the world and make my mark... And I did just that, me and that little red book."

- *Patricia Rooney Lally*

"For the last 50 years, I have appreciated the fact that a school district utilized a "tracking" system. This allowed us to reach our maximal potential, and to be simulated by our classmates. My children were not tracked, to their detriment. Our Math Chairman Mr. George Lenchner founded "Mathletes" on Long Island which has since spread through the US and the world. It has become a world championship event held in different cities throughout the world."

   *- Mark Salita (Retired Rocket Scientist)*

"The teaching staff, in retrospect, was probably one of the greatest treasures of our youth."

   *- Neil Simon*

"For me, the memories of Valley Stream North are joyous and sweet. It is always rewarding to reconnect with old classmates. Educationally, being challenged by teachers like Mr. Gamerman, Miss Lehman, Miss Cottone, Mr. Mann, Mr. Diamond, Mrs. Siegel, and many others prepared me well for life, at Cornell and NYU."

   *- Peter Sperber*

These are just a few classmates' testimonies about our teachers who were much more than just classroom teachers. Can you imagine teachers today giving you a ride home in their sports car with the top down? Lending you their sports car on the weekend? Allowing you to babysit for their children? Having you over for dinner and to sleep over? Taking you places you have never been, or to meet people that were different than you? Take you on trips, out to dinner, or an opera? Inviting you to be counselors at their summer camp? Hiring you to paint their apartment for some extra money? They would probably all be brought up on charges today. This was indeed a special time when parents trusted their children's teachers with their total education inside and outside of the classroom.

Reading over the testimonials given by my classmates made me stop and think. Although I didn't appreciate it at the time, in looking back I can see what a terrific education was being presented at North High through the many diversified classes and the extremely dedicated teachers. Thankfully, I absorbed more knowledge than was reflected on my report cards, even though some, I believe, were through the process of osmosis. This knowledge stayed hidden within my mind and didn't make an appearance until much later in my life.

Mrs. Lehman was an excellent teacher who tried her best to teach me Spanish. It was I who failed her and not she who failed me. I'm so happy that some of those lessons stayed with me as I use some of the Spanish language when talking with Spanish-speaking students who board my bus for a ride to school each day. I also understand more than I can speak which is also a big help to me at work. Who would have believed that in 1957 there would be a need to speak and understand Spanish today on Long Island?

My baseball coach Mr. Suprina taught me respect for the game and the right way to play it. In my senior year, we won the Division Championship under his direction.

My basketball coach Mr. Shannon, who was also the

special education teacher at North, was very special to me. He made time to teach me many lessons about life in a way that only a dedicated and caring teacher could. He took me into his home where his beautiful wife, who was his high school sweetheart, made us dinner. He took us to youth centers that he managed in his other job for the City of New York. Teachers didn't get paid enough back in the 1950s so most of them had other part-time jobs. He showed me what life was like in the projects. I learned about gangs, violence, and what it meant to grow up with no family, not even parents. To meet other youth my age who didn't have the comfort of family to grow up with or a quality education was an eye-opening experience.

| Joe Shannon

He also taught me what it was like to give back to the community by helping young boys in their greatest time of need. As teenagers standing at a crossroads deciding which path in life to take was a very important time in their life. Mr. Shannon would try to help them choose the road to success and not the other road that led to prison or death which was unfortunately all too common in that area at that time. I experienced this first-hand, having spoken to a young man my age one day at a basketball game only to learn that he had been murdered the following week with a baseball bat for a dollar. I'm sure that the lives of many other kids in that center were saved by the work of youth counselors like Joe Shannon. His love for the kids and his passion for the work he was doing were very easy to see.

Mr. Shannon had four children and two jobs, three if you count coaching, but still found time to spend time with us and teach us about life. He ran clubs after school on a volunteer basis and loved every minute of it. One of his sons became a chef and, like his dad, served underprivileged kids by cooking for them at The Hole in the Wall Gang Camp founded by Paul Newman. One day Joe met Paul Newman at the camp and left with the feeling that Paul loved to help kids just as much as he did.

I too always loved sports and kids, so my wife and I volunteered our time and talents to start the Catholic Youth Organization (CYO) basketball program for children in our parish from second grade through high school. With the help of many others, we got it off the ground and running very well. One day I went to visit my old coach Joe Shannon to reminisce about the old days. I told him about what we were accomplishing at St. Catherine's and gave him one of

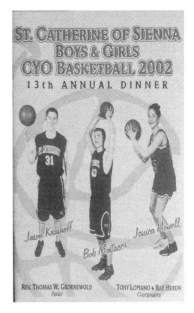

St. Catherine's of Sienna
Annual Program, 2002

the annual programs we had printed which included pictures of each team organized by age group on the glossy magazine pages inside. He smiled as he looked through the program, and proudly said to me,

> "Great job! Some people might think you're doing all of this for free, but you're getting paid by giving back."

I believe that Joe Shannon did as much as he could for everyone that he touched in his life because he believed God had spared him during the Korean War. As he tells the story, he was supposed to get on a plane to return home after the fighting ended, but he missed that flight, so he had to take a different plane home. On the long flight back, he received devastating news that the plane he was supposed to be on crashed and that all on board had been killed in the crash. Many of his fellow soldiers that he fought with side-by-side were now gone. But by the grace of God and the mix-up that occurred causing him to miss the flight, his life was spared.

Another classmate Susan Lewis Levine sums up it best in her following testimonial about why we still love to get together over 50 years later to relive our special teenage years at Valley Stream North.

> "I have wonderful memories of North High. Many teachers remained memorable for their teaching skills and wonderful personalities. But what stays with me to this day are the fabulous friendships that were made

and formed in that journey from seventh to twelfth grade. Those "kids" taught me lifelong lessons about friendship, patience, loyalty, and optimistic attitudes. We learned how to work, play hard, and have fun. Thank you to my forever friends!"

Still to this day, those of us who are left meet at annual reunions and experience time travel as our minds take us on a joyous ride. Seeing our classmates and friends after many years apart instantly transports us back to our high school years all over again, making each reunion we have a very special and thoroughly joyful time. The environment that the North High School faculty provided was fueled by our parent's full support and was filled with safety, diverse learning experiences, and love. It was because of this environment that we naturally formed so many life-long friendships, still getting together to reminisce about that magical time and share updates on what's currently happening in our lives.

Join me on a journey back to October of 2011 to our 50-year high school reunion weekend so you can experience the joy in its people, and the labor of love in the committee who arranged the wonderful event. Then, we will journey further back to 1960 during the week of the big championship North-South football game as seen through the eyes of a teenage boy who loved that time in his life at North High and the many friends he made that would last a lifetime. Let's begin!

| Valley Stream North High School

L to R: Bernie Havern and I in front of my famous '49 Buick circa 1961

# NORTH: THE JOURNEY

## HIGH SCHOOL FRIENDSHIPS THAT LASTED A LIFETIME

RAYMOND PHILIP HERON II

# 1

## THE REUNION WEEKEND BEGINS

My story opens on a beautiful October night in 2011 at the 50<sup>th</sup> High School Reunion for the Valley Stream North class of '61. I was on the reunion committee and had been chosen as the Master of Ceremonies, so I had the honor of delivering the welcome speech. It was so hard to believe that it had been 50 years since graduation from high school. The festivities were scheduled to start on Friday at 9pm with an informal gathering at a local bar and grill. However, a few of us started celebrating earlier that night at a Molloy College awards dinner honoring one of our classmates, Bernie Havern, who was being inducted into their sports hall of fame after a lengthy career as the Head Baseball Coach.

Bernie was my oldest friend and had been since we met in church when we were six years old. We introduced ourselves as Bernie and Ray, so then I teased him by calling him *burn-up*.

Feeling insulted, he demanded that we step outside, which we did, and we wound up rolling around in the grass fighting like six-year-olds would. After a few minutes, we got up shook hands, and remained very close ever since.

Bernie giving his Molloy College Athletics Hall of Fame acceptance speech

At the Molloy College awards dinner, Bernie was honored for single-handedly starting and elevating the baseball program at Molloy College into one of the most respected programs in the NCAA Division II. Every detail of the field was immaculate because Bernie always believed that the boys should have a big-league field to play on and that having such a gorgeous facility would bring out the best in his team. Somehow Bernie managed to build an entirely new baseball field with dugouts right in the middle of campus and got his players all new uniforms which were the best looking in the division. His teams always played the right way whether they won or lost, playing with respect for the game and their opponents.

Bernie made a very long Hall of Fame acceptance speech to thank everyone with whom he had contact during his 22 years at Molloy College. He made sure to mention everyone and express his appreciation for the part they all played in building the baseball program into a Division II powerhouse throughout the years. For Bernie to give a thorough and heart-felt speech was not surprising because of his naturally very charismatic and caring nature, but as it would turn out there was also another reason he made sure to thank each and every person. Unbeknownst to most of us at the time, Bernie thought that this speech might be his last chance to recognize all the people he worked with because he just received a diagnosis of advanced prostate cancer.

The ceremony ran later than expected so we didn't get to Monahan's Bar & Grill until later that night at 10pm. Unfortunately, by the time we arrived most of our classmates had already left. We were sorry to have missed them, but we had such a fun time with those who had stayed, laughing and exchanging stories about our high school days until 2am. As 60-year-olds, most in our group were no longer night owls like many of us were in the old high school days. However, we were so glad to have fully enjoyed the special time we shared that night despite having to be up early the next morning to continue our reunion weekend festivities.

I finally got home and slept for a few hours, but before I knew it Saturday morning had arrived. It felt just like being back in high school trying to get up and go to class after a long night out with friends. But this time, unlike high school, I couldn't simply shut off the alarm clock and go back to sleep. Our first officially scheduled event of the reunion weekend, a morning tour down the hallways of our Alma Mater, would be starting soon!

Upon arrival, the group began to gather and grow larger as carloads of old classmates continued to trickle in. A security guard who was also serving as our tour guide commented that he had never seen so many people attend a reunion like this before. He was amazed that so many people from one class were getting together after 50 years. We explained that our class formed a special bond and that we enjoyed each others' company whenever we got together. With that, the tour began outside where North High didn't seem to have changed much over the last 50 years, though a couple of changes were immediately noticeable. The old wooden stands had been replaced with new metal bleachers while the track was upgraded to a new green composite surface with white markings. The old, open courtyard had been closed off to become a closed-in space surrounded by new classroom buildings.

L to R: Bernie and I in our high school
championship baseball team picture

Our first stop inside was the gym, where I was happy to see that pictures of all the championship teams were still hanging. I smiled looking at our old championship baseball, football, and rifle teams. I wore jersey number 13 on the baseball team and played right field because I had a strong arm. For football, I wore number 27 and played receiving tight end. Our football team formed very special and close bonds which we still, over 50 years after high school, continue to celebrate annually at football team reunions. Like the current North High 50-year reunion, our annual football get-togethers were full of love, laughs, and old stories that came to life through their retelling, each time with new wrinkles that only time can bring.

Looking at the picture of the championship rifle club also brought back memories even though I was not a member. I felt sad that the sport of marksmanship, which was at one time vital for survival and feeding one's family, is now a treasured part of human history quickly getting lost over time and misunderstanding. My Uncle Tom, a war hero and expert rifleman, taught me how to shoot both a rifle and a pistol when I was about fourteen years old. He had seen young men die during his service in World War II and he had even killed a few enemy soldiers himself, so he couldn't emphasize safety enough. The first thing he taught me was respect for weapons and important shooting safety procedures before, during, and after using a firearm. Most importantly, he taught me never to point a gun at anyone unless my life was in danger, and I fully intended to fire the weapon.

Because of the many gun safety lessons I learned at an early age from an expert war veteran, I believe that potential gun owners should have to complete a certified safety course, pass a test, and receive a license before being permitted to own any size firearm. The rifle club in high school would be a perfect place to learn gun safety and the correct way to use a weapon, similar to how driver's education prepares young adults to operate a vehicle. It is a shame that as firearms become less and less socially acceptable, they grow in popularity for the wrong reasons, all too often falling into the wrong hands of young, influential, untrained individuals who desire their power to commit crimes. On top of growing gun violence, the many stories of careless, self-inflicted wounds and accidental deaths caused by guns constantly seen in the news continue to solidify my beliefs.

Continuing into the classroom hallways, the subject of our tour shifted to our old classes, teachers, and academic achievements. I took advantage of this opportunity to play a joke on one of the brightest students in our class, Barbara Benson Kaplan, who went on to become an Urban Planner for the City of Philadelphia. Kidding around with her, I advised her that there was an unforeseen oversight when calculating final class GPAs and that she had finished ranked third in our class GPA, not second. Imagine how this extraordinarily intelligent and gifted woman, one who oversaw the development and planning of a major US city for seventeen years, looked at this announcement from someone who had failed Mrs. Gold's math class! She wondered in amazement how I could arrive at this ridiculous conclusion. I then proceeded to explain how I figured this out using math skills I learned in Mrs. Gold's advanced Math class: My GPA of 73% was earned despite my being there only 73% of the time. So, if adding in another 27% which I feel I would have earned if I had been there every day, the total would be 100% while the highest ranked Dan Prener's GPA and the GPA of Barbara were only in the high 90s. Relieved, she then realized I was just joking and smiled.

I was honored that Dan Prener, a software designer for IBM who was first in our class with the highest GPA, said I could keep the GPA award based on my mathematical calculations. At IBM, Dan worked with others to develop the IBM Cloud System one of the largest in the world. It's a virtual server performing two billion calculations per second and its technology helps the world in almost every phase of life. Even though his genius didn't rub off me, it was an honor to sit with him in Mrs. Gold's advanced math class on the occasions when I was there.

Later in the tour, I discovered that the school had a third floor where the library was located. As a student at North, I was only concerned with the first floor where the cafeteria, auditorium, and gymnasium could be found. The rest of the school remained a mystery to me until now, walking the halls 50 years later. One such mystery that was solved on the tour was why I never got to know Miriam Pisk until after high school at our reunions. Immediately upon entering the third floor for the first time, a floor I previously never knew existed, it became clear to me why Miriam and I never crossed paths in any significant way during our high school years. Miriam spent most of her free time in the library, and I spent most of my free time down on the first floor. So as it turned out, our reunions weren't only a fantastic way to catch up with old friends but were also an opportunity to form new friendships with classmates who had different interests or hung out with a different crowd back in high school.

During my high school days, I could mostly be found on the football field, baseball field, basketball court, or outside of school riding around in my '49 Buick. On the tour, I found myself explaining the reasons why my classmates didn't remember seeing me around in the hallways or in class consistently. I rarely attended Monday classes because, after a long, hard weekend, I needed Monday for relaxation. On other weekdays, in my world, the school day didn't start until around 11am and that was only because I had to be on time for lunch!

My mother would give me 35 cents for lunch and three cents for milk, so I figured a good night's sleep and a hot meal would prepare me for afternoon classes and playing ball after school.

I always got extra food at lunch because I had a big appetite and became friendly with the cafeteria workers who served the food. The wonderful ladies behind the lunch counter looked at me as a young, tall, skinny drink of water and thought I could use some meat on my bones. I always got large, heavy-handed portions amounting to more than 35 cents worth of food, but I would manage to get second helpings when my favorite, roast beef, mashed potatoes, and gravy, was being served. Unfortunately, despite their best efforts, the lunch ladies' plan to help me bulk up was unsuccessful as I burned up every calorie that I consumed playing sports every day.

In addition to reminding me of the lunch ladies, arriving at the cafeteria on our tour also reminded me of Tony DiBenedetto's mother, "Mrs. DB" as we called her, who cooked delicious Italian meals for her family almost every night. Mrs. DB would pack Tony's leftovers for lunch in a brown paper bag and the aroma from his delicious Italian meals would drift down the hallway getting the attention of many hungry classmates. Others offered bribes and promises in exchange for Tony's lunch, but Tony was never going to give up the lunch his mother had made for him with great love. Then once, on a very chilly winter day when the hot roast beef & mashed potatoes lunch was being served, Tony gave in and sold the lunch he had brought from home, enjoyed having something different for a change, and made a profit too!

As our walk continued, Barbara Cohen and Ed Simms extended an invitation for us to visit them in Nevada next summer. From what I understand, temperatures can frequently reach 115° or higher, but they said not to worry, that it is a dry heat. Steve Hachtman, on the other hand, invited us to go ice fishing with him in Minnesota in the winter, where the temperature often gets down to twenty degrees below zero. Not wanting to find myself in a hot Nevada oven or on the other extreme getting frostbite, I respectfully declined both invitations.

John Belluardo and his lovely wife Barbara made it all the way to Long Island from Ohio in John's small plane. With John at the controls and a strong tailwind to push them along, they made it to the reunion safely in no time at all and thankfully also made it back home safely to their home in Dayton afterward. John is an excellent pilot who fought and reversed the effects of heart disease successfully, his

John Belluardo's Amazing Story, *How I Reversed Heart Disease*

newfound clean bill of health allowing him to keep his pilot's license. He later wrote a book *How I Reversed Heart Disease* to help others conquer this condition through exercise and diet.

When I found out that my wife's friend's husband was dealing with heart issues, I suggested he read the book and later was overjoyed to hear that he found the book uplifting, had recovered, and was enjoying life. I am sure John's book had a similar effect on many others and their families as well. I believe that we are meant to share our knowledge and successes with others, and John's book is an example of how doing so really can make the world a better place for everybody, one person at a time.

Looking at Josephine Rauch for the first time in 50 years I noticed right away that the years had not diminished the beauty of her violet eyes. Seeing Jo brought back memories of driving around with Bernie and the boys passing her house and yelling her name out of the windows. Being young, awkward, and shy around girls, we never worked up the nerve to talk to her directly in school so we never found out if she saw or heard those crazy guys making a racket outside her home as only young teens can. Telling Josephine about those episodes during our walk-through brought a smile to her face.

Those of us who were there really enjoyed the walking tour of good old North High. Seeing our old classrooms, lockers, gym, fields, cafeteria, and auditorium made our cherished memories come alive in a way that only being there could make possible.

# THE REUNION CONTINUES AT CORAL HOUSE

L ater that day the reunion continued at Coral House, a catering hall located in Baldwin, NY, where we gathered to celebrate for a night of dinner, dancing, and catching up with old friends. The party was filled with so many people, some of whom hadn't seen each other in 50 years, all greeting one another with big smiles, animated conversations, laughs, and hugs. The room was filled with beautiful decorations, a delicious buffet, and a DJ getting ready to play some of our favorite songs from yesteryear when we were teenagers. My graduation picture, which was blown up and hung on the wall with the rest of the class, never looked so good. Upon entry, everyone received a CD and a commemorative booklet showing pictures of each student and a brief description of what they've been doing during the past 50 years. A fellow student named Noel Fox had put together the book and CD, both of which will last a lifetime. I was very impressed with everyone who worked so hard to plan an excellent event, their mission was most certainly accomplished.

After taking it all in, I began to work my way around the room saying a round of hellos. As had been the case for past reunions, teachers who had a positive influence on our lives at North were also invited to attend. Now, members of the class of '61 were in our late 60s, and the teachers were in their 70s and 80s so only a few teachers could be present. Even though I wasn't in their classes, I approached teachers Mrs. Marion Vinci and Mrs. Charlotte Cascio to say hello and introduce myself. They were having such a wonderful time, happily sharing all their great classroom memories from half a century ago so I was glad they made it and that I was able to make their acquaintance at the reunion.

Letters of regret from some teachers not able to attend were also on display, their words were wonderful examples of the close bonds that remained intact between the teachers and student body 50 years later. The following are two examples of such letters that stood out to me:

"Thank you so much for your kind invitation to attend the 50th reunion of the Valley Stream North High School class of 1961. Regretfully I cannot attend, but I didn't want the occasion to pass without sharing the following thoughts with all the members of the class of 1961.

As a physical education teacher and coach at North

from 1958 through 1962, I was blessed in many ways. The school had great spirit because the students worked hard to be successful in every endeavor. Achievement in the classrooms, extracurricular activities, and athletic competition was pursued with vigor. The young men and women who attended, North were filled with a zest for life that made them a joy to teach and coach. I learned a great deal from my experiences at North that were very valuable throughout my almost 40-year career in education.

Many of my professional colleagues at North influenced my life, just as they did yours. Fellow teachers and coaches like John Miele, Phil Banks, Frank LoPresti, Don Fleming, Holly Whitacre, Ted Tanzi, Ralph Jansson, and Sherm Pohl, among so many others, made working at North High School a daily treat. Their insight and educational practices helped me attain success as a high school principal and superintendent of schools.

Coaching championship teams in football and baseball at North was a thrill. The energy, talents, and commitment to excellence of the young men who played on the teams I coached was truly something special. It was an honor to be their coach.

I hope that the years have been good to you all, the entire class of 1961, and your loved ones. It is gratifying to learn of the success so many of you have had in your lives to date. Best wishes for a wonderful reunion and that the future is filled with good health and happiness for you all. Thank you, Spartans, for the great memories of the class of 1961."

*- Dr. Richard Suprina,*
*Physical Education Teacher and Coach*

"Dear Valley Stream North High School committee members and class members,

Unfortunately, Lil and I will not be able to attend the class of 1961 reunion. We have a previous commitment that we cannot break. We wish all members of the class of 1961 continued success in the best of health to celebrate your 50th reunion. By now, you and yours have not only your success to celebrate but the success of younger members of your family as well. God bless you all!

Nothing but positive memories fill Lil and I of the good times and experiences that we had at Valley Stream North High School. Good luck and best wishes for a great celebration and many best wishes for the future.

With our love and best wishes,
Lil & Holly Whitacre"

*- Mr. George Holly Whitacre*

Barbara Cohen Simms and I dancing together
again at the reunion

I continued my walk through the room and said hello to as many people as I could before starting my welcome speech. As I watched everyone having such a wonderful time, my mind flashed back to high school and I still couldn't wrap my head around the fact that it had been 50 years since graduation. Of course, I had noticed physical changes that took place in my classmates over the last 50 years, but inside, I still found the same people smiling back at me. We spoke to each other as though time had stood still. Old friendships were strengthened and new friendships were still being formed 50 years later. This beautiful celebration seemed like it was taking place right after high school graduation. 1961 felt like just yesterday; it seemed as though time had stopped immediately after our graduation and that it was just now continuing as we shared stories of what had happened in our lives over the last half-century.

I then had just enough time to greet a few more classmates while grabbing a drink and something to munch on before it was time to take the podium on the stage. On my way to the podium, I noticed Barbara Cohen, my first high school crush. When my sports commitments didn't interfere, I used to walk her home from school carrying her big stack of books. The weight of her books wasn't difficult for me to manage though because my books were almost always left behind in my locker anyway. Given her commitment to studying and doing home-work after school every day, it was no surprise that Barbara did very well in school and that she was a member of the National Honor Society. Her dedication to academics was like my dedi-cation to sports, each of us choosing to put in the time and effort necessary to succeed in the things we loved to do. I found those memories to be bittersweet, however, as I realized that the hard work and preparation we once held in high regard were becoming yet another lost art, over time, as gener-ations progress.

Another significant contrast between generations I then began to contemplate was how differently we amused ourselves in our younger days. Back then, most families in our neighborhood didn't have much money, so we all found ways to have fun at little or no cost. One such way was going to a good old-fashioned sock hop, which was a dance that took place in the school gym. Hundreds of teens dancing on the gym floor while wearing fancy shoes would've scratched up the floor, so shoes were not permitted. Instead, everyone danced in socks, hence the name "sock hop." I loved to dance and practiced often with my twin sister Linda at home doing crazy moves to fast music. We laughed as we went along, figuring out which moves would or would not work. Linda and I were so good at dancing together that we once won a swing-style dance contest called a Lindy Hop Contest that was held during one of our high school dances.

Linda and I showing off our Easter outfits on the front page of Newsday, 1956

But dancing wasn't our only claim to fame. Linda and I appeared on the front page of our local paper *Newsday*, on March 31, 1956, at the age of thirteen. Also unlike today, back then newspapers used to prioritize good news in the form of human-interest stories. *Newsday* decided to feature a front-page article about the upcoming Malverne Easter Fashion Parade to help generate interest in the event. Because tall, photogenic, boy/girl fraternal twins were a rarity, Linda and I were selected to be leaders in that parade, and the clothes we would wear in the parade to take place on the following day were the headline of the article. Believe it or not, I was shy and didn't want to be on the front page of the paper. But my mother thought it would be a good opportunity for Linda, and without me, *Newsday* couldn't run the front-page story they were planning, so I agreed to appear in the photoshoot as well. Outside of the big Easter Parade front page story, Linda and I also appeared together in Newsday to promote the opening of the new Malverne Library in 1954 and I also appeared on the front page at six years old to help reunite a lost dog with its owner.

My beautiful twin sister Linda in her VS north yearbook picture, 1960

As a result of the newspaper appearances, Linda and I drew interest from modeling agencies, but our mom always declined their offers. Linda was tall, thin, and beautiful so looking back years later I realized why she was sought after as a model. But our mom didn't want our lives to be disturbed by the glitz and glamor that go along with the modeling lifestyle, not to mention the contracts, responsibilities, time allotments, and demands of the industry which could be over-whelming. Money was never important to us growing up; instead, family, well-being, and enjoying life together were always the top priorities. So, our modeling career consisted of just a few unpaid appearances for *Newsday* but nothing further. It was just as well though, because I preferred to spend most of my free time outside of school concentrating on playing three varsity sports rather than modeling. My dedication to sports also took priority over my love of dancing, so the competitive dancing career Linda and I had started also ended, though we still enjoyed dancing together just for fun many times throughout the rest of our high school years.

Unfortunately, Linda wasn't in attendance at the reunion as she had just lost a battle with cancer the year before, leaving behind her husband Joe and her son Joey. While reunions are mostly a time to celebrate accomplishments with old friends, they are also a time to share memories of those like my twin sister and the many other classmates who are no longer with us. I still remember how it felt when we lost my close friend and classmate Tommy Scibelli in 1969 who was killed in action serving our country in the Vietnam War. My heart and prayers went out to his family and to the families of each of the other classmates who passed away since then just the same. But I am sure many of those families would agree that our loved ones continue to live on in their succeeding generations in

My VS north yearbook picture, 1960

ways they probably never could have imagined. As one of those types of ironic twists would have it, Linda's son Joey wound up moving out west to work as a color scientist in the Hollywood movie industry, the exact scene my mom prevented Linda and I from joining for our good. Thankfully, rather than getting swept up in the Hollywood lifestyle, Joey thrived in his career, married, and together with his wife is raising two sons in their beautiful Sherman Oaks home.

All of those thoughts and memories crossed my mind as I continued to make my way across the room until I finally approached Barbara. As we smiled and hugged, the 50 years it had been since we last saw each other in high school melted away instantly. The band was playing a slow song, so I asked her to dance. Once again, she accepted and we danced just like we did 55 years ago, as the feelings of my first-ever date with Barbara at the eighth-grade sock hop came rushing back all at once. As I looked at the very wide smile on her face, I could tell she must have been reliving our first date at that very moment too.

| Sergeant Thomas Scibelli

Later, we danced to an up-tempo song, and she remembered the dance contest I had won with my sister back in high school. I couldn't believe she remembered! Barbara was always a very special person in my life. She was my first date, my favorite dance partner second only to my mom and sister, and she is a friend who can still make me smile any time we talk, write, text, or e-mail to keep in touch as we have been doing for the past 60 years. Barbara and I stopped seeing each other in the ninth grade as I wasn't ready for a steady relationship at fourteen years old. Soon after, Barbara began dating a classmate named Eddie Simms who would turn out to be her husband. I was very happy for them both and felt that they would have a wonderful life together as I watched their relationship continue throughout their high school years eventually leading to a happy and long-lasting marriage.

Another classmate Marilyn, a member of the reunion committee, then looked my way and called me over as the time for my speech was nearing. We greeted each other with smiles and talked about how we could already tell that the reunion was a huge success even though it had barely just begun. Marilyn, like I was back then, wasn't motivated to do much more in school than the minimum necessary to pass so we wondered why we weren't in more classes together. She then told me a story about why we were never in the same math class because she talked her way into advanced algebra. To avoid staying in class with a boring and strange algebra teacher who, because of her tiny stature had an irrational fear that students might throw her out of the window one day, Marilyn begged the guidance counselor to switch her class. The relief she felt from escaping her prior teacher was immediately erased by the rude awakening of undecipherable complex equations covering three chalkboards that she found upon entering advanced algebra for the first time. After a few minutes of frantically trying to copy notes, she raised her hand intending to go back to the guidance office to be switched to a different math class again. However, instead of calling on her, the teacher turned back around towards the chalkboard and thanked Marilyn for pointing out an error that he had made! She put her hand back down and for the next two years never again thought about switching math classes again. Advanced algebra was a subject I would have done anything to avoid, so it was easy to see why we never shared the same math class.

Miriam, who was also on the reunion committee, then motioned to me that it was finally time for me to officially begin the evening. It was time to pause the mingling, talking, and laughing that filled the room by calling everyone to attention and toasting the class of 1961. I took the podium to begin my speech of love and respect for every one of our classmates, both those present on this special night as well those who could not attend.

# 3

## THE REUNION WELCOME SPEECH

I was very honored to be chosen as the Master of Ceremonies entrusted with delivering the welcome speech to the class of 1961. I started by thanking everyone, above all God, for filling my high school years with unbelievable joy and excitement. Surely, only God could have put us together in this awesome class, which had given us all a lifetime of friendships filled with love, parties, and get-togethers. I explained the emotions I felt walking through the room and how even though it had been 50 years since many of us last saw each other, after talking for just a few minutes it seemed like we were never apart at all. I talked about how the bond we all felt as a class was formed long before North, many of us first meeting in grade school and growing up together in the same village.

I then spent some time describing my memories of the

good old days that we were so blessed by God to experience, the special decade of our youth we affectionately call the '50s. The USA was not involved in any wars between 1955 and 1961, neither divorce nor abortion was the norm, drugs didn't have a place in our lives, and people practiced their faith regularly. Back then, Churches were filled with Christians on Sundays, and Temples were filled with Jewish people on Saturdays. More people attended services in those days not only because faith was highly valued in the family, but also because religion was prioritized in society. This will seem hard to believe to younger people these days, but up until 1976, New York State had a set of laws called the "Blue Laws" which banned businesses other than pharmacies from opening on Sundays so that people could keep holy the Sabbath Day. As far as technology goes, families usually had just one electronic device in their home, a small black-and-white TV, so life didn't revolve around cell phones, computers, and televisions like it does today. Without such distractions, life was easier because it moved at a slower pace, had less stress, and was also more personal because most times the only way we could communicate with each other was face to face. Life was also a lot more centered around family, especially at dinner time, and relatives were mostly involved in leisure time weekend activities.

Of course, I had some fun interjecting jokes, and borrowed a line from King Henry VIII who once said to his wife, Anne Boleyn, "I won't keep you long!" I got a few laughs when I joked about how the *ten years* I spent at North High played such an important part in my life. Many also laughed when during the piece about changes in life and technology, I mentioned how our main concern in grade school was not anything like social media, but instead, we would worry about how hiding under the desk during air raid drills would protect us from an atomic bomb!

I thanked everyone, my teachers, classmates, and teammates for being part of such a very special time in my life and let them all know that our days at North will always have a special place in my heart. I went on to commend my classmates for proving that a good education and the support of family and friends bring much success in life as exemplified by the amazing variety of accomplishments our class went on to achieve after high school. Some of us had become teachers, coaches, authors, lawyers, doctors, Ph.D., police detectives, youth ministers, rocket scientists, psychiatrists, therapists, hypnotists, city planners, business owners, CEOs, managers, construction foremen, activists for women's rights, authors, commercial pilots, and even fighter pilots, just like Top Gun! I told stories of how every one of us, through the magnificent work we had done in our professions, touched the lives of others and changed the world in significant ways.

Although I described many specific successes, I was particularly proud to tell stories of sacrifice and country. I honored classmates who served in the Armed Forces fighting in wars thousands of miles away from home, and Roger Olsen for leading a construction crew that helped to rebuild the World Trade Center North Tower after the 1993 bombing. I also highlighted two classmates who were involved in creating marvels of modern technology, Mark Salita who worked for NASA designing rockets, and John Belluardo who while working at National Cash Register (now known as the NCR Corporation) consulted on projects with Paul Allen and Bill Gates before they started Microsoft. John then started his own tech company Bass Inc. where he designed and manufactured the first portable wireless barcode scanning system which revolutionized the supermarket industry and was the foundation for the technology still in use at supermarkets across the world today.

And finally, I explained why I was so proud of all that our class turned out to be, and that we owed it all to having been born during a very fortuitous point in time. We were children of "the greatest generation" who fought not only for our freedom but also to ensure that we could have a simple life in which everything revolved around family and friendships. They raised us to be respectful, unafraid, challenging, and God-fearing. We learned by their example to always maintain a deep respect for each other regardless of religious beliefs or political affiliations, which in our diverse community were many. We were taught that we could become whatever we wanted to be, whether male or female, as evidenced by some of the success stories I had previously mentioned to the crowd. I expressed how thankful I was to be part of our generation and part of the North High class of '61 which has given me so much over the years. As my speech progressed, it was heartwarming to see smiles, hear laughter, and feel the love radiating from the audience. I mentioned how great it was to see how many of us had not only made it to the reunion but had made it there still having so many working parts even if some were bionic.

If Thomas Wolfe had been part of this class he would never have written, "You can't go home again." For home is where the heart is, and that night we were home again, reunited with each other. Unlike Thomas Wolfe, Victor Hugo knew our class, and was referring to us when he wrote, "The future belongs even more to the hearts than to minds." It's what was in our hearts that brought each person to the reunion that night after so many years and despite so many miles. I wondered how many 50-year reunions were so well attended but I didn't think many could match ours. As it turned out, 65 of the 195 North High class of 1961 graduates were in attendance at the reunion. If lessons from Mrs. Gold's advanced math class sank incorrectly, that would mean 33% of our class was present. We had gathered from thirteen states as far west as California, as far south as Florida and Texas, and as far north as Maine. It was wonderful that so many people had attended, some leaving families, children, grandchildren, and pets to travel at great expense. But whether each classmate traveled from afar or still lived locally and simply got into their car and drove to the venue from home, each was there, and that said it all.

I then found myself ending the speech by making a promise to give back to this extraordinary class by writing this very book! It would tell the story of a journey through high school, seen through the eyes of a teenage boy who traveled to the beat of his own drum. The story would be funny, and warm, and make the case that the world was much better off in the '50s without any electronics and much less money both of which create a lot of distractions and problems in today's day and age. The story will open at the reunion and flashback to the boy's beginnings before returning to our high school days mostly detailing the big North-South varsity football game, and the week-long series of festivities leading up to the game including a float parade and bonfire, before concluding with my later years and what those high school years and friendships meant to me later in life. I promised updates throughout the next year and warned that everyone should expect many phone calls and emails from me in attempting to collect the information necessary for the book.

I ended my speech with my version of an old Irish blessing: May the road of life rise to meet you, may the winds of trouble always be at your back, may the sunshine warm upon your face, and until we meet again may the good Lord hold you in the palm of his hand. Even though the official speech was completed, the crowd was just getting warmed up for the next part of my act. I decided to have some fun with the audience by making comical announcements, some at the expense of unsuspecting classmates.

Unbeknownst to anyone in the room, not even the subjects of the announcement themselves, I offered my condolences to Joan Havern and Pat DiBenedetto, the wives of Bernie and Tony respectively, as their husbands would soon be leaving them... for each other! Tony, a gourmet cook, and Bernie, a meticulous groundskeeper who also kept the inside of his home clean as a whistle made the perfect "couple." They both loved sports and Tony would always follow Bernie around like a faithful sidekick. There were no arguments because whenever Bernie spoke, Tony would listen and whatever Bernie wanted done, Tony would do without ever questioning any of Bernie's plans. I invited them both to stand and take a bow!

Next, I announced that my wife Lois wasn't present because, after the stunt I pulled at her last reunion, we agreed that it would be better to attend future reunions alone. Walking into her reunion after mostly everyone else had arrived, there were only a few name badges left on the check-in table. Because I didn't know anyone in Lois' class, I decided to have some fun by becoming Jeff Heller, who my wife said was a writer who had been aloof for some time. I clipped the correct Ray Heron name tag on my sports jacket and put Jeff's name tag in my pocket. When my wife became distracted in conversation with some of her old friends, I switched name tags and slowly walked away. At last, I could finally find some excitement at my wife's reunion, but I had no idea how much excitement there would be!

The first person I met Herman Hoffman said, "You've gotten taller since school! How'd that happen, Jeff?" I told him that I was wearing special elevator shoes and asked how he was doing wanting to divert attention away from myself. Joel Halpern, the person standing next to him, said he didn't recognize my face because it had changed so much. I explained that after a fire, they had to do reconstructive surgery on my face and asked how I looked. He said I looked fantastic then I asked how he was doing again trying to move the conversation away from myself. But refusing to take the bait, Joel said life had been good to me, meaning Jeff, then said something I had not counted on before and would almost definitely blow my cover.

Joel mentioned that a classmate named Karen Kramer would love to see me again. He asked if after such a long time being away writing, perhaps I'd forgotten about Karen who was my flame in high school. I, Jeff Heller, had an affair with Karen before disappearing and she'd been wondering all these years what happened to me and why I left without a word. Joel spotted Karen and said he was going to get her. With that, I quickly walked over to my wife Lois and told her that I wasn't feeling well so I'd be waiting in the car. Meanwhile, inside the reunion, chaos ensued as Karen frantically searched the room for her lost lover Jeff Heller who had disappeared again. Lois was left by herself to explain why she was with Jeff Heller, where he went, and why her last name was Heron. It took a long time for Lois to find me in the car and it was a long and very noisy car ride back home. So much for using the old wrong name badge prank, and needless to say, that was the end of reunions for us as a couple.

With the audience laughing, I thanked them for their generous response to my attempts at humor. I then stepped down from the podium, ready to venture back into the crowd and visit more classmates. As I exited the stage, Miriam thanked me for being the Master of Ceremonies, for making the opening speech, and for my funny stories. She said she knew that I'd make a great emcee which made me smile and I thanked her for her confidence in me. I found that compliment to be extra special coming from someone who I hadn't gotten to know until after high school. At that moment, I realized that friendships like ours which developed only after graduating are what validated the hard work that went into organizing this and every previous reunion the class of 1961 ever had.

Next, I grabbed something to drink and took a breather as I prepared to continue making the rounds and talking to as many people as possible into the fading night.

# 4

## MAKING THE ROUNDS

As I walked through the crowd, the committee members thanked me, and others commented on how much they enjoyed my speech. My emcee responsibilities now complete, I was free to enjoy the rest of the evening with classmates that I hadn't seen in many years. First, I saw Noel Fox who has been very successful in life. I asked him if he could spare an extra 2.1 million to help improve my current financial situation because my portfolio was in a negative position. Without missing a beat, he smiled and asked if I preferred cash or check, and with that Roger Olsen almost fell to the floor in laughter.

Roger, a big man at 6'3" and 275 pounds was a very hard-working carpenter who eventually worked his way up to Foreman for one the largest construction companies in America. Over time, upwards of 180 carpenters and some of the biggest projects in New York State including JFK Airport were put under his supervision. After the 1993 bombing of the World Trade Center, Roger was among the first contractors called to shore up the massive 60-foot hole that the bomb had made in the foundation. Upon arriving to survey the damage, Roger realized that two truckloads of massive 12" x 12" girders, beams, and columns up to sixteen feet in length would be needed immediately to prevent the building from collapse or further damage. After receiving approval from his supervisors, he called his supplier explaining he would need the lumber the following day. But the supplier, which was located near the Canadian border, said they needed at least a week to deliver the amount of lumber Roger and his crew so desperately needed. Roger asked them to put a second driver on the trucks and drive all night as this was a major disaster that needed immediate remediation. Although it would raise costs significantly, Roger's supervisors approved the extra expenses and because Roger wouldn't accept any delay in shoring up the World Trade Center, the lumber arrived in just two days. The repairs were completed in record time because Roger got several different unions to work together towards the common goal of completing the job as quickly and safely as possible. The World Trade Center stood proud and without any further issues until September 11, 2001, when it was attacked again.

I then walked over to another classmate, smiled, and told him that I heard he had died a few years ago but that he shouldn't worry because he looked terrific for a dead guy. His name has been intentionally omitted because a few years after our reunion, he sadly passed away. I remember how good he looked, his big smile, and how we both laughed loudly at my joke when we talked. I am glad that our last interaction left me with good memories of him happily enjoying his life.

Our favorite high school hangout, the famous La Stella Pizzeria parking lot circa 1960

Next, I saw Barry Seedman, a very interesting fellow who I hadn't seen since high school. Talking to Barry reminded me of one of our favorite hangouts, a little shopping center with a gas station and La Stella Pizzeria on Dogwood Ave in Franklin Square where most of the kids went for a soda and a slice after school. When Barry was in eleventh grade, he and his good buddy John Belluardo would sometimes hot wire the gas station owner's car, go for a joy ride, and then put gas back in the car so the owner never knew it was being used. One thing

Barry and I had in common was often missing school. As for me, I was usually home sleeping after staying out late at a party the night before. But Barry didn't ditch school to stay home and rest. He'd often be at the horse track making bets until one day when he got caught at the races by the truant officer, Assistant Principal Mr. Bergesen. Instead of trying to avoid him, Barry should have asked Mr. Bergesen what he was doing at the track and who he liked in the next race to make light of the situation. But that's not how it went and so after learning of Barry's whereabouts from Mr. Bergesen, Barry's father, a former NYPD Chief of Detectives who wrote the best-selling book *Chief*, transferred him to a private school and we never saw him again.

Even though Barry and his good buddy John, who also finished his education in another school, didn't graduate with us, they turned out to be two of the smartest guys I have ever known. Barry went on to earn a Ph.D. in psychology where he focused on hypnosis to cure patients. While we chatted, I asked if he had any advice that I could use to help my grandson who was frequently having nightmares about monsters and spiders crawling underneath his bed. The doctor smiled and assured me that it was an easy problem to solve by simply cutting the legs off the bed and showing my grandson that there was no more room for monsters and spiders under-neath! For the cure, Barry asked me whether I'd be paying the sum of $600 by cash or check. His justification was that such a cure would typically take ten consultations at the 50% discounted rate he'd charge for an old friend, $60 each. I told him that he should be arrested for stealing and that my payment to him would be a round of golf when I eventually made it out to visit him in Phoenix, AZ. We both laughed and shook hands on the deal.

I then found Frank Morelli and Benny Franquiz in the bar area, of course, surrounded by a crowd telling jokes as usual. I guess the stories they were telling were very funny judging by the laughter surrounding them. Seeing Benny reminded me about our good old days in the Omega Gamma Delta fraternity. North High, like most other high schools, didn't support any fraternities but they couldn't prevent us from joining them. Instead, school leadership took other measures to attempt to silence our groups, downplay our existence, and prevent perceived affiliations with our organizations. We felt that it wasn't right for the school to judge us for how we lived our personal lives outside of North, but they still denied fraternities the right to purchase yearbook ads or wear clothing bearing fraternity symbols on school property. Unlike how we were viewed by the school administration, we saw ourselves as fun-loving young men enjoying our high school years and doing good for society. So, we would proudly wear our black and gold fraternity sweaters and jackets everywhere including to North High, just without the skull and crossbones patch that signified Omega Gamma Delta when on school grounds.

Because fraternities were not regulated by the school or supervised by adult Hi-Y clubs that were affiliated with the school, we were free to do whatever we wanted. A group of wild high school boys left to their own devices meant that some decisions, like pledging, were made in poor judgment by the older members of the fraternity. New pledges like Benny and I, who entered the fraternity together, had to endure a few weeks of proving our worth by doing anything a particular older fraternity member asked. I was assigned to pledge for Bill Scheezer who required that I keep his car clean and report to him early every morning for a ride to school. The North High teachers and administrators were very happy to see me on time for school, bright and early every day for three weeks straight during the time I pledged!

At the end of the pledge period was the final test, a difficult rite of passage that fraternities called "hell night." As if getting up early to go to class many mornings in a row wasn't enough to prove my commitment, still wanting to join Omega Gamma Delta after "hell night" sure was. For our particular initiation, Benny and I were beaten up and then dumped in the woods somewhere out on Eastern Long Island. I still have no idea where I was or how I got home, but I do remember regretting my decision to join the fraternity at that time. Violence has no place anywhere in society, especially not among a group of so-called "brothers" so I don't understand why our initiation, like that of so many others at that time, had to be so brutal. As I look back, I now realize that while most things were better back in the days when life was simpler, increased oversight of groups like fraternities and athletic teams along with growing awareness of and prevention against important issues like bullying and hazing make the world a better place for the youth of today.

Though I don't suggest that anyone go through a "hell night" to join such a group today, Benny and I did eventually wind up having a lot of fun in the fraternity. Back then, the nationwide governing body of Omega Gamma Delta would sponsor an annual meeting in NYC which was always a wild time. Hundreds of teens would engage in all kinds of partying and mischief like our tradition of throwing water balloons out of the 23$^{rd}$-floor hotel windows where the event was held. Since then, Omega Gamma Delta has celebrated the 100$^{th}$ anniversary of its founding, and while I'm sure they're still up to similar hijinks, one can only hope that getting into the fraternity nowadays has evolved with the times.

In our chapter, we threw many house parties, but they were nothing like the famous movie Animal House. There was booze and some kissing, but I never witnessed anything like drugs or wild sex during any of our high school fraternity shindigs. Our meetings were mostly in good clean fun like one night when we were watching the famous movie, Doctor Yankem. At one point in the movie, the dentist puts a female patient to sleep with gas so she won't feel any pain during the drilling procedure and then starts to take off her clothes. After a few minutes, the doctor worked up a sweat trying to take the clothes off his sedated patient before starting to drill her cavity. I then called out, "I'm never going to be a dentist. Preparing to drill a cavity is way too much work," bringing the house down with laughter.

We were a bunch of jolly jocks who held no prejudices and didn't harm anyone except pledges during hell week. The fraternity was primarily made up of athletes who loved the excitement of being on the playing field, the gym, or the wrestling mats. We were part of championship football and baseball teams who loved having a fun time and being part of a society of brothers who worked so well together because we cared about each other. The challenge of competition and the thrill of victory were the driving forces that untied us and provided the motivation we needed to persevere through the hard work that achieving excellence required.

But we were more than just a bunch of rebellious, fun-loving jocks united by the sports we loved. We also realized that our physical abilities and talents were a blessing, so part of our organized activities included doing charitable work for those less fortunate. We raised money for Sister Elizabeth Kenny, a self-trained Australian bush nurse who opened a clinic in 1942 where she developed a new approach to treating victims of Polio that she called rehabilitation medicine. At that time, Polio emerged as a new virus destroying nerve cells in the spinal cord, causing muscle weakening and in extreme cases total paralysis. It was soon discovered that Polio was not passed from person to person but instead, it was picked up from consuming contaminated food or water. Like all viruses, if Polio was contracted it could only be managed but not cured. However, thankfully scientists also found that Polio could be prevented through a vaccine. Given that contracting this dangerous virus could happen suddenly and unexpectedly to almost anyone, anywhere, the time from when Polio was first discovered until a vaccine was developed was very scary for us all. We felt so fortunate to have made it through the epidemic with our full physical capabilities still intact, so we felt that giving back to the less fortunate living with physically debilitating conditions for the rest of their lives was a very worthwhile cause. I felt particularly happy to support an organization whose work was very close to my heart ever since my younger brother Michael was struck with Polio. Thankfully, Michael was lucky enough to recover most of his physical functions to the credit of an aggressive approach outside of mainstream thinking applied by a Russian Doctor. But back in the mid '50s, the disease and possible treatments were still being studied and few were as fortunate as Michael, so helping Sister Kenny's foundation in my small way was very fulfilling to me.

But despite their physical limitations, many people who suffered from Polio like our classmate Georg Minkoff who I ran into next at the reunion, were still able to live very successful lives and served as an inspiration to others. When spending some time with George, I was so glad that I had a chance to tell him personally that, in retrospect, he was my high school hero. At the

George Minkoff

age of six, George contracted Polio which would debilitate him for the rest of his life. However, he was always in class, worked hard, had a great sense of humor, and never made any excuses. Whenever I face complications in life, I smile and think of people like George who succeed despite facing numerous daily obstacles that most others don't have to endure. Reading stories about how others battle through difficult circumstances to accomplish goals can be inspirational, but as a teenager witnessing my classmate George persevere every day put my determination to overcome challenges into a new perspective.

| Mr. Pohl

George also didn't let his disability get in the way of his sense of humor, so when others would joke or pull pranks at his expense, he would take it lightly. I never saw George get angry, not even when another wild class-mate, Steve, threatened to unleash termites on George's wooden crutches or entered George's name into a 100-meter dash claiming that he would race on all fours. Maybe George was able to keep his cool because he knew that often others would come to his defense and get angry at the pranksters on his behalf. One such example of someone who defended George was our gym teacher, Mr. Pohl. Only two times in my years at North did I witness Mr. Pohl lose it, screaming until his face turned red, demanding that someone claim responsibility for what had gotten him so angry. The first time was when someone kicked all of the kick balls up onto the roof of the school. Nobody ever fessed up to that prank, but when George's name was entered into the race, Mr. Pohl wouldn't give up until he found out who would do such a thing. Steve later apologized to everyone for what he thought was a silly prank. Although it's difficult for anyone who couldn't walk, much less run, to find humor in the prank, we all learned a lesson in forgiveness from George when he graciously accepted Steve's apology.

Despite his physical disabilities, George never allowed himself to feel limited and led a full life. He was a member of the National Honor Society and after North went on to excel in college, get married, have children, become a published author of many novels, and start his own business working with rare books. He took the time to personally autograph his three-novel trilogy for me: *The Weight of Smoke*, *The Dragons of the Storm*, and *The Leaves of Fate*. The novels were so well-written that a Hollywood producer purchased the rights and plans to make a movie or TV series about these books which tell the story of Capt. John Smith and his role in the establishment of the first permanent English settlement in America, the colony at Jamestown. After announcing my plans to write this book at the reunion, George

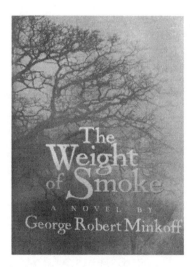

One of George's Novels,
*The Weight of Smoke*

offered to help if needed. It was very encouraging and comforting to know that I had such an accomplished author in my corner ready to assist!

Thinking of George's success despite his challenges made me hope that many others with Polio went on to lead lives as successful as his, perhaps helped even if just a little by the work our Omega Gamma Delta chapter had done supporting Sister Kenny's foundation many years prior. Another pair of classmates who overcame a different set of challenges to eventually become very successful were Noel and his beautiful wife Mary who I ran into next. Noel, whose real first name is James, was a transfer student from a New York City Catholic school who came to his first day at North dressed in what he always wore to school, a jacket and tie. He stood out from the crowd but after a brief time, he joined our fraternity, assimilated to the Omega Gamma Delta environment, and lost the jacket along with everything else he learned in parochial school except generosity. Soon after, Noel and Mary began dating but Mary's parents didn't like Noel very much because they thought he would never turn out to be very successful in life. Even though Mary's parents didn't want them to date, Noel wouldn't give up on Mary, and with the help of his good friend and frat brother Sal, he was able to continue dating his high school sweetheart.

Sal was a hustler, always thinking ahead with a plan for everything in life. If there was something that he wanted to do like buy a car, be with a certain girl, or play his favorite position on the baseball team, he would figure out a way, often devising genius plans to pull off the impossible. Sal started hustling and a very young age when he and his friend Roger would take early morning bike rides through the neighborhood picking up empty bottles and cans to return for nickels and old newspapers to turn into recycling centers, payable by the pound. As he got older, he earned some extra money by helping his father deliver beverages on the soda route he owned. Drawing from his lifelong experience as a hustler, it wasn't difficult for Sal to solve Noel and Mary's dilemma so that they could go to their high school prom together after just a few dates.

The plan was for Sal to go to Mary's home and tell her parents he was there to pick up Mary for a date. Then Sal and Mary would meet up with Noel, and Sal would leave the couple together to enjoy their time together. At the end of their date, Noel and Mary would meet with Sal at a prearranged time and location so that Sal could bring Mary home. Brilliant! What could go wrong with that plan? Although Mary's parents wondered why their five-foot-ten-inch daughter was dating a little Italian guy who stood no taller than five foot seven, the plan worked, and Noel got to take Mary to the prom. After high school, Noel and Mary went in different directions each getting married and starting families of their own. Noel went to college and worked his way up to become a Vice President at IBM. Then, 30 years after graduation they found each other again, got married, and moved to Japan for two years where they started what would become a very successful film processing company.

I then ran into Lou and Pat, another senior-year romance, this one a success story from the start. Lou, one of the sharpest members of the Omega Gamma Delta fraternity, was a rare individual who was able to combine being a jock with being highly intelligent at the same time. With a different, more sophisticated point of view than the rest of the group, Lou would often respond to questions in a way that nobody would expect. So, I was prepared for an interesting response when I asked him to tell me about his favorite high school memory. He went on to tell me all of the fun times that came rushing back to his mind: the candy store Ickle & Bickle, games on the firemen's field, the delicious German potato salad at the deli, the aroma of greasy hamburgers and fries at Benny's, buying the Gump and me a slice at Poppy's after our PBC ball game, the great Malverne vs Franklin Square stickball games under a canopy of beautiful Norwegian Maple trees when Vinny Morris, Danny Cash, Bernie Havern and myself would go up against the likes of Charlie Marker, Ralph Zanchelli and Lou Martorello from Franklin Square. Life was great and the memories in those small doses will last forever.

After chatting for a while, I leave Lou and Pat smiling and confused as always. They were two very cerebral individuals who looked at things much differently than I did which would explain how Pat and I could have been in school together from first through twelfth grade without ever being in the same class together. Looking back, I'm glad we weren't in the same class when I had a crush on her. Had that been the case, I probably would have failed sixth grade due to a lack of concentration and as a result, would have been left back, and then wouldn't have been part of the North High class of 1961 that I grew to love so much.

Speaking of North High love stories, the fraternity brother for whom I pledged, Bill Scheezer, went on to marry our beautiful homecoming queen Chris Beuttenmueller. Chris was a wonderful person, well-liked, and involved in everything during high school. She was a cheerleader, played sports, and was a member of the German Honor Society, Leaders Club, honor roll, and so much more. I hadn't seen Chris much until we became part of the committee to plan the 50-year reunion. We worked for weeks meeting in various locations but mostly in Marilyn's home. It was so good to once again re-experience her beautiful smile, positivity, effervescent, upbeat personality, and wonderful sense of humor that everyone always loved about her since high school. Chris' note to me in my North High yearbook read,

"I've known you well since the ninth grade when we had all those crazy parties. Now as seniors, we repeated those great times ten times over. I wish you and Sue the best of everything, you both deserve it. God bless you, Love, Chris."

Chris was close friends with my girlfriend Sue Zanto in our senior year and they remained friends throughout their lives.

Along with Marilyn Grispin, they formed the three amigas who often got together for girl trips on weekends.

Next, I saw my good friend Joe Corea and his beautiful wife Mary Jeanne. I was in their wedding party, and I was also the last one in the group who had not gotten married yet. At that time, I was living in a three-room apartment in Long Beach one block from the ocean, driving a Corvette hardtop convertible, still playing ball and bowling for money, so the last thing on my mind was marriage. Mary Jeanne tried to fix me up at her wedding and remained persistent in her mission to make sure I was a happily married man for the next three years until she successfully introduced me to my future wife Lois at their pregame bar league football house party on October 26, 1973.

I must've been on dates with fifteen different young ladies before I met Lois. The longest relationships I had previously were with Susan for five years and then with Maureen for about a year when we realized that the relationship wasn't right for either of us and we mutually agreed to stop seeing each other. So as the last single person in the group, all of my married friends were determined to set me up with the perfect woman. There were blind dates, meetings in bars, friends of friends, and someone at work, but all to no avail until Mary Jeanne did the impossible by matching me up with Lois. But more on that later.

By this time in the reunion it was getting late, and most people were beginning to leave the party. But as I stayed behind a while longer allowing the wonderful North High memories to sink in, I started to realize just how interconnected all of life is. As the night wound down, I pondered the incredible chain of events that brought my beautiful wife into my life through North High friendships that were formed many years before Lois and I were introduced to each other. I then found myself reflecting on the occurrences of my family history which brought my family and I to Malverne and eventually brought me to North High as part of the class of 1961.

| North High Class of 1961 at our reunion October 22, 2011

# 5

# MY BEGINNINGS

My mom Gertrude Mackey was nineteen years old when she married my dad Raymond Philip Heron who was 23, on June 7, 1941.

My parents had originally settled in an apartment in Brooklyn before my father, who was a member of the Army Air Force, was assigned to a base in Colorado. Exactly six months after their wedding, Pearl Harbor was attacked on December 7, 1941, triggering World War II. So, my mom who was pregnant with twins was forced to live alone in their apartment which did not

Wedding picture of my mom and dad June 7, 1941

have air conditioning during hot summer months while our country was in the midst of a world war. But my mother was always very strong, smart, and independent, so she made the best of her situation. She was relieved when her efforts of carrying two large twins eventually paid off on August 13, 1942, the day she gave birth to two healthy children, my twin sister Linda Rea-Ann Heron and myself, Raymond Philip Heron II.

Our family began in our apartment located at 500 Chauncey St. Brooklyn, NY 11223. Jackie Gleason lived down the block, but at that time he was just a neighbor and nobody knew that he would become world-famous for starring as Ralph Kramden in the hit television show The Honeymooners. The show was based on living on our very street in Brooklyn, so if you were to watch The Honeymooners, you'd get an idea of the type of apartment and neighborhood where my sister and I spent the first two years of our lives.

My mom and dad in front of the Capitol Building in Denver, Colorado circa 1945

I was two years old when we finally moved down to Colorado and we all got to be together as a family. Before then, my father came home to visit as often as he could but for the most part, my mother raised her infant twins all by herself. Being so very young, the only thing I remember about the moving was the dark black smoke coming from the smokestack of the locomotive pulling the train on which we traveled. Back then, trains did not run on electricity but were powered by steam engines fueled by coal furnace heat. An engineer would shovel mounds of coal into the furnace to increase power when needed but would also carefully monitor the system's temperature to prevent overheating.

We didn't stay in Colorado very long because the Army wanted my father to work on a special high-priority assignment in Texas. My father was put on a team charged with developing new technology for a bombsight that could pinpoint a target. Developing the new bombsight was urgent because at the same time, other units were hard at work developing an atomic bomb and the Army wanted to be very accurate with where it would land when it was ready to be dropped. Improving on an earlier design developed by Carl Norden, the new technology became known as the Norden Bombsight which automatically measured aircraft speed and direction relative to the ground, which older bombsights could only estimate after lengthy manual calculations. The Norden Bombsight also improved on previous designs by using an early version of a computer to continuously recalculate and automatically readjust the projected impact point based on changing flight conditions, wind, and other environmental factors. The technology was so advanced at the time, that pilots were under orders to instantly destroy the bombsight if their plane went down to prevent enemy forces from discovering the secrets to this impactful new technology. The Army's plans all came to fruition in early August of 1945 when two atomic bombs were dropped in Japan. Because of its devastating strength, this new type of bomb put an abrupt end to World War II on September 2, 1945, and the accuracy of the newly developed bombsight saved thousands of innocent lives.

While my father was immersed in this special project on his home soil, his brother Tom who was stationed in the mountains of Italy fighting off the Germans, eventually became a war hero for his efforts in a specific battle. My Uncle Tom and his men were asked to hold back the Germans while the Allied forces prepared for the invasion of Normandy. 220 Allied soldiers marched up a mountain in Italy to hold off German forces, and 30 days later only Uncle Tom and eighteen of his fellow soldiers made it back down the mountain after completing their mission. Uncle Tom spent the next six months in a hospital recovering from frostbite and other injuries before returning home. He was later awarded several medals including a Purple Heart and a Bronze Star.

But recovering from his physical injuries was only the first step in the long road to recovery for Uncle Tom. Back then, there was no treatment for battle fatigue or Post Traumatic Stress Disorder (PTSD) so returning soldiers had no choice but to overcome it by themselves or succumb to its effects. Having comrades fall to enemy fire and others freeze to death attempting to keep the night watch on top of the frigid mountain was a very traumatic experience. Upon returning home and trying to process what had taken place without professional help, it took Uncle Tom ten years to get over the horrors of war and another 40 years to be able to begin talking about what he had experienced and seen. Like so many other veterans in "the greatest generation", Uncle Tom paid a tremendous price to protect the United States of America, its people, and their freedom.

Many years later, I asked Uncle Tom why he and my father wound up with such different roles in the war. Uncle Tom explained that when joining the Army, an IQ test was given to determine placement. My father had scored a genius level 155, so he was designated for special projects rather than combat. Uncle Tom's IQ score was not too far behind at 135, but he wasn't interested in any special projects. He preferred to remain a Private throughout his tenure with the Army, so he turned down many offers of promotion to a higher rank.

My father never told me how he wound up working on the important Norden Bombsight project, but when I found out, I understood why he demanded that I take college entrance courses in eleventh grade like Mrs. Gold's Math class. Despite the poor marks and attendance records he had seen on each of my freshman and sophomore year report cards, he must have concluded that because I was his

World War II hero, my uncle Thomas Heron

son, my IQ should also be high.

So, figuring I needed to be challenged for my true intellect to show, he met with my guidance counselor and insisted that I be enrolled in rigorous college preparation courses for junior year. Unfortunately, the experiment failed and so for senior year, it was back to a much easier curriculum of Gym, Art, Driver Ed., General Wood Shop, Mechanical Drawing, English, and a Health class that I needed to take twice because I failed that mandatory requirement the first time around. Thankfully it was much easier on the second attempt. But more on that later...

So it was Dad's high IQ that kept him from combat overseas, allowed our family the good fortune to stay together during the latter part of World War II, and led us to Texas where he worked on the bombsight project. In Texas, we started by settling into 1403 S. Abe St located on the Goodfellow Air Force Base in San Angelo, Texas. I remember thinking it was strange that every bunkbed had a gas mask on the headboard even though we were out in the wide-open Texas countryside. We only stayed on the base for a short time before moving into a nice big house in 1945. I can't recall much about living in that house except for the memories that looking at pictures sometimes conjures up. However, I do remember the beautiful pool area, the heat, and my father saying that he needed to carry a gun because of the rattlesnakes which were very active in springtime.

Later that year, coinciding with the end of World War II, an epidemic of polio broke out in Texas and many other parts of the South. In late 1945, a Polio vaccination had not yet been developed, so my parents decided to move the family back up north where we lived with my mother's brother, two sisters, and both of her parents in Queens. That made nine of us sharing my grandparents' small, three-bedroom, one-bathroom house with a tenth resident, the big black family guard dog who was trained to defend anyone who was being attacked unless my grandma called him off. We were glad to be safe from the Polio epidemic and happily shared the cramped accommodations while my parents decided what to do next.

My twin sister Linda and I in Texas, 1945

We were many people living in a very small house, but we were a family so we made it work. Living with so many family members was a real treat to my sister and I. Being only three or four years old at the time, it was fun to have so many people to play with, read to us, and help us at home every day. I do not have many memories of that house, but I do remember the joy I felt living with extended family members like my grandfather William Mackey and how he would take my sister and I down to the corner pub to play shuffleboard sometimes. Grandpa was an accomplished metal worker whose crowning achievement was getting to work at the top of the Statue of Liberty to repair damaged metal plates in the area around the head. His expert craftsmanship skills would later be used on our family's new home in Malverne when he installed solid copper leaders and gutters that were so strong we could hang from them. Then there was my Uncle Dave who was only 7 years older than us, so living with him was more like living with a big brother. As an eleven-year-old, when he was left to look after us, we would always have a lot of fun.

After about a year of living together, in 1946 Uncle Tom found a bargain on a foreclosed 40'x100' plot of land in a small Nassau County village called Malverne, NY. Knowing that we couldn't afford it, Uncle Tom paid the $35 in back taxes that were owed on the foreclosed property to purchase it as a surprise for our family. To put things in perspective, average pay in 1946 was approximately $8 per day, so $35 was no small sum of money.

Uncle Tom was a very special man in so many more ways than just being a war hero or buying us a plot of land where we eventually wound up settling and establishing our roots as a family. It was his kindness, and ability to connect with young children like my sister and I that stole our hearts. I still remember the time he bought me my first train set when I was six years old, and how excited I was when I woke up that Christmas morning and found it all set up under the tree! I will also never forget when as a young teenager, he began to teach me the marksmanship skills he learned in the Army, especially the correct ways to shoot both pistols and rifles. But my fondest childhood memories of Uncle Tom are reflecting on the times he would take Linda and I to the beach. We would at times go to the beach with my mom, dad, and other family members, but when it was just the three of us going to Jones Beach, Uncle Tom treated Linda and I very special so we were always very excited when he would take us by ourselves. We would play on the sand and swim in the ocean, having a great time. Linda and I would watch in amazement as Uncle Tom, who was a very strong swimmer, would go way out past the breaking waves and swim great distances.

Then, the fun would continue on the Jones Beach boardwalk which back then was filled with attractions and food vendors. There was something very special about a hot dog, fries, and a cold drink for a young child after a day at the beach, of course, finished off with a nice, cold, ice cream cone. Back then, we had rectangular ice cream cones that held scoops of ice cream side by side instead of being stacked vertically atop one another. The old-fashioned rectangle top ice cream cone was a great idea because the ice cream melted down into the base of the cone rather than quickly dripping down the sides of a vertical cone on a hot summer's day. The seating area, shower area, and pool area with diving boards and beautiful, cool, clear water also made Jones Beach very memorable for Linda and I.

One of our favorite boardwalk attractions was the Native American Village where authentic Native Peoples dressed in traditional garb performed ancient rituals, and dances, sold handmade items, and showed us how they made their teepees. There was also lots more to do like miniature golf, bowling games, and a roller-skating rink. My Aunt Elaine, Uncle Tom's sister who liked to be called "Blondie", loved to roller skate. On occasion, she would take us to the Jones Beach skating rink bringing her own skates and renting pairs of skates for Linda and I. Those summer nights at the beach roller skating under the stars in the cool ocean breeze could not be beaten.

Those times at Jones Beach and the views of the ocean were like a dream come true for a small boy and his sister. In my heart, Jones Beach lived up to its billing as the "Eighth Wonder of the World" thanks to my Uncle Tom, who was a hero not only to our country and to our family, but also to my sister and I as children. Back then, we just knew him as our fun and loving Uncle Tom. As children, we never realized the difficulties he faced reintegrating into civilian life after his heroic Army service. But looking back, it is truly amazing that despite all he went through, he was still able to create such special, lasting memories for my sister and I on those hot summer days.

L to R: Myself, mom, dad and Linda back in NY, 1945 circa 1947

# 6

## MOVING INTO MALVERNE

My Uncle Tom was living on Twelve Aberdeen St in Malverne at the time, which is how he found the plot of land he purchased for my family so we too could have more space and a better life out in the countryside. My father immediately began working on a design and with the help of my uncles, grandfathers, and a couple of friends, they began to build a small cape-style house on the property.

Our home in Malverne being built by family &
friends, 1946

To afford the construction materials, my father took out a
special loan available to US Armed Forces veterans through
the GI Bill. When funds started to run low, he took out a
second loan using the GI Bill this time causing a red flag with
the bank. One Sunday morning two bank managers sat and
talked with my father over cigars at the kitchen table, with the
second loan at stake. After getting an understanding of my
father's poor financial situation and how he planned to use the
money, they decided to let him retain both loans so as not to
put a US Army veteran and his young family in dire financial
straits. Thanks to his high level of intelligence and willingness
to push boundaries when necessary, my father was always
good at finding creative ways to solve problems like this one,
which kept our home, and our family, afloat.

The front of the house faced Linden St and the back of the house faced Orbach Ave where a driveway led to a garage tucked in under the house next to the basement. We moved into our house after my family finished building it at the beginning of 1947. I was only five years old and don't remember too much about the construction except that the nails came in a large wooden keg, and I couldn't believe how many nails were needed to build a house. Today, nails come in one-pound cardboard boxes for small jobs and a keg of nails would probably cost a small fortune.

On the first floor of the house was an eat-in kitchen, bathroom, den, large living room, and a master bedroom. The kitchen window over the sink looked out into the woods next to our house. Dad added hinges to the side of the big kitchen window converting it into a Dutch window that swung wide open sideways just like a door. He also made the back door a Dutch door with the top opening up bringing fresh air into the kitchen. The kitchen walls and cabinets were finished in knotty pine planks giving the kitchen a country look to go along with an airy feeling created by the Dutch door and window.

On the second floor, there was a small bedroom for my sister and a large, unfinished open space for my brother and I. The basement remained unfinished because my dad ran out of money to complete the rest of the house. Instead of the standard three-to-one sand-to-cement mix ratio as it should have been, to cut costs the basement floor became a ten-to-one mix but somehow managed to hold up all the years we were there.

In the early days of our new home, the roads were paved but there were no sidewalks or streetlights and the houses had cesspools because there were no sewers. There was no TV, only a radio, and one black rotary phone hooked up to a party line that was only used in case of an emergency. Back then, a party line was a single phone line that served several nearby households so when we picked up the phone to make a call, there could be someone else who lived nearby on the line already having a conversation and you'd have to wait for them to finish to make a call. One day as a young boy, I remember listening to a neighbor's conversation and they must have known I was eavesdropping because they started telling a very scary story which made me hang up quickly! Another day, my father was trying to call from the grocery store to ask for a ride home but couldn't get through because the line was in use by another neighbor, so he had to ask the operator to interrupt that call so he could reach my mother. Even when raising my children in the era before cell phones, there was only one phone line in each house which had to be shared among the family. My how things have changed since the inception of cell phones with call waiting and how having phone lines tied up and inaccessible, like many other things, have become a thing of the past!

We later closed off the garage and made it part of the basement as a weightlifting area. My father dug a pit to create additional clearance needed to perform overhead Olympic-style lifting techniques like one of my father's favorites, the snatch. My father, having been a weightlifter most of his life and competing against the York Barbell Club, tried out for the Olympics in his 145-pound weight class. He qualified for the Olympics but during his test to become a New York City firefighter, he ruptured his Achilles tendon climbing over an eight-foot wall, so he unfortunately never made it to the Olympics or the fire department.

The other half of the basement was originally unfinished, but later would be converted into a very nice entertainment area. When the family came over in the winter to visit for the day we would go downstairs where we had plenty of room. We had many parties in that basement with both family and friends. Many of Linda and I's high school friends would come over often and we had some great times.

My dad at 148lbs lifting 258lbs during a weightlifting competition circa 1939

The laundry room was in the basement, and Dad had built a laundry chute that went from the bathroom directly to a bin in the laundry room. We loved that simple chute because when we took a shower or changed clothes, we just threw our dirty laundry down the chute, and then the clothes mysteriously found their way into our drawers in the bedroom all clean and smelling fresh. God Bless Mom!

The way we got and stored food was very different back then. We didn't have a refrigerator, but we did have an ice box which was an insulated container kept cold with dry ice delivered by a truck that passed through the neighborhood each week. The ice box kept the eggs, milk, meat, and vegetables fresh. The ice box couldn't keep anything frozen, so we had no frozen items at all.

Fresh bread and eggs were also delivered by trucks during the week. We couldn't afford too many deliveries so this nice delivery man Murray would give us eggs with cracked shells that were still good enough to eat at no charge. We would buy some additional eggs that we could afford, and others he would give us for free. We kept the cracked eggs in the coldest part of the icebox and ate them first so they didn't go bad.

Murray the egg-man was from the island of Jamaica and had a beautiful accent that I still remember. He was so friendly and always had a smile, so we got to know him well over the years. He had a chicken farm out east which he invited us to visit, so one day when I was little, we took him up on his offer. I couldn't believe how big it was and how many chickens lived on the farm. He took the time to show us around and explain the process of how an egg starts inside the chicken and winds up in a carton for delivery to houses like ours. I always remember how happy he was in his work and how he spread the joy of living every day to everybody he encountered.

Another of my favorite delivery men was the milkman. I loved waiting for his early morning deliveries of glass bottles filled with fresh cold milk which had thick cream floating on top. I loved that he allowed me to ride on his little delivery truck and he made me feel like I was his helper. He was such a good man with the patience of a saint for letting me ride with him down the block. It was an exciting time for a young kid who looked forward to his visit each week. I can still to this day remember being a youngster and enjoying the taste of the sweet cold cream on a hot summer's day. The milk truck also delivered butter, cream, cheese, and other dairy products that we could not afford at the time so Mom would go to the local supermarket and buy them at a lower price. In later years, we would go to Gowz Cows on Dutch Broadway in Elmont for fresh milk, juice, eggs, butter, bread, and other dairy products. This was the first time I learned about prices being different for the same product at different places. The emergence of more accessible markets and food stores would end the delivery truck service and my rides down the street; another simple activity lost in time, never to be found again in today's busy, technological, security-conscious world of mass production and instant gratification.

Malverne was a small friendly village with its police department. In the summer I would walk all around the village dressed in only shorts and shoes. I don't remember having sneakers when I was young. The first pair of new sneakers that I remember getting was when I made my high school basketball team and the coach issued all the players a brand-new pair of high-top basketball sneakers.

As a six-year-old, I liked to walk around looking for adventure. I found it one summer day when a policeman in the village asked if I was lost. I don't remember saying I was, but the next moment I found myself in the police station. They sat me down, put a police hat on me, and brought over a dog that they had recently found roaming the neighborhood. A reporter from a local paper, The Newsday who happened to be at the police station took a picture of the dog and me. The nice policeman said thank you for helping the lost dog to find his owner and then took me home in a police car which was a very exciting day for a six-year-old! Fortunately, that was the only time I was inside a police car in my life.

The next day my picture with the dog was on the front page of the newspaper with this caption: " SOMEBODY'S PUP has been picked up for loitering by the Malverne police and, although he captured the supposedly hard hearts of those stewards, he has been sent to the pound. Raymond Heron, 6, is willing to adopt him but his owners must be found. (Story on page 9)"

I also liked to walk west down Linden Street to the end where the creek was usually filled with running water. Looking up past the creek, corn fields stretched seemingly forever to the six-year-old boy who would stare at them in amazement. I loved living there surrounded by the woods, cornfields, and a flowing creek that as far as I could tell extended endlessly in both directions with no beginning or end.

We ran free in the woods next to our house as if it were part of our property. Dad had cleaned out a large area of the woods and made a table and benches for us so that we could eat outside under the trees which we loved to do on summer days. In those woods, there was a large tree near the picnic area where my dad built a tree house. We loved to climb up to the treehouse and had a lot of fun playing there. I had a dog, the woods, a tree house, the creek to explore, and the beautiful cornfields to look at. I felt like I was in heaven! How can it be any better than this? Not knowing anything about money or finances, I believed we were very rich. Oh, the life of a small boy living in the country without a care in the world was like living in a fairy tale. Still today, I remember those beautiful summer days with great appreciation, fondness, and thankfulness for my parents giving us that very special time in our lives.

Me at six years old appearing on the front page of Newsday with a lost dog, 1949

Parties and get-togethers were always big in my family, and started with my parents inviting some family who lived in the city to spend the weekends with us in what was back then, the country. My mother's sister Aunt Ellie and my Godmother along with her family would come out from Brooklyn on many weekends during the summers. They would pick up my grandmother who lived in Queens on the way in because she had lost her husband, my grandfather, when I was only in the fourth grade.

Most of the time we would then go down to the beaches between Point Lookout and Long Beach because they were all open at the time and you could do anything you wanted. There were no restrictions of any kind. You could drive right up on the beach, make a fire, go swimming, play ball, or fly airplanes. It was a child's dream.

We would park on the beach and camp there all day. The waves were high because the jetties were not yet built, and we would ride our inner tubes, which were large inflatable tubes about the size of car tires, on those big waves. We invented a game sort of like baseball that everyone could play... girls, guys, older people, and younger people included. We used a beach ball instead of a baseball and guys had to bat opposite from the way they normally would swing. One of my cousins' hobbies was flying gas-powered airplanes so they would bring the airplanes to the beach to fly in the open sky. Back then, there were no remote controls, instead, steel wires attached to handles were used to guide the planes. My cousins understood the airplanes' engine mechanics and could repair anything on the plane or the controlling apparatus, so they were very good at flying them. For a twelve-year-old boy to spend those kinds of summer days with his aunts, uncles, grandma, and cousins, life didn't get any better than that. But the party didn't end there when the sun started to go down, because spending summer nights together as a family was always a lot of fun too.

After all the fun during the day, if we wanted to stay at the beach for supper, the adults would start a fire and cook up a meal. On other days, especially when we would fill up bushel baskets of the large crabs we would catch in the bay at low tide, we would all head back to my parent's house for dinner. We would bring the crabs home still alive, cook them up, and enjoy a fresh crab meal with corn on the cob, of course, washed down with cold beers by the adults, on a beautiful summer night in the woods next to our home. I loved those freshly cooked crabs; the blue claw crabs were especially delicious!

On many occasions, the party continued after dinner when my cousins and their families would stay over on Saturday nights before heading home on Sundays. My brother, sister, and my three cousins Dickie, Billy, and Barbara would go upstairs and sleep on the floor. The adults would stay downstairs watching movies, eating cold cuts, and drinking beer. We loved having the family together for the weekend enjoying the simple things in life. At some point during the height of the festivities, my Uncle Dick would bring laughs and smiles to the crowd with his famous saying, "I wonder what the poor people are doing tonight?" Even though we didn't have much, we felt like the richest people in the world enjoying the simple things in life with family.

As a young boy, I experienced how bringing people together to do simple things brought so much joy. This, combined with how much family meant to us all growing up, became the foundation for the parties and get-togethers I've hosted with my friends and family over the many years since then. I can still feel that same childhood joy today when people are together having a good time sharing a meal, drinks, smiles, and laughter. It warms my heart, brings peace to my soul, and a feeling of accomplishment that I was a small part of bringing joy to others by simply bringing people together. My oldest friend Bernie was raised the same way, and between us, we had many great get-togethers and parties over our lifetime.

Even when life wasn't always a party, we were still very thankful to have settled in Malverne during difficult times because of the helpful neighbors and friends, like the great Dr. Cornelius Savitsky who lived just down the street with his daughter and her family. As it would turn out my little brother Michael, the subject of the first exciting event to take place in our new house when he was born on April 8, 1947, would be especially glad we moved into our Linden St Malverne home just before he was born. During the polio outbreak, we all got the vaccine which spared us all from contracting the disease except for my little brother Michael, who got a mild case of polio at seven years old. Our family doctor had taken x-rays of Michael's spine and said he would never walk again. My father, unhappy with that prognosis, took Michael to see Dr. Savitsky who was a chiropractor. Dr. Savitsky had escaped from Russia during the 1917 revolution and we were blessed that like us, he also wound up settling on Linden St, in Malverne, NY.

When the good Doctor Savitsky came to America after escaping the Russian Revolution, he tried to continue his profession. However, his license from Russia did not meet the necessary requirements to practice in the United States so he would have needed to go to medical school for a while to start practicing the same type of medicine. Unfortunately, as he had just escaped with his life, the clothes on his back, and only a few dollars, this was not an option for him. He then discovered that he could be a certified and licensed chiropractor with his existing background in medicine because there weren't that many restrictions for being a chiropractor at the time. There weren't that many chiropractors in the area, so figuring it was the best possible way to earn a living in the field of medicine that he loved, he rented an office in the neighboring town of Rockville Centre, hung a shingle "Dr. Savitsky Chiropractor," and began to practice.

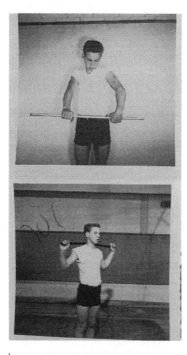

My brother Michael Heron demonstrating exercises to appear in David Cook's fitness book

With the help of Dr. Savitsky, Michael was saved from being crippled. It took several months and many adjustments to repair damage to his spine, but the treatments were successful and his spine was made straight again. When the sessions with Dr. Savitsky were finished, he took another x-ray and we were all amazed to see what a tremendous improvement had been made. Michael had no trouble walking, but he was never able to run as fast as he could before contracting the disease. Although Michael never played sports again, thanks to Dr. Savitsky, he was able to walk, swim, and lift weights. Pictures of Michael demonstrating how to properly exercise with weights were even featured in a book written by author David Cook. Michael was very strong, but sports weren't his thing like they were for me. He preferred hands-on projects like working on cars, and anything mechanical, or electrical appliances.

When my father told the family doctor what had transpired, he could not believe it and asked to see the X-rays. After reviewing the X-rays, he was astonished at the transformation that had occurred in Michael's spine. The doctor and the chiropractor got together and subsequently became lifelong friends.

When people went to visit Dr. Savitsky, they didn't have to tell him which body part required attention. After a little while adjusting the patient, Dr. Savitsky would tell the patient what was wrong and would work on the area for the better part of an hour to heal whatever condition it might be. He would often send patients home with special herbs and instructions to brew the herbs into a tea, drink it, and lay down for an hour to allow the body to heal. The treatment, tea, and rest always seemed to work miracles for me as I was able to bounce back from injuries, quickly returning to complete the sports I loved to play.

One time, I was playing basketball at Seaford High School against Jim Valvano (who went on to win the NCAA basketball championship at N. Carolina State as their coach) and his coach/father Rocky Valvano who attended Newtown High School in Queens. My father and uncle also attended Newton with Rocky, a 1933 graduate. My father graduated in 1936 so he attended with Rocky for one year, although I am not sure if they knew each other. But I digress, now back to the game!

Our center had broken his foot earlier in the season and even though I was only six feet two inches tall, I could really get up so I was moved to the center, going head-to-head against the tallest guys in the league. During the game, I went up for a rebound, got hit from both sides, and was injured to the point where I couldn't raise my right arm above my waist without tremendous pain like a knife sticking in my shoulder. Wanting to stay in the game, I decided not to tell Coach so I continued to play and began to shoot lefty. I was then taken out of the game because Coach thought I was clowning around so I then admitted that I couldn't move my shoulder. The following day, I went to see Dr. Savitsky who worked on me for 45 minutes and had me back on the court playing good as new two days later.

## 7

---

# MY TRANSPORTATION

My first means of transportation was walking, running, and jumping to get from one place to another. I had strong legs and loved to keep moving. I always wanted to find out where the cornfields ended where the creek came from and where it was going. One summer day, still not ten years old, I walked down to the corn fields and the creek. Linden Street, the road I lived on, stopped at the creek. It had not been extended because there was no development started in that area yet. The creek was wide and deep with water, so I decided to walk further to find an easier crossing to the corn fields. I followed the creek to Valley Stream, behind Central High School, where the creek went under Merrick Road. At that age, I thought that's where it ended, and my trip had been a partial success since I found where the creek ended. I still hadn't found where it began or got to the corn fields yet, but that would be another day.

My second mode of transportation was a bicycle, which I needed to get to school. We had a school bus that took us to Wheeler Avenue School in Valley Stream. However, after building Corona Avenue School, we had to either walk or take a bike. Starting in the third grade, there was no more school bus for us. There were no car rides from Mom, as there was usually only one car per household at this time. Using my bike expanded the distance I could travel. New schools were being built, and cornfields were gone, replaced by new homes. The illusion of living in the woods vanished as houses were constructed on both sides of my home. The picnic area and the treehouse were gone, but not the memories of my fairytale childhood.

Up until this time, I mostly spent time with my oldest friend, Bernie, who lived several blocks over on Doncaster Road. Another of my early childhood hangouts was the Cash's who owned the only TV in the neighborhood. There, Terry, Danny, and Bobbie would let us come over to watch the Six Gun Playhouse, a television program that showed old Western movies. There was also my twin sister, Linda, and her friends, Jody and Pat, who both lived nearby. Sometimes we played together on the swings in the empty yard across the street from us next to the Rosenberg's house, singing songs or playing hide and seek.

However, new construction popping up in the area also

brought new friendships. The first new house was one block over, where the Hoffmans moved in. Butch and his much older brother, Lawrence, lived there. Butch's father, an interesting man, started out sweeping the floors in a machine shop and later bought the business after years of saving and smart investments. He even took us to see the Yankees play at Yankee Stadium. Butch's father had also asked him to check stock prices in the New York Times one morning when he was driving us to a ball game. That was the first time I had heard of the stock market.

One day, Butch introduced me to English muffins. We toasted them and buttered them with sweet butter, and they melted in our mouths. Mrs. Hoffman, a very sweet woman, made them for us, and they were delicious. I had never tasted anything like that before. We were used to plain white bread toasted with regular butter. Funny how such a small thing can stick with you from childhood.

Around the block lived Jeff Wala, who didn't play with us much. He did show us a baseball bat that was used by Babe Ruth. I remember how big and heavy it was. My only other memory of Jeff was when he playfully threw some pebbles at me, chipping my front tooth. We were just kids fooling around, and I didn't think much of it until I got home and my mom asked what happened. I looked in the mirror and said, "Wow, how did that happen?" I had that chipped tooth for many years until I had it fixed later when I had the money.

The next development of houses a couple of blocks away

from Linden St brought the Halpern family. Kenny and Gary Halpern were brothers, one year apart, with an older sister named Gail. I met Ken on the corner of Linden Street and Legion Place. I don't know how it started, but there we were, two ten-year-olds in a fisticuffs fight. We went at it for a while, with other kids cheering us on. They didn't seem to care who won, as long as the fight continued, they were entertained. It was a memorable bout between Ken and me.

I would say that although Kenny was bloody and looked like he lost, it was my stomachache that gave the fight to Ken as I lay on my couch recovering. Kenny had the jaw of a Marine; there was no way I was going to knock him out. He worked my midsection like it was Swiss cheese as I covered my face. We became the best of friends with great respect for each other. We loved to play ball together, no matter the type—football, basketball, baseball, punch ball. Any game, any time, was good for us.

The next development, next to the creek, was where Michael Griffith lived. He was an only child, friendly and sports-loving. Tall, strong, and very fast, he often joined us for football, basketball, and other games. My circle of friends was growing, thanks to my improved means of transportation. As the houses expanded, the action picked up. Football in the street, wiffleball in the backyard, ice hockey in front of Hoffman's house, and basketball in the street at the vacant lot. Bike rides to Valley Stream, Ickle & Bickle's candy store, Malverne town, to the little league baseball games in Malverne. We had bike rides with friends everywhere. If it was fun, we'd go, regardless of the distance. We explored movies, pools, beaches, ball fields, and schools until the time came to get a driver's license.

Finally, I had transportation that allowed me to go anywhere, no matter the conditions of the day. Rain, snow, wind, or a hot summer's day couldn't stop me. At last, freedom, I thought with excitement! I could travel around town, picking up my friends for school, in my beautiful 1949 Buick straight-eight two-door sedan. It had plenty of room inside, and I could bring more friends along if needed.

As I entered my junior year, I was seventeen and legally allowed to drive. I had obtained my driving permit the year before, at sixteen.

However, there were conditions my father insisted I meet before I could obtain this vehicle. He agreed to provide the car if I paid for the insurance. Being a teenage boy in a high-risk pool, insurance was expensive, costing $353. I was seventeen years old during the summer, so I was old enough for a full license but short $350. I did have three dollars. It was clear: I needed to get a job.

The Hill Supermarket on Franklin Avenue in Franklin Square had recently opened that year, and they were hiring. I secured a job as one of the stock handlers and needed to work a full six weeks to earn enough money to pay for my insurance. Back then, there were no timecards; we didn't punch in, we just signed in. However, there were many new employees, and we had a new assistant manager each week. Some of the guys would come in, sign in for the whole week, and not return until the following week. Joe, one of the employees, did this, working only one day a week but getting paid for five.

After two weeks, I was called into the office and told they had to let me go. I asked if everything was okay, as I was the only one working all week. They said they'd investigate it and asked me to come back the next day. When I returned, they gave me a promotion as a cashier, working the cash register. It was a great relief, as I had now made enough money to cover my car insurance and was in the perfect position to host some memorable and affordable parties.

One time, my old friend Bernie worked for Tron's Meats, and for our party, he brought 27 pounds of cold cuts. With everyone else contributing to the ingredients, we managed to have a fantastic party without spending much. What a great summer that was.

My dad informed me that I would only need to pay $303 for insurance if I took a driver's education course. Even though I had been driving for a couple of years, I signed up for driver's ed. Thank goodness it was an afternoon class; otherwise, I wouldn't have made it to many of the morning sessions.

The driver's ed. teacher was very serious about teaching the correct way to drive an automobile safely. While none of the other kids in the class had my experience, which was probably a good thing, I wasn't exactly safety-focused. One day, Carol, a classmate, was behind the wheel and attempted to parallel park in front of the school, which had a high curb. Nervous about being close enough to the curb, she ended up parking on top of it, with the car leaning to the left. She turned to the teacher and asked if she was close enough. I burst into laughter, unable to control myself.

Finally, I completed the driver's ed class and was free to continue wandering wherever my old, faithful, '49 Buick would take me. Enduring the class wasn't so bad and I had a lot of laughs, so it was well worth the discounted insurance rate.

# 8

## MONDAY: WEEK OF THE NORTH-SOUTH GAME

It's 7am, and my dad is calling me to wake up for school. I yell downstairs that I'm not feeling well and will sleep a little longer, maybe able to go to school later or tomorrow. Now my twin sister, Linda, who's in another room, says she's coming down now, and she heads to school later. It wasn't always like that with Linda; whenever Dad called, she used to say she would be right down and then go back to sleep. But one morning, when she didn't immediately respond, Dad went up with a big pitcher of water and poured it on her. After that, she always came down right away.

Dad was always ahead of us with his simple, straightforward responses to anything we did contrary to what he thought was best for us. He didn't engage in lengthy conversations with Linda about the importance of getting up when called. He didn't inquire why she hadn't gotten up or why she stayed up late. He took a direct approach and removed any ambiguity from his message. She knew that if she didn't come down in a reasonable time, the cold water would follow. The uncertainty of when the water would arrive motivated her to hurry downstairs. Brilliant!

During dinner, if we disliked the food or weren't hungry, he didn't argue. He only made one statement, especially when our favorite dessert was in the background: "Whatever you can't finish, you'll have for breakfast tomorrow morning. And, if you can't eat your dinner, you won't have room for dessert tonight." I would slip the vegetables I didn't like to my dog under the table, like lima beans. After that, there was only one instance when I had dinner for breakfast, an unforgettable memory. Dad never wasted food, knowing that there were people in the world who had nothing to eat. Genius!

Later in life, when I returned home from college, feeling smart after a philosophy class, I decided to ask my father a question I thought he couldn't answer: "Prove that you exist and that you're here now." He smiled, raised his hand, and gently slapped me in the face. Then he asked, "If I'm not here, who hit you?" He was the master of mind games. I felt deflated but learned my lesson: never try to outsmart the mastermind. I was fortunate to have him guide me on my life journey. He had a unique perspective, approaching things with simplicity, an open mind, and no barriers to his thinking. Thank you, Dad.

To illustrate how my thinking differed from mainstream ideas, I decided to retire after high school. I thought that waiting until 65 years old to enjoy my "golden years" would leave me too old to truly enjoy them. I opted to have those golden years while I was still young to fully relish them. But I digress.

Weekends were challenging for me. Friday nights were for parties, gathering at someone's house to hang out. Some of the best parties happened at my place. My parents enjoyed having people over, and our friends were always welcome. At one party, a wrestling match broke out in our living room, and the boys accidentally broke my mom's favorite piece of furniture, a tea cart with a beautiful lamp on top. I managed to fix the broken leg so it didn't appear damaged. Moms seem to know everything. She spotted it immediately and inquired about what happened. I told her the truth. Why didn't I make up a story, you might ask?

When I was around ten years old, I smashed my piggy bank to get money for candy at the store. Upon returning home, my mom asked me about the broken piggy bank. I feigned innocence, asking why she thought something was wrong. Her reply was, "A little birdie told me." Then my father taught me a lesson I've never forgotten. He said, "Son, it's crucial to always tell the truth. Someday, when all evidence points against you, and your word is all you have, people will believe you because you're known for honesty." It was a time when your word was your bond, and your handshake was your contract. How times have changed; one's word and the truth have become estranged. We now live lost in a sad world of self-centeredness and greed, in a time when peoples' words have lost significance and handshakes have lost their meaning.

Another time, my parents were out late, and we all fell asleep on the living room floor. When they came home, my dad told my mom to gently step over us. He reassured her that we were safe and that he would wake us in the morning. Dad always saw the positive side of situations.

Then there was the day I answered the front door and a severed pig's head rolled into my house. Bernie brought it, a gift from his job on the meat truck. We all laughed; it was still frozen, so there was no blood on the floor or rug. The only time I saw Kenny Halpern truly frightened was when we were leaving a party one night. Bernie had gotten his hands on another frozen pig's head and during the party snuck out and hung it from the rearview mirror of Kenny's car. After the party upon returning to his car, Kenny opened the door, sat down in the driver's seat, and as he glanced to his right noticing the pig head staring him back in the face, his screams could be heard miles away. We all found it hilarious, but Kenny didn't share our sentiment.

One time, my sister had friends over from out of town who we didn't know, while I had my gang over. Before long, words were exchanged and Sal claimed that Tony could box the ears off the troublemaker from the other group. Tony then chimed in, saying the only thing he ever boxed was oranges. Laughter filled the room, diffusing the tension. These are just a few party highlights; there were numerous tales, and they continued even after high school. We had dances and pizza nights, and sometimes we just roamed town in my 1949 Buick. There are many stories about that car and its wild driver, some exaggerated. Although driving around the house or on sidewalks hitting garbage cans might be embellished details. Football games took place on Saturdays, and we almost always won, except once when we were missing players and recovering from a long party the night before.

When we approached the South game, winning was the only option if we aimed to secure the divisional championship. Saturday night was dedicated to celebrations that often continued into Sunday morning, but mass was also important, so we had to plan when would attend Sunday services in advance. Back then, masses were only held on Sundays, but not Saturday evenings except for a midnight Mass every Saturday night at the airport. So, we attended midnight mass at the airport to ensure we wouldn't miss mass on days when we wanted to party late into the night. Following mass, an early breakfast awaited us at the famous diner on Franklin Avenue, next to the greasy Carol's hamburger place. For a dollar, you could enjoy eggs, bacon, home fries, orange juice, and coffee. The diner was bustling even at 2am, with drag races on Franklin Avenue right in front of it.

Once, I brought a six-foot ladder to the middle of Franklin Ave and used it to start races before the light turned green. Races started at the red light in front of Carol's and ended with a roar. The Saturday night action was invigorating. Given the late night, attending Sunday morning mass seemed improbable. I would inform my mom that we went on Saturday night to avoid being woken up on Sunday morning.

I slept in on Sunday and hung out with friends in the

evening. Mondays were reserved for catching up on sleep and recharging for the week ahead. I was ahead of my time, perhaps the pioneer of the four-day workweek. But this Monday held exceptional significance due to the impending championship game on Saturday. I made it in time for my favorite class, hot lunch. Attending classes wasn't my top priority in high school, the driving force for my education was sports. If not for playing a variety of sports (end in football, forward/center in basketball, and right-fielder in baseball) I might have considered dropping out, a choice that would have been a mistake. My books remained pristine in a locker provided by the school for the term. Opening them would have meant studying, writing reports, or working on class projects, which would have taken time away from practice, fraternity meetings, dates, hanging out, and parties.

Nevertheless, this Monday was exceptional, as everyone buzzed about the upcoming float parade, bonfire pep rally, and the game. I aimed to be on time for lunch so I could enjoy some of the festivities before practice.

Walking through the halls after my usual double portion of hot lunch on my way to study hall, I passed by a few of the advanced classes I had taken last year at my dad's request. I was so glad to have gotten back into my comfortable slower learning track classes which had lower expectations so I could coast by under the radar and enjoy my last year of high school focusing on sports. I embraced this situation since it meant less time devoted to schoolwork, avoiding class as much as possible, but still finding a way to pass.

Before junior year, I had originally been placed on the slower learning track, a fact of which I wasn't initially aware. There were signs of this differentiation; in seventh-grade English, I was asked to read aloud from the textbook. Not having my book with me, I stated that we didn't read. The teacher continued with the reading and never asked anyone to read aloud again. I recall thinking, "That was easy, I wonder if other classes will be similar."

Then my father, and his 155 IQ, decided that I should take all college entrance courses. After setting up a meeting with the class guidance counselor, Mr. Jonathan Monastery, we discovered he was the same person who administered a test to determine our career aspirations years earlier. Supposedly, those tests scientifically indicated our future paths and my results indicated I would become a forest ranger. I had no inkling of what a forest ranger did; wandering in forests held no appeal, and I favored athletic fields. Mr. Monastery placed me in slower learning track classes, likely influenced by some forgotten test results suggesting slower-paced learning. This was fine with me since I was focused on sports. But that was not ok with my father. When he finally met with the guidance counselor, Mr. Monastery needed nursing assistance to recover from a fit of laughter. My father's request for me to take all college entrance courses was so amusing that Mr. Monastery fell off his chair in amusement. However, my dad was persuasive, and for my junior year, I found myself in advanced Math, advanced Chemistry, and regular-paced English, History, Social Studies, and Health classes. These replaced my previous slower learning track courses in Art, Woodworking, and Study Hall. I received new books with homework assignments and that was how I ended up sitting at the back of the classroom alongside Dan Prener, the smartest kid in school. Thanks, Dad!

Passing by Mrs. Gold's Advanced Math class which I had taken in junior year because of my dad's intervention, I recalled a funny memory of when Mrs. Gold questioned me about a particular previous absence stating that I would be receiving a zero for that class. Surprisingly, I thanked her and explained my rationale. I reminded her that the single zero sounded good compared to the four zeros I received the last time I was in her class. One for unfinished homework, one for a quiz, one for speaking out, and one for altering Dan Prener's proof. Mrs. Gold didn't appreciate my response and informed me that I was on track to be the first person in New York State history to receive a negative mark on a report card. I told her that wouldn't reflect well on her, as I intended to pass the Regents exam. She laughed and said, "Good luck with that." Our exchange was interrupted by someone sliding a toy set of chattering teeth across the floor that stopped at her desk just as the class was about to end. The eruption of laughter continued as the bell rang and everyone left without Mrs. Gold catching the student responsible for the prank. Despite taking yet another zero and eventually failing the class and having to repeat it in summer school, I still look back on it with good memories like this which was the most memorable Math class of junior year.

I then walked by a Chemistry class taught by the eccentric

professor Mr. Snow who I also had the pleasure of entertaining during my junior year, again thanks to my dad. He was
a Canadian who kept students engaged by randomly tossing
small novelty explosive balls onto the floor, he said, to demonstrate spontaneous combustion. This sure kept us awake in his
chemistry class. Despite my sporadic attendance, Mr. Snow
recognized me and inquired about my absences from Monday
morning classes. I responded by suggesting that I deserved
extra credit for conducting a scientific experiment at home on
those mornings. Intrigued, he asked for an explanation. I
shared that regardless of Sunday night's indulgences or late
hours, I would always place my science book under my pillow
before passing out. This experiment aimed to prove or
disprove the theory of osmosis. Mr. Snow questioned my
experiment's progress, and I replied that it was too early to
determine. I assured him I would present my findings by the
term's end. Judging by my final grades, I can definitively state
that osmosis, as hypothesized in this experiment, was unequiv-
ocally disproven. After explaining my osmosis experiment to
the class, I then proceeded to conduct my own chemistry
experiment. I formed a concoction of random substances
whose properties I didn't understand just to see what would
happen, resulting in a noxious cloud of gas being released into
the classroom. Mr. Snow set aside his explosive balls and
inquired about the chemicals I mixed to elicit this reaction. I
explained that I was experimenting with new compounds.
Approaching the mixture he suddenly exclaimed, "You lunatic!
These compounds produce a toxic gas when combined!" He

shouted for everyone to evacuate while opening the windows. Fortunately, my evacuation from the class was permanent, and my foray into college-level experimentation concluded. The silver lining of the dissipating cloud of chemical gas was an early departure from class, sparing me from ever being welcome back to Advanced Chemistry class again.

Passing those classrooms brought back enjoyable memories, and also made me feel so good not to have to take those classes again. Study hall awaited; a chance for an afternoon nap to sleep off my extra-large lunch and leave rejuvenated for afternoon football practice.

Passing the elevator from the third floor, I saw George disembarking, moving quickly with the aid of crutches. I stopped to inquire about his well-being and destination. He responded with a smile, expressing gratitude for asking. He shared that he was doing well and had an excellent day. He had just come from the library, conducting research for an English class. I looked at George and told him they were looking for him, grinning. He asked who, puzzled. I replied, "Two squirrels looking for a nut." George, with a great sense of humor, burst into laughter. It was heartening to see him laugh despite his physical limitations. He asked about my plans, and I mentioned football practice, one of my favorite classes. His laughter followed me as I waved goodbye, thanking him and hoping for a good outcome.

# 9

# TUESDAY: GOING TO CLASS

D ad didn't need to wake me up this morning; the excitement of the upcoming activities ensured I was wide awake. I had a restful night's sleep and was eager to get to school. North High was buzzing with preparations for the big game, float parade, and bonfire. After a quick breakfast, I hopped into my trusty '49 Buick, a vehicle that always started up no matter how much I pushed its limits. My first stop was Bernie's place, followed by a swing around the block to pick up Joe Corea. Next, I left Malverne and headed over to Valley Stream to collect Tony and Steve Due. It was a rarity that I managed to pick everyone up on time. Tony and Steve, living near the high school usually chose to walk, unwilling to conform to my sometimes-erratic schedule. I parked the car in the student lot adjacent to my favorite place, the gym. The guys were already immersed in discussion about the upcoming weekend and the imperative to win the championship. We exchanged thoughts about being televised for the first time as the "game of the week." Typically, this title was reserved for major city teams, making us wonder how they could pass up the opportunity to broadcast the iconic North-South rivalry. The contest would take place on neutral turf, accompanied by a float parade, marching bands, bonfire, pep rally, and thousands of fans lining the roadways and the stadium, all witnessing the grandeur of the parade and the intensity of the game. We were confident that victory was ours.

With the guys heading inside, I took a moment to inspect my car and ensure all my tools were in the trunk. Over time, I found myself in a few fender benders in this parking lot. I always carried a small sledgehammer, a pry bar, a large screwdriver, and a hefty pair of vise grips—my toolkit for addressing any damage I might cause to other cars, or they might inflict upon mine. Occasionally, I would unintentionally back into another car that had parked behind me. In such cases, I'd simply crawl beneath their car's fender and gently hammer out the dents from the inside. Sometimes a pry bar or large screwdriver was required to fix the dents. Thankfully, these older vehicles posed no issue due to their robust steel construction. Confident in my preparedness for any parking lot mishap, I locked up the car.

Entering homeroom, Mr. Disend greeted me warmly, pleased to see my punctuality. He mentioned the importance of my being on time for football practice later that day, emphasizing the extensive preparations required for the game on

Saturday. Assuring him that I was prepared for anything the week held, I sensed his knowing smile before the bell marked the beginning of my day. My journey commenced with a visit to my favorite class, Physical Education. This early workout would energize me for the rest of the day, and I planned to conclude with a refreshing shower before heading to English class. I held a silent hope that my teacher wouldn't single me out today; I hadn't managed any reading over the weekend due to my packed schedule. Thankfully, Mr. Schmidt had never doled out a failing grade on my report card, a courtesy some other teachers had overlooked. Although I'd admit that I occasionally deserved a failing mark, my focus now was to pass English IV and ensure I graduated.

As I walked towards gym class, I spotted a group of students outside the principal's office, their animated chatter suggesting that a fellow classmate was in trouble. It turned out that one of my fraternity brothers, Al, had called the school posing as his father and said, "This is Mr. Larsen, I am sick and I won't be in today," attempting to excuse his absence for the day. Al's amusing charade earned him time in the assistant principal's office. I recalled how Al used to frequent the Blue Lounge Bar and Grill on Franklin Avenue in Franklin Square, often enjoying some beer and a burger. On his eighteenth birthday, we all joined him to celebrate taking advantage of the legal drinking age which was eighteen years old at that time. During that celebration, the bartender, who was also the owner, asked Al which birthday he was celebrating. Al turned around with a big grin on his face and said, "My eighteenth!"

The bartender looked at Al and asked, "How can that be, you've been coming here for years?" Al said in reply, "You're right, I've been coming here since I was sixteen," then everybody started laughing like crazy.

I could smell the unique aroma radiating from the locker room as I was approaching my favorite class, gym! Our gym teacher, Mr. Pohl, was known for his straightforward demeanor and his insistence on adherence to the rules. As I entered the class, Mr. Pohl was searching for the dodgeballs he planned to use for class that day. Little did I know that some of the guys had managed to kick all the dodgeballs onto the roof before Mr. Pohl emerged from his office to start class. Despite his usual composed nature, Mr. Pohl's face turned red, and his temper flared as he demanded, "Where are my balls?" The situation spiraled into hilarity, with all of us breaking into fits of laughter. One brave soul admitted that the balls were on the roof, which we had inadvertently launched up there when we were tossing them around before class not realizing our own strength. Mr. Pohl knew exactly who was responsible; he didn't need a list to identify the culprits. The class was canceled, but we had to wait until the bell rang for the next class to begin. Later, a custodian was tasked with retrieving the scattered balls from the roof, ensuring that we could play dodgeball during our next gym class.

As the bell signaled the transition, I moved to my next class: Mr. Schmidt's English class. The music room on the way was strangely silent, which I later discovered was due to a prank. Some mischievous students had relocated Mr. Bennett's piano down a hallway, stashing it in a storage closet. When the custodians denied moving the piano, Mr. Bennett's quest to locate it further added to his already troubled day. Matters escalated when he entered the auditorium to practice with the orchestra and discovered paper-stuffed tubes and trumpets. The revelation of this escapade took place during practice, and his exasperated shout reached my ears before I proceeded to class. Mr. Bennett's piano-playing abilities were also a source of income, as he performed at nightclubs to supplement his earnings. Our discovery of this fact occurred one night when we visited the Sands Club. Watching Mr. Bennett expertly tickling the ivories, we gave him a standing ovation. His surprise at seeing high school students under the age of eighteen at the club prompted a lighthearted agreement to keep his nightlife endeavors a secret. We cherished the night's memory and his lively performance.

I had heard rumors of a significant English test scheduled for today, but fortunately, my class with Mr. Schmidt was exempt. Roger, however, was faced with passing the test to secure his spot in the upcoming Saturday game. Bernie took it upon himself to assist Roger by orchestrating a system where Roger could compare his answers with Bernie's during the test. This method ensured Roger could verify his responses against Bernie's to avoid any mistakes that might cost him the game. Bernie had always been an exceptional English student, consistently earning excellent grades throughout high school. In contrast, Roger excelled in carpentry and football but struggled with academics. Bernie cleverly positioned himself to the left, while Roger mirrored the movement to the left, creating an effective communication channel. Bernie leaned back, and Roger leaned forward—this synchronized routine lasted for the duration of the test. Roger's contented smile indicated that the plan was working flawlessly. When the teacher announced the end of the test, and the requirement to put down pencils and submit papers, Roger, engrossed in his answers, implored for a few more minutes to complete the exam saying, "We're almost done." The teacher's stern response demanded immediate submission of test papers. Surprisingly, they both passed, leading us to believe that their rapport with the teacher had played a role in this outcome.

Reflecting on Roger and Bernie's test predicament, I couldn't help but wonder if Mr. Schmidt had planned an English test for our class that day. The possibility of failure and the subsequent exclusion from Saturday's game nagged at my thoughts. Unlike Math class, if I skipped English class I wouldn't receive a zero, but I questioned whether skipping could result in being sidelined from the game. The dilemma bore an uncanny resemblance to Shakespeare's famous line: "To be or not to be." In my case, it was "To be in class or not to be in class." Shakespeare must have understood the gravity of such decisions when he penned those words. I contemplated his potential academic performance while traversing the halls on my way to class, contemplating whether to attend or not.

Tony descended the stairs from the second floor just as I was making my way to English class on the first floor. He had just concluded his health class and was still chuckling as he caught up to me. Tony had a penchant for enjoying health class, an appreciation that I only grasped much later in life. I inquired about the source of his amusement, but he struggled to respond immediately, laughter still seizing his speech. Eventually, he managed to convey the anecdote: Richie Barone had stumped the health teacher by responding with a protracted silence when asked about the consequences of sperm meeting egg. With a satisfied grin, Richie's reaction and his expressive sigh of, "Aaaahhh," brought the class to an uncontrollable fit of laughter. A quick chat with Tony revealed that this incident had occurred during Mr. Bennett's piano removal caper, temporarily relieving me of my musings as I arrived at Mr. Schmidt's English class. He greeted me warmly, and I felt a sense of relief knowing that no test awaited me today. Unlike Hamlet's soliloquy, which revealed his tragic flaw of indecision and inaction, my decision was clear: I would attend class and avoid a fate akin to Hamlet's demise.

Exiting the classroom with my head held high and no academic blemishes, I realized it was time to pause for a day. Avoiding overexertion, I decided to pay a visit to Marilyn's place, where the garage served as a hub for float construction using papier-mâché. The girls, eager to complete their float for the upcoming parade, had opted to skip school. However, this truancy came to the attention of the assistant principal's truant officer, leading to an unexpected visit to Marilyn's front door. Our strategy was simple: we hid in the garage, hoping that the officer would leave, unaware of our presence, thus allowing the float-building process to continue unhindered. The parade was a spirited competition among different grades, each crafting their own float. Judged by the faculty, the winner would be announced at the game, following the parade. Our evasion proved successful as the assistant principal eventually departed, believing the house to be empty. With renewed dedication, work resumed on the float. Having bid farewell to my friends, I made my way back to school.

One class remained on my agenda for the day—an art class with my wonderful girlfriend, Sue. Stepping into the classroom, I spotted Sue sitting by the window. Her smile radiated warmth, lighting up my face as I responded with a hearty wave. She was the highlight of my school day, rivaling only the excitement of football, which would follow the academic portion. Typically, we weren't permitted to sit together, but today's special project allowed us to collaborate at a spacious table. Strangely, despite attending North High together since seventh grade, Sue and I hadn't noticed each other until this year's art class. She later revealed that she knew about me during my time with Roberta in tenth grade, as her awareness of me stemmed from our shared connection. My active presence in school sports and local news coverage made me somewhat public. However, I had no inkling about Sue's interests, her companions, or her experiences throughout those years. Only upon receiving the yearbook did I discover that she had dated Richard, an older student previously. Showcasing her artistic humor on the art page of the yearbook, Sue drew eyeglasses and the phrase "I only have eyes for you," which included her name in one lens and Richard's name in the other lens of the glasses. I later learned that we had shared the chemistry class I was in briefly, though I had failed to notice her presence because I was too busy mixing random concoctions of chemicals and as a result getting kicked out of the class before too long. Despite my musings on our past, our current connection grew stronger, and our shared experiences cemented our bond. Watching scary movies on Thursday nights, a tradition initiated by Sue, became one of my cherished activities, providing us a chance to unwind after demanding school days. This newfound shared interest became a regular highlight of my week, offering a welcome reprieve.

With the school bell marking the end of the academic day, I prepared to transition into the realm of after-school sports. Football practice beckoned, with the impending big game on Saturday demanding our focus. Sue and I strolled out together, engaging in conversation before parting ways. Aware of my impending practice, we shared a goodbye kiss, mindful of the limited time to drive her home. A call or a post-practice visit was in the cards if energy permitted. As practice loomed, I mentally braced myself for the forthcoming football session.

## 10

## WEDNESDAY: MY GIRLFRIENDS

This morning I had to get up early and be on time because my girlfriend Sue Zanto wanted me to pick her up and talk to me before school. I had no idea what this would be about, but recently we've been getting along well so I thought it had to be a good thing. Thinking back as I drove over to Sue's house on the other side of town in Valley Stream, I never understood why I had any girlfriends in my life since I was always shy when it came to talking to girls.

When I was eight years old in the third grade, there was Jody. She was one of my sister's first friends when we first moved into Malverne in 1947. She lived around the corner from us in a big white farmhouse that had a coal bin and cast-iron stove in the basement used to heat the house. We were going to get married someday as two eight-year-olds would dream. She had an older brother Bobby and a sister Carol who much later in life went out with my uncle Dave. It's funny how certain little things like this stand out as vivid memories later in life. We drifted apart as I got to make other friends in the neighborhood with whom I would play sports in the streets until our parents would call us in for supper.

A perfect example of how shy I was around girls was when at twelve years old I had such a crush on one of my sister's close friends who lived on the same block a few houses down, Pat Everly, who was one year younger than my sister and I. Jody, Pat and Linda were very close friends so I would see Pat around a lot. I saw Pat as gorgeous, smart, talented, and a real tomboy because she did all the things boys would do like play sports, wrestle, climb trees, or just horse around. She played

| Jody

the violin and I used to walk past her house to listen to her practice even though I never knew any of the classical music songs she would be playing. She had an athletic build with long dark black hair and seeing her beautiful smile up close would make my heart pound out of my chest. Sometimes I thought I would melt because of the chills that would run down my back.

I saw Pat often from the time we moved into Malverne when I was five years old until I was eighteen years old, graduating from high school. The Everlys had moved into their home in 1946, just before my family and I moved into Malverne in early 1947. It may have been because Jody and I were going to get married that I wasn't origi- nally interested in Pat at that time. I guess the hormones started to kick in at age twelve when I realized that I liked girls in a very new way, but I was afraid to start expressing those feelings just yet. Pat, Linda, and I would sometimes play golf in the hallway of my house just putting the golf ball down the long

| Pat

hallway which ran from the kitchen to the living room. When the ball would roll to the right because the house was leaning that way, we laughed. I was so shy and nervous around Pat because she had a smile that would light up the world around me. It was easy to make her laugh and she was always fun to be around, but I didn't get the courage to tell her how she made me feel until 50 years later.

When we were in the ninth grade, she started going out with Lou Martorello. The couple, both mature for their ages, would walk down the street behind my house very happily holding hands. I would watch them go by from my backyard and smile happily for them both seeing how in love they were and how perfect they seemed for each other. One evening as teenagers, Lou picked up Pat in his car and they parked in a quiet spot to be alone and make out in the back seat. A policeman came over and tapped on the window to see if everything was ok because the windows were fogged up and they were parked on a street where nobody recognized the vehicle. Even though they answered the knock right away and were fully clothed, the policeman was tough on them, took their names and addresses, and said he was going to send a letter to their parents. Being young and worried about what their parents might do, they changed their plans that summer and made sure they got to the mailbox every day before their parents did, but letters from the police officer never arrived at either house. Pat and Lou have been happily married ever since.

| Barbara

As a fourteen-year-old in the eighth grade, I had my second crush on a classmate named Barbara Cohen. Her smile was so beautiful that I couldn't keep my eyes off of her. But I was also so shy that I would look at the ground or turn my head in another direction to hide the fact that I liked her any time she would look my way. Finally, I thought I could break the ice by offering to walk her home from school and carry some of her books. What amazed me about Barbara was her ability to maintain honor roll grades while playing more sports than I did. I was a three-sport athlete, but she played four sports: volleyball, basketball, bowling, and tennis all while still maintaining her high academic marks.

Then one day I got up the courage to ask her out on my first ever real date, a sock hop in the gymnasium. She said yes and we always had a great time together because she was fun to be with, had a great sense of humor, and boy could she dance! Unfortunately, sports were my first love so my life in high school revolved around my sports schedule and I stopped seeing her. She thought I was upset with her which was never the case as she could do no wrong in my eyes. I should have explained that it was all my fault and apologized for not being more upfront with her in the first place, but I was only fourteen years old, so I was too young to realize that expressing how I felt would've been the best course of action. I guess she didn't hold a grudge because upon graduating she wrote in my yearbook, "I hope we can be friends always." We got exactly what we wished for, remaining friends forever, still to this day. Though we live in different parts of the country, we stay in touch via text and e-mail, we talk by phone sometimes, and I will always love Barbara like a sister.

In tenth grade, there was Roberta "Bobbie" Natalie, a cheerleader who played sports, was very athletic, and a lot of fun to be with. She let it be known that she liked me which made it much easier for me to ask her out. On many occasions over the next few years, Bobbie and her squad would be cheering on our team from the sidelines, so we got to see a lot of each other over the next couple of years. Her mother had a strict rule which forbade her from having visitors over after school because both of her parents were working. Full disclosure, I was never informed of the rules, however, it wouldn't have made a difference... if Bobbie asked me to come over, I would be there! One afternoon at Bobbie's house, we were

| Bobbie

studying science: the effects of kissing and the rise of the temperature in the human body. This was a fun, firsthand way to study science up close and personal. No book could describe the changes and feelings in one's body during this type of firsthand experience. If school learning involved experiments like this, my attendance record would have skyrocketed. The exchange of kissing may not sound exciting, but for two young teens, the feeling was utopia. We decided to conduct this experiment in her kitchen where we could get a drink of ice water to cool things off on this very warm day which our experiment made feel even hotter.

Then suddenly, her aunt unexpectedly arrived at the front door! Bobbie told me to go hide while she answered the door, so I ran upstairs and hid in one of the bedrooms. Bobbie let in her aunt, and they exchanged greetings and talked for a while until her aunt finally left and went to her car. Whew, a bullet dodged, or so I thought. Hearing Bobbie saying goodbye as the aunt left, the front door closed, and I took a quick look out the window. As my luck would have it, she happened to look up at the window at the same time and saw the top of my head quickly disappear below the window as I ducked. Why did I look out the window I thought to myself?! Bobbie's aunt quickly returned inside visually upset like she just caught a burglar. She came flying back into the house galloping up the stairs two at a time and sprinted down the hall to the bedroom where I was hiding. She didn't see me at first, so she hurried around the bedroom looking everywhere for the intruder she had seen through the window. She searched under the bed and behind the drapes to no avail, but she knew I was there so she didn't give up. Then, she finally found my hiding spot when she slid open the closet door just like an elevator. Standing face to face with her very distressed aunt, I smiled, looked her straight in the eyes, and said "Going down," like an elevator attendant!

I usually say the first thing that comes into my mind without thinking. My lack of a filter has been an issue for most of my life. To make matters worse, I have no idea what words will come flying out of my mouth when I'm under pressure. During stressful moments, words just seem to formulate like a volcano and bypass my brain with any limits or censorship of any kind, though thankfully I do not curse or use foul language. I don't think this is what our forefathers meant when they wrote the First Amendment to the Constitution protecting freedom of speech. Rather, I think my wife sums it up best in one of the famous sayings she says when she is frustrated with me, "Open your mouth and outcome to the words."

My words are often as surprising to me as they are to the people around me who hear them. This time in Bobbie's closet, my words flabbergasted her aunt and not knowing what to say, she turned and yelled at Bobbie. I then went downstairs, apologized to Bobbie for causing her so much trouble, and left her home with her aunt hoping she wouldn't get in much trouble, which she didn't. It might have been my smile and clever remark that eased the tension of the situation and got Bobbie off the hook, but either way, Bobbie told the story to her friends and the story spread throughout the school. Before long, other kids would walk up to me with a smile and just say, "Going down!" Now looking back 50 years later, she says I should have hidden in the backyard, but I think you would agree hiding in the closet made for a much funnier story.

Then one day, the carnival was in town and I told Bobbie I was going to win her a large teddy bear in the baseball throw. Having played right field because of my strong, accurate arm, I believed I would easily win the game on the first or second throw. The big teddy bear would cost me almost nothing, like a gift for my girlfriend I thought. I went to the carnival and found the hit the cans off the platform baseball toss game. Inside the carnival booth, among the prizes winners could choose from sat a big teddy bear that I knew she would love. To make things better, the game only cost a dollar for three balls. So far, this plan was going to perfection, a chance to win a big, beautiful teddy bear for only a buck, by throwing baseballs. What a steal, I thought to myself as I confidently stepped up to the booth. So, after five dollars I'm sweating now and realize the game is either fixed or set up in such a way that makes it almost impossible to win. These carnival guys are no fools, they arranged the games in their favor percentage-wise, just like the way slots in Las Vegas are programmed. With just two dollars left, I start to focus on these barrels and why they aren't all going off the platform for my prize. On my sixth dollar, I experiment with my three throws to set up exactly what I'm going it do with my seventh and last dollar. I give the man my last dollar, say a prayer, and throw as hard as I can on the first two throws but still no prize. Then on my third and final throw, I hit them in the only place that will take down all the barrels. Hallelujah, they all came tumbling off the platform and that big teddy bear was mine to bring to my girlfriend! I excitedly went over to see Bobbie that evening so I could give her the prize I had promised. She loved the big teddy bear and gave me a big kiss. She then wondered aloud what we should name him, and I said without missing a beat "Bankruptcy." She then asked me why I chose such a strange name for the teddy bear, so I explained that the game took all my money, and I was bankrupted trying to win it for her. Well, that got me a big hug and a kiss so the seven dollars I spent was well worth it.

Bobbie and I always had a good time together, but being in the tenth grade and not wanting to get into a more serious relationship at just fifteen years old, I just stopped seeing her and would avoid her at various functions if she was also in attendance. I just didn't know how to say what I was feeling or what else I should do to end the relationship. She did nothing wrong, but I didn't want to hurt her by continuing to stay in a relationship that I could not commit to as passionately as she could.

In my life, I have always found that things work out for the best. I have always trusted in God, and in my whole life, I have only missed Sunday Mass on purpose two times when I decided to go bowling instead. I felt so guilty and sorry, that I never made that same mistake to miss Mass intentionally ever again. God has been so generous with His love for me over the years in my journey through life, that it would take a lifetime to count all of the great blessings He bestowed upon me. The breakup with Bobby was no exception. Richie Barone, my fraternity brother came over to me one day in the hallway at school and asked me if I was going out with Roberta. I told him that we were no longer seeing each other, so then Richie asked me if it would be okay if he asked Roberta to go out on a date with him. I asked why he wanted to go out with Bobbie and he just said he had always liked her. I told him that he should go ahead and ask her out, but not to mess around with her feelings because she was having a hard time getting over what had just happened with me. I loved Roberta as a friend and didn't want her to get hurt in a bad relationship, so it made me feel better when Richie promised that he would always treat her well. They dated through high school, married a couple of years later, and had three beautiful daughters. Richie's air-conditioning/refrigeration business took off and he built a beautiful house out on Eastern Long Island for himself, Bobbie, and their family where they lived happily ever after just like a fairytale.

Now arriving at my girlfriend Sue's house, I got out of the car, knocked on the door and her mom answered saying, "Good morning, Ray." I smiled and said, "Good morning to you Mrs. Z. Is Sue ready to go?" Mrs. Zanto said that Sue would be down in a minute and while I was waiting, Sue's younger sister Linda who was in the tenth grade asked if she could come with us.

| Sue

Normally I would have been glad to take Linda with us, but this time keeping in mind that Sue wanted to talk with me this morning, I told Linda that she would have to check with her sister. Sue then came down, and along with Linda who had gotten permission to come with us, we all headed to the car.

Figuring that the subject of our talk wasn't that serious, I was relieved that I wouldn't be in any trouble with my girl-friend to start this day. Sue and I kissed good morning and then she told me to make sure that I came over to her house the following night at 8pm so we could watch our usual Thursday night Boris Karloff's Horror Series TV show together, which I had missed the prior week. She loved watching that show and snuggling up on the couch with me while the monsters attempted to scare the daylights out of the show's viewers. It was not a show that I enjoyed, but I was young and in love, so I would rarely miss an opportunity to be near Sue, hold her tight, and make her happy which made me feel really good too. Any excuse to be with Sue one night a week after school was a good one for me! I promised that I wouldn't miss tomorrow night for the world and told her I'd be there, ready to be scared. At first, being shy, I sat on one end of the couch and Sue on the other. Later in our relationship, her mother told me how cute my shyness and innocence were when she would watch me let Sue take her seat first, and then I would sit on the other side of the couch. I think perhaps Sue started to like to watch scary movies with me so that she would have a good reason to come to my side of the couch and cuddle up with me. After a few weeks of gradually moving closer, we got used to cuddling up on the couch and did so for most of our senior year.

Even though we were together at the time, we didn't go to our prom because Susan had gone to the junior prom with her previous boyfriend Richard, and she didn't want to go again in senior year. Richard was a year older than us, and he had since graduated and went into the Army by the time we were seniors. She never talked about him, and I never asked any questions. Their relationship had ended for some reason, but I wasn't interested in finding out the details. Back then in the '50s proms were no big deal. They were held in the gym like a fancy sock hop only with beautiful decorations, a live band, shoes, suits for the guys, and fancy dresses for the girls. I didn't own a suit, and skipping the prom would save my parents' money which we didn't have a lot of anyway, so I gladly agreed with Sue when she suggested that we pass on the prom. Instead, we decided to meet the gang at the beach afterward. There were no nightclubs or fancy restaurants in our area during the '50s, so the Jones Beach Boardwalk was my friends' after-prom party location of choice. I picked up Sue, we rode around, made out for a little while, and then headed to the beach to meet up with the other couples coming from the prom. It was a cool and windy night, so prepared always, I whipped out a blanket to cover Sue. We snuggled up, watching and listening to the waves crashing onto the darkened shoreline, and looking at the stars above which always looked even brighter in the sheer black nighttime sky at the beach.

Sue and I dated on and off for five years before we realized it wouldn't work between us. We discovered that neither one of us loved each other enough to make the difficult sacrifices that would be required, or to endure through the many difficult challenges life would have in store for us ahead if we decided to stay together forever. Sue wanted to be the most important thing in my life, and I wanted her to trust that she was my number one priority. But I had many friends and still played football, softball, and two different bowling teams on top of bowling for money late into the night once a week. She had only a few close friends and not too many activities outside of work, so she needed more of my time than I could give. Realizing that our two visions for the relationship didn't quite align with each other, we decided it would be best to break up. I guess the real reason I stopped seeing Barbara, Roberta, and Susan was that I just wasn't ready for a serious relationship that had marriage on the horizon so early on in life. I didn't get serious about someone until late 1973, twelve years after high school when I met Lois who would become my wife. Looking back, I am happy that I waited until I felt ready to settle down before committing to a serious relationship because while breaking up with those special girlfriends was difficult at the time, things turned out for the best for us all in the end.

Writing about my love life and girlfriends reminded me of an English professor I once had when I was taking college classes later in life. He posed this very interesting question to the class; "Do you know why you married the person you married and not someone else along the way?" He described people falling in love and getting married in terms of internal biological clocks that tell people when the time is right for them to do certain things in life. If a couple is together and both internal clocks are ticking on the same timetable, then they will naturally get married and probably live a happy life together. So, in his opinion, it is the combination of the right timing of two biological clocks, rather than the combination of the right two individuals, that made for a successful marriage. While it felt so right to be with my ex-girlfriends, all of whom were, and still are wonderful people, our clocks just didn't synch up. I am glad that they each found someone else whose clock was ticking in rhythm with theirs and that they all turned out to have happy family lives. As for me, I am glad I found someone special whose clock was ticking on my timetable, even though my clock was set several years behind the clocks of most other people my age.

Finally, Susan, Linda, and I pulled into the North High student parking lot ready to go to school for the day. Linda got out and ran to meet her friends before going into class. I asked Sue if she just wanted to talk about coming over to watch TV, and she said that she just wanted me to know how important it was that we watch our show together the next night and that I must be on time. She grabbed me and gave me a big hug and a kiss to last the whole day. I kissed her goodbye, and then off to class we went.

# 11

## YEARBOOK LOVE LETTER

In high school, Sue and I shared a deep and passionate love for each other. Our senior year was a journey of ups and downs, but as it drew to a close, our bond had grown stronger than ever. Sue penned a heartfelt love letter in my yearbook on the final two green pages, encapsulating our year together and our aspirations for the future. Outside of my family, it stands as one of the most beautiful tributes ever dedicated to me. I was humbled by her eloquent words and the depth of her affection. I yearned to live up to the image she held of me, to be as remarkable as she believed I was.

*My Dear Ray,*
*It is very amusing that when I think back over the years and realize that we never really met each other until this year. I do remember when you were going out*

with Roberta and everyone said she was so lucky. I didn't understand why, but that was only because I didn't know you. When I think that you were in my Chem. class, I can just about laugh myself sick, because we never noticed each other. I'll never forget some of the silly things we did this year and how much trouble we could have gotten into (the day before the north-south game). But needless to say, I'm glad those wild times are over, (for me anyway).

I'll always be thankful to North High School for giving me many, many good times and things. The most important of which is you (and my diploma). Graduation isn't the end for us as it will be for others but only the beginning of new and more wonderful things.

I'll always be grateful to you for the good things you have introduced to me, (such as church, and other things which you know I never thought possible). I can only hope you feel the same way as I do. And though no one could (or would) deny that things didn't go very smoothly for us until recently. They have worked themselves out finally. It would take me ages to tell you what you mean to me and I think you know. But I will say that you are the kindest, most understanding, and dearest person in the world. You have a way about you that no one could compare to and I love you for it and many other reasons.

*Yours, Sue*

*P.S. I don't know how you put up with some of the things I do. But I hope you will never tire of it.*

As time went on, Sue married and was blessed with three beautiful children, while I eventually embarked on marriage and the joy of raising three wonderful children of my own. Our paths diverged after high school, leading us to unique and fulfilling lives. Despite the twists and turns, Sue and I maintained a steadfast friendship that endured through the years. Though I held onto my high school yearbook throughout the decades, it was only in the process of writing this book that I truly immersed myself in its contents. I used it as a resource for facts and details concerning various individuals and events. Rediscovering Sue's letter after all these years transported me back to the moments we shared and kindled a multitude of memories. But it also revealed new insights that I hadn't considered before.

I never knew that girls who were dating discussed their relationships so extensively with other girls. I can't help but wonder what they might have divulged. Upon reading Sue's reflections about my relationship with Roberta during our sophomore year, it seems that there are no boundaries in their conversations about relationships. In contrast, boys rarely, if ever, shared such matters. At least that was my experience, never participated in or overheard any such type of conversation.

I also didn't realize that Sue was in my Chemistry class. However, I assume this oversight stemmed from my limited time in the class, which was abruptly curtailed after the incident involving poison gas. Sue's statement about me enduring her quirks and actions is inaccurate. To clarify, she never exhibited any behavior that warranted patience or tolerance. Being with her was uncomplicated and enjoyable; we relished each other's company, and our relationship was marked by harmony. Any differences we had related more to my time commitments. Between sports and hanging out with friends, my schedule often left little time for her preference for spending time together alone with me.

During our high school years, Sue's family did not attend church regularly. Her mother was a non-practicing Catholic, while her father, originally from Wisconsin, was a non-practicing Lutheran. I appreciated accompanying Sue to church on Sunday mornings from time to time, as it was an experience she valued. Given that she hadn't been able to attend church with her family, I was pleased to share that experience with her and I was elated that she mentioned Church as one of the positive things she associated with me in her letter.

Reconnecting at our 40-year reunion brought us back in touch, and we exchanged a few emails thereafter. She even shared a picture with me, one I had never seen before: A snapshot of Artie and me standing in front of my 1949 Buick, all decked out following the North-South football game. The picture was taken outside her home, and receiving a copy of it was a pleasant surprise, albeit four decades after the fact.

My last email to Sue was sent shortly before she passed away. I encouraged her to communicate directly with God, offering heartfelt words in her own way. I assured her that He would forgive her for any transgressions and wrongdoings, regardless of the gravity, if she was sincerely repentant. I had no inkling that she was in the final stages of cancer when I sent that message. God's ways are often enigmatic to us, and we may not always understand His plans. However, His intentions are always rooted in our best interests. I sincerely hope that she found solace in connecting with God before her passing and finding peace from the torment of cancer that ultimately claimed her life at the age of 72, the same affliction that had taken her father when he was also 72 years old.

Sue remains in my prayers, alongside the other classmates who have passed on from this world. I feel their absence keenly, especially that of my dear twin sister, Linda.

# 12

## THURSDAY: A FULL DAY OF CLASSES

Wow, it was already Thursday morning, and there was so much to do before the big game. We had to paint the '49 Buck with all our fighting slogans. I needed the team for that. Yes, Dad, I knew what time it was and came down right away. I hurried downstairs, grabbed a piece of toast, and a glass of orange juice, and wished my dad a good day.

My mom had already left for work as an executive secretary for Mr. Sperry at Sperry Gyroscope in Lake Success. It is now Unisys, part of Honeywell after merging with Burroughs in 1986. My dad worked for them back in 1955 when it was an Aerospace Defense company. While working at that job, my father had attended some top-secret meetings in Washington D.C. at the Pentagon. I'll never forget when he came home from a particular trip to Washington when I was thirteen years old. He told me, "Don't worry about UFOs, they're ours." My dad was an industrial engineering consultant who worked for himself. Other companies looking to reduce their overhead and increase their productivity hired him for a short term to make recommendations to improve both. He had worked for both the government and private institutions. His focus was in the area of increased production, and he was home now because he was between contracts.

I headed out the back door to my car. I was going in on time and picking the guys up on the way in. I hopped into my car and headed over to my best and oldest friend's home, Bernie, just a few blocks over in the same town we both grew up in, Malverne. I pulled up in front of 34 Doncaster Road and honked my horn. Bernie came running out and said, "I can't believe you're here and even on time." I asked him if we were all set for the car painting on Friday with the team. He said, "Don't worry, I'll take care of all the small details. You have that bucket of bolts out in the parking lot, and I'll have the paint and the guys ready to go."

Then we swung around to Joe's house on the next block. Joe was new to us, as he had only moved here in the tenth grade, but what a great guy and a terrific teammate. Joe had been through a lot in his young life. He lost his mom when he was young. He had an older sister and himself with his biological mother and a younger brother with his new mom as his dad had remarried. Joe's dad had also moved a few times, upgrading the home after each move. His dad worked the night shift, and his mom worked the day shift. He got to see his mom at night and his dad in the afternoon and evenings. You would never know there were any major changes in Joe's life because he was always happy and upbeat. He was great to hang out with. I pulled up, honked the horn, and Joe came running out, smiling, thinking this was only a mirage since I was never on time.

Then it was off to Tony's house, who lived in Franklin Square on the other side of town near the school. We pulled up, and Bernie got out to go get Tony. After a few minutes, they both came out, both laughing. I said, "What's so funny?" They both said, "We're all together and on time. It's a miracle; anything can happen, a great sign for a win against South this weekend."

So now I looked at the gas gauge; it was, of course, on empty. I said, "Fellas, we've got to make a stop at the gas station." Back then, gas cost twenty-five cents per gallon and the going rate for reconstituted oil was twenty cents per quart. Everyone chipped in a quarter apiece, and we had enough to buy three gallons of gasoline and a quart of oil because this Buick burned a lot of oil. I parked my car in the student parking lot, and into school, we went. The guys were still laughing as we went to our homeroom class, all of us in disbelief that we had made it to school on time after staying out very late, and getting very little sleep, the night before.

My first class was earth science, and our class projects were due that day. We had to present the projects and give an oral report explaining the reason for the topic we chose and its scientific significance. I, of course, was called on first and asked for an extension for my presentation to Tuesday of next week. The teacher, Miss Earthly, knew full well that the odds of me turning in any project at any time were very high, if not impossible. She wanted to encourage me and said she would allow me this extension, but it would be graded with a ten percent deduction in points. If not presented on Tuesday of next week, I will receive a zero. I thanked her for her generosity and belief that I would turn something in. The next person she called was Lee Lasala. After having six weeks to work on the final science project, Lee proudly walked up to the front of the room and unrolled a large oak tag with the oak leaf taped to the center of it. He then clipped it to the front blackboard. In large black letters on top of the oak tag, the project was simply titled "Large Oak Leaf." When Miss Earthly asked Lee where the report was in a written and verbal form describing his exhibit, his reply was "It speaks for itself." Upon further questioning by Miss Earthly, Lee became frustrated and confused and finally questioned the teacher. "Did you want me to bring in the whole oak tree?" Which brought down the class with laughter. I thought to myself if the classes were this much fun, maybe I should come to school more often.

Walking to my next class on the first floor, I looked out the window and spied someone hanging out a third-floor window. Upon further observation, I noticed it was Steve Wildman. It looked like the teacher was trying to get him in the classroom before he fell. Now Steve was only halfway out the window, and there was no way he could fall unless Steve wanted to go all the way out the window, which, if you knew Steve, was not likely since he was on the football team and didn't want to miss any games due to injury.

At that time, the windows could open fully. Steve had figured out what to do when you received a failing grade on a test, and your classroom was on the third floor. He was putting pressure on the teacher to give him a makeup test by shouting, "I'm going to jump!" Naturally, Mrs. Easy, his teacher, was frightened and tried to coach him back with the promise of a makeup exam. Steve reluctantly accepted the offer, really hoping for a change in his mark. He feared his father would remove him from the football team if he brought home a failing mark, hence the unorthodox and urgent actions.

I was already tired after just one class, having gotten to school on time after picking up the guys. We were out late last night and didn't get much sleep. Some of the guys, not part of our group, had the ingenious idea of playing a prank on our biology teacher Mrs. Disend. They snuck into the school through the gym doors, which one of the guys had fixed so it wouldn't lock. Then they sneaked into the biology lab where dead frogs to be used for experiments were preserved in refrigerators. The guys took the frogs out, cut them open, took out their innards, and replaced them with fresh worms they had brought in with them. Then they sewed up the frogs and put them back in the refrigerator. You can imagine how excited they were to get to biology class that day. But it was they, the pranksters, who got the big surprise. Mrs. Disend was not in, so Mr. Disend, her husband, happened to be substituting for her in biology that day. Mr. Disend was a retired professional football player for the Green Bay Packers who would bang his massive hands and arms on the desk and declare that there would be no nonsense in his class. With that, the kids were ready to leave the room, but he said to be seated and started the class. The first experiment was to dissect the frogs and identify their insides.

Mr. Disend: homeroom teacher, coach and former Green Bay Packer

Now, they were thinking, "Holy crap, are we in trouble?" That's because Mr. Disend was also the football team's line coach. Some students came up and began to cut open the frogs. Then the worms, which were still alive, started to crawl out of the frogs. The kids who were cutting the frogs had no idea what was happening because they weren't part of the break-in the night before. Then all hell broke loose when Mr. Disend saw all the worms coming out of the frogs and crawling around the table. His face contorted in disbelief, his eyes almost bulging out of their sockets in astonishment as he forcibly demanded in a loud voice, "Who did this?" You could hear a pin drop in that room, with everyone hoping the bell would ring so they could escape the fury of Mr. Disend. They looked around and said, "We have no idea how anyone could do this. It's much too sophisticated for us to undertake." Luckily, he believed that another advanced class was responsible.

My next class was mechanical drawing with Mr. Fleming, one of my favorite classes. We had to design and draw the prints for a house. Mr. Fleming was a young teacher, well-liked, and one of my favorites. He cared about teaching but didn't put undue pressure on you. It was a laid-back atmosphere where he said, "Just do your best and don't worry about the grades." We had to draw the house to scale and then

Mechanical Drawing teacher Mr. Fleming

actually build one. In other words, one inch would be the equivalent of ten feet in scale. So, the house was 30 feet wide by 60 feet deep, but on this scale, it was just 3" x 6". When I finished building my house to scale, it didn't look like it would stand up, but somehow it did because there was no breeze from the windows in the classroom. Somehow, I managed to pass that class with the help of a very generous teacher in his grading system. He had a great sense of humor, as demonstrated in his comments in my yearbook: "We didn't learn much, but it's been fun."

One more class before lunch, Spanish One with Mrs. Lehman. I had some difficulty with the language, but not with the very good teacher. I spent four years in Spanish One, never advancing to Spanish Two, Three, or Four. Amazingly, many of the Spanish words stayed with me, and I used them in later years especially when working with people from Spanish-speaking countries. *Muchas gracias, Señora Lehman. ¡Aleluya!* Maybe osmosis does work; it just takes decades for it to manifest itself in my exceedingly sluggish brain.

Then it was off to the required Health class with Mr. Miele, our football coach. This course was only one semester, so I could take it twice in one year, which unfortunately I had to do since they gave me a failing mark the first time. This course was required to graduate. One of the girls, Sharon, in the class, thanked me for my funny comments in class. She said they kept her awake during this extremely boring class. Another girl, Joan Dini, stood up to make a presentation. I started with my funny comments, and this young lady, usually very quiet, snapped. She told me in a very forceful, loud voice that woke up the rest of the class to shut up! Well, that sure got my attention and everyone else's as she proceeded with her presentation without any further interruptions. I hope it was good, and she received a good mark. I wouldn't know because I was lost after she said her topic was the circulatory system.

Today, Mr. Miele was going to show us a film on the long-term effects of smoking. I wasn't a smoker since I had tried to be cool a while back and almost had an accident. While driving my car with my collar up and a cigarette on my lips, thinking I was cool, the smoke from the cigarette teared my eyes up and blocked my vision, almost causing an accident. I wondered how people could smoke with a cigarette or cigar in their mouths while driving a car. It was mind-baffling to me at the time. Now I wonder how women can put on an array of makeup while still driving, and I don't understand how they don't get into accidents. That incident was the last time I smoked while driving my car. Unfortunately, there were still a lot of kids in school who smoked, and this film was aimed at frightening them into giving up smoking. As the film began, it showed a person on an operating table in the hospital who had smoked all his life and now had lung cancer. The camera zoomed in on the man's chest as they cut it open and pushed apart his ribs to get at his cancerous lungs. Then they went in to cut part of his lungs out, and that's when some of the kids asked to leave the room. It was a brutal film that made the smokers in the room very nervous. They left and went outside to have a smoke to calm themselves down. The film did scare the smokers but not enough to make them stop. It had the opposite effect.

You should have seen all the cigarette butts by the tennis courts. Some of the kids who had no idea what tennis was all about but wanted to grab a smoke volunteered to go over and play tennis. The gym teachers were excited to see some students who would rather be in auto-mechanics playing tennis in the tennis area. Why the tennis area? Because it was the farthest from the school where people could smoke without getting caught. Most of the after-school parties were filled with smoke. At one particular party, I remember drinking and chain-smoking all night. Then the next day, I couldn't get out of bed all day not because of the booze, but because of all the cigarette smoke I inhaled the night before. I had gotten nicotine poisoning and felt ill for a few days until the poison cleared out of my system. What a great lesson I learned about the dangers of nicotine and how it can poison many of the body's systems besides the lungs so quickly and profoundly. Thankfully for me, that was the last time I ever smoked. Some people take years to realize that quitting smoking would be best, but unfortunately, by then much damage has been done and it is very difficult to stop because they are already hooked on nicotine which can be more addictive than heroin. I have lost close friends to that terrible drug and smoking, most of whom would still be here today if it weren't for cigarettes.

Speaking of parties, I took my girlfriend Sue to a fraternity party at one of the guy's homes where there was, of course, drinking, smoking, slow dancing, and several couples making out. Marilyn and Jo came to the party together with dates but found the party boring because of the guys they brought. So, they devised a diabolical plan to ditch their dates and come back later. It seemed like a small-minded, immature, but fun thing to do! There were a lot of cool people at the party, so they preferred to be loose rather than tied down to their dates. The guys were okay, but they were just someone to go to the fraternity party with. Now that Marilyn and Jo were there, they wanted to mingle with the crowd and dance with different single guys. So, they told the guys that they had to be home by ten o'clock and then the guys took them on the short walk home, only a block away from the party. The girls were hysterically laughing as soon as their guys left, and they didn't take a chance on returning thinking that the guys probably went back to the party themselves. I wondered why they left the party so early and didn't find out why they left so early until much later.

# 13

# FRIDAY: A TRIP TO THE PRINCIPAL'S OFFICE

At last, it was Friday, and now all the excitement of our biggest weekend was here. Dad didn't even have to call me that morning as I flew out of bed and got dressed. I rushed downstairs to wash up and grabbed a banana and some juice. It was time to pick up the guys and plan the day. I picked up Bernie first and asked him when he had arranged for us to paint the car. He said, "Get your bucket of bolts to the teacher's parking lot under the lights next to the shop right after practice." So, we coordinated our schedule for the day. Classes went on until 2:30pm, followed by football practice until 4:30pm, car painting from 4:45 to 6:00pm, and then setting up the bonfire from 7:00 to 9:00pm. At 9:30pm, we'd start the bonfire and pep rally with the football team, cheerleaders, and all the students. Wow, how exciting!

I swung around the block to pick up Joe who had moved

here when we were in the tenth grade. Joe's father was home during the days as he worked the night shift, but he was usually sleeping in the morning. Joe was one of the toughest guys I played football with. In one game, he got a concussion but played the whole game as if nothing had happened. He wouldn't say anything and definitely wouldn't come out of the game. We knew he had a concussion because he couldn't remember what happened in the game afterward. We were losing the game 6-0 at the time against New Hyde Park, and we wanted to go undefeated for the year. We had been unscored upon so far after three games, having upset powerhouse Wantagh High School 13 to 0, Malverne High School 26 to 0, and E. Rockaway 26 to 0. Having lost our unscored-upon record, we didn't want to lose our undefeated record as well.

I remembered that Wantagh game like it was yesterday because they had a big write-up in Newsday about how big and strong they were, thanks to their advanced weightlifting program. They were way ahead of the other schools that didn't have the same weight program as Wantagh High School. As our bus pulled up to the field, we had an indescribable feeling, something you can't put into words. We were all pumped up, adrenaline flowing, and the general feeling was that we were going to whip Wantagh from the starting whistle. Everybody had picked Wantagh to win, which only gave us more motivation. On the first play, our center, Steve Due, blocked their middle linebacker ten yards down the field, carrying him on his shoulder. It set the tone for the game as both our offensive and defensive lines dominated, bringing us victory.

Joe played defense, halfback, and safety and wasn't coming out, period. We were missing our starting center, Steve, who I had driven to a bus stop at the state border with his girlfriend, Pat. They were very much in love and were running away to get married. He had asked me for a ride to the bus, which I gave him. I wished them good luck as this was going to be a tremendous change in their lives, and high school life would be over. We were also missing all-league halfback Ken Halpern and one of our captains, all-league guard Bernie Havern, due to injuries.

This was our toughest game because due to a wild party the night before, the guys weren't in their peak playing condition. We had been at a house party at one of our teammate's homes. As teenagers, you don't realize how much you can drink without it affecting you the next day. The party had guys out with injuries and our star center running away to get married. Well, we sure did find out what drinking can do that day, as it became the only blemish on our record. The final score was VS North 0 New Hyde Park 12, the first time we had been scored upon and our first loss. But with a win against South tomorrow, we would be league champions, and that New Hyde Park game would only be a blur in our memories. We had to win the South game now.

Afterward, it was over to Tony's, which we called the "Gump." I don't know how he got his nickname, but he liked it. Now, Tony was one tough kid for a little guy. He had wrestled the New York State defending champion in the 125-pound weight class as a freshman and knocked him out as he swung his arm across his face to grab his shoulder; he hit his nose, and there was blood all over the place. They had to stop the match and declare his opponent the winner because of the infraction, which wasn't on purpose. His uncle Charlie, a Navy wrestling champion, was in his corner and trained Tony to be an outstanding wrestler. When Tony tried out for the football team, the line coach and retired Green Bay Packer Leo Disend looked at him and said, "The tennis courts are over there, son." Tony, not one to ever quit or back down, said, "Give me a shot, coach."

The coach said, "Okay, put on your helmet and let me see you get past those two guys," which were Roger Olsen and Dick Zucker, both over six feet and 230 pounds, our biggest linemen. I guess he thought the size of them would discourage Tony from even trying. He had no idea of the heart Tony DiBenedetto possessed or how quick he was. He got past those big guys, and the coach smiled and said, "Congratulations, you made the team." Tony wasn't playing now because he had broken his wrist, and it wasn't healing fast enough for him to get back on the field. It was killing him not to play with the guys, but there was nothing he could do about it. He came to all the practices to watch and encourage the team.

I pulled up into the students' parking lot, which was on the south side of the school next to the gym. We said goodbye and made plans to meet on the football field for our final practice for the big game. I arrived in homeroom early for attendance. Mr. Disend, my homeroom teacher, was happy and surprised to see me there early. He pulled me aside and told me that I had to report to Mr. Woods, the principal. So, I got up and walked slowly to report to the principal's office, not knowing what punishment awaited me. I hoped this wouldn't affect my playing in the biggest game ever at school. What infraction had they come up with? My mind started to race, thinking about all the pranks I had been part of, the classes I had cut, my lateness, or my general attendance. I wondered what excuse I could come up with. Having miraculously escaped being called to the principal all my years at North, you can imagine how astounded I was when the summons finally came the day before the championship game.

When I arrived at Mr. Woods office, he said, "Good morning, please have a seat." All this made me nervous, so I sat down and smiled, saying, "Good morning, Mr. Woods. How are you? You know, I've never been in your office before and always wondered just what you did here at North?" His response, with a smile, was, "To make sure all the students here get the best, well-rounded education possible in a safe, friendly environment." I replied, "Well, Mr. Woods, I give you an 'A' for this very friendly environment here at North, and I always feel safe whenever I'm on school grounds. I'm still working on the educational aspect and my performance in my various classes. I have always believed in a well-rounded education. To emphasize that in my senior year, I'm taking the following classes to prepare myself for life after North High School: Gym, Diver's Education, Basic Art, Mechanical Drawing, Health, Woodworking, English, and playing on the sports teams. This combination of classes will do the following for me in the future: Gym will keep me in shape, Diver's Education will reduce my insurance, save money, and allow me the independence to get around safely. Basic Art will enable me to draw my visions on paper to see more clearly. Mechanical Drawing will allow me to get a job as a drafter. Health class will provide me with the information to stay healthy by understanding the different systems in my body and how they work independently or together. Woodworking class will enable me to build furniture and someday my own house, coupled with the Mechanical Drawing class. English allows me to express my thoughts and beliefs on paper for others to read and understand. Finally, competitive sports will teach me teamwork, discipline, hard work, and what it takes to be a winner. Maybe someday I'll write a book about all this."

Mr. Woods looked at me with amazement and said, "No one has ever described the benefits of those courses the way you just did. If you, as a student, were a report card on me, I would have to give myself an 'A' in education." I thought to myself that this was just a line to soften the punishment that I believed was coming to me. I didn't believe one word of that until years later when I realized what a complete education I did receive at North, coupled with the experiences I had outside the classrooms and the friendships that were made during my days at North H.S. and after. Thank you very much, Mr. Woods.

Then, Mr. Woods started to explain the reason for my visit to his office that morning. My mind said to me, "Oh boy, here it comes." He advised me that the time had come for me to sign up for the draft. I had just turned eighteen at the start of the school year, and the law required that every male who turned eighteen had to sign up for the draft. I said that I wasn't interested in joining the Army because I had no desire to get up early, engage in the rigorous physical training that would be required, or eat army food! He replied that I had no option. When I asked about going to college, my less-than-stellar scholastic performance undoubtedly flashed across his mind as he smiled and wished me well with

| Mr. Woods

that, but I still had to sign up for the draft. I signed the papers, and Mr. Woods and I were both happy. He was happy for me to sign, and I was happy to avoid any punishment. So ended my only trip to the principal's office in all my days attending North High School.

I left the principal's office smiling and so relieved that I could continue my day and the weekend without being concerned about any distractions that could prevent the success of my mission. My mission was to do everything I could to enhance the bonfire, pep rally, the game, and parties on Friday night, Saturday, and Sunday. I had my schedule for the day, so it was off to the class I went to. Because of the extra time I spent in the principal's office, I missed most of my mechanical drawing class. I walked in, and the teacher, Mr. Fleming, asked why I was so late. I handed him my pass from the office and said, "Looks like I'll be in the army soon." He said, excitedly, "That's just the place for you. The Army has a way to straighten out guys like you without any difficulty. This is what they do!" He looked at me sternly and added, "Try coming to class once in a while; that would certainly be helpful in your case," with a grin. Mr. Fleming was a young teacher in his twenties and very nice. He was helpful, caring, and patient in his teaching. He made connections with students and was one of my favorite teachers. I loved being in his class, he had a great sense of humor and even laughed occasionally at some of my funny lines.

I had one more class before lunch period, so now it was off to English class. In the hallway, I met up with Richie Baron, my fraternity brother, who was always in a good mood. I asked him how it was going with Bobbie. He smiled and responded, "Couldn't be better; everything is great, thank you, Ray." Then off to class. Today, I would be in all my classes, so I couldn't get into any trouble this close to the weekend festivities.

I took my seat in the back of the classroom next to Big Bruce Nylund, who was truly big, standing at 6' 6" and weighing two hundred and fifty pounds. Whenever we ran out onto the football field, all the big guys would run out first, led by Bruce. The opposition would look at the size of our big guys, led by Bruce, and be very concerned. Sitting on my left was Roger Angrisani, another fraternity brother. He turned to me and asked if I could remember anything about the party we attended the other day. I responded, "Not much; why?" He said, "It brought back memories of the wild parties we had before freshman football games." I said, "The party was that good to bring back old memories?" He loved coming to Mr. Schmidt's English class because he could catch up on all the after-school parties and other activities that were happening or would happen. Then he could just fall asleep because he worked after school and nights in his family's restaurant. The teacher sometimes read from the textbook, which made it very easy to doze off. I fell asleep and was awakened by the bell, so now it was off to lunch to meet up with some of the guys in the cafeteria.

I smelled the aroma of food cooking from the lunchroom. Perfect timing as I headed to the lunchroom for a hot meal. They knew me behind the counter as I always remarked about what a great job they were doing serving this delicious food. I had learned early on that if you want something in life, it is important to be nice. It's not about what you know, but who you know, and you catch more flies with honey than with vinegar. The people in the cafeteria were always the most important people for me to get to know.

I found a seat next to Tommy Scibelli, an excellent athlete who was on the football team with me. He didn't play baseball or basketball with me on the high school teams but did outside of school. He ran on the school track team. He was much faster than me. He grew up without a father as his dad was killed in action on the beaches of Normandy, France, in 1944 when

Tommy was only one year old, and his brother Bobby was still in his mother's womb. His mom never remarried, so her dad, Tommy's grandfather, became his "acting father" to help raise the boys. They lived on the top floor of a house in a rented apartment. As kids, we never thought about any of this. He was one of the guys, a fraternity brother who liked to have fun and compete in sports. He seemed always happy and enjoying life as best a teenager could without a dad to be there for him when needed. His mom was there for him and was very understanding when we guys came around. She was easygoing and wanted us to have fun, but she had no idea about some of the parties we attended, until one night. The night after a fraternity party at Dominick's house, I had to push Tommy up the stairs to get him inside his home. I don't know what happened once inside because it was very late or early in the morning, but I'm sure Mrs. Scibelli knew some of the parties were wild. Tommy had too much to drink. Maybe it was because he had no father or because his girlfriend had moved to Ohio.

Sitting next to Tommy at the lunch table was Artie Schnitzer. Now, why Artie hung out with us is mind-boggling. Why, you ask? Well, for one, he was very smart and a member of the National Honor Society, the German Honor Society, and Sigma Beta Phi Hi-Y. We, on the other hand, had trouble just passing regular classes, much less honor classes. Most of us were in the fraternity and were on many of the school sports teams. He was in classes with all the "eggheads," discussing philosophy, trigonometry, and speaking German in his German class. Meanwhile, we discussed the party from the night before in English, barely recognized by our English teachers, much less any foreign language taken in school. Math? Well, just ask Mrs. Gold about my ability to comprehend simple formulas. So, on the surface, there was nothing in common between us. He did run cross-country track and played on the football teams when he was younger. We loved him because of his wonderful sense of humor, with the best hearty laugh that was contagious. He also could mix drinks with the best of them. When making his famous punch, he never diluted it with the punch juice. He always made sure to empty the whole bottle of booze into the punch bowl. When you had a few of Artie's drinks, you felt relaxed. One of the side effects was that you didn't remember too much of what happened the day after. Tommy and Artie were very close friends who lived close to each other and grew up together. They asked, "What time is the painting of your bomb today?" I informed them it was right after football practice. They said, "We'll be there; wouldn't miss this event for the world." I told Artie, "No punch bowl tonight; we have to be in good shape to face South on Saturday. You sure can make a big bowl after we win the game."

The lunch bell rang, and it was down the hall and up the stairs to the second-floor Art class for me, one of the few classes I didn't want to miss. Mrs. Silverman was always good to me and very generous with her grades as I earned, or let's say, was given, a 75 as my final grade. There was no homework, and I wasn't forced to do any projects, although there must have been some, but I just don't remember. I remember very little about the class and the homework because I was sitting next to my girlfriend, Sue, who had all my attention. We talked about what was happening after school and the plans we had together when we weren't in class. I walked into class, headed right to my seat, and hoped there were no pop quizzes or projects due that day. It was my lucky day as the teacher told us to break up into groups. Of course, I was going to go with my Susan. She was smiling and happy to see me this afternoon. This was the last class for the day, so we were both excited that the school day was almost over. She started to draw a picture of us at the bonfire, which was pretty good. She could draw, but I couldn't if my life depended on it, much less to do work worthy of art class. I scribbled, "I love you, see you at the bonfire tonight," on the paper, and we smiled at each other and spent the rest of the class talking about the drawing and the plans for that night.

As the school day was ending, the excitement was building for our big night ahead. We couldn't wait for school to be over so we could start getting ready for the bonfire, the pep rally, and then the big game tomorrow. Sue and I were looking forward to spending the evening together, and nothing could dampen our spirits. I had a feeling that this weekend was going to be one to remember. The final bell rang signaling the end of the school day, and the weekend we had all been waiting for was about to begin!

## 14

## PAINTING THE '49 BUICK

The afternoon classes flew by, and it was time for football practice. As I walked into the gym, I noticed the ABC news crew, including Marty Glickman, exiting. They had spent the day meeting with the coaching staff, going over player names and numbers, and discussing what to expect during the game. Seeing them leave our gym filled me with the realization and excitement that the big game was finally here. It was being televised for the first time in North High School's short history. Our class had started in seventh grade and was now finishing twelfth grade, having grown together through our very formative adolescent years. North High opened in 1955, and we graduated in 1961, making our high school years spanning from 1955 to 1961, free from war.

The TV coverage planned interviews with both coaching staffs from Valley Stream North and Valley Stream South before the game. They aimed to synchronize the timing of the float parade with the game's start for TV viewers. The game was scheduled for 1pm, but the float parade, featuring cheerleaders and the marching band, was set to begin two hours earlier. They hoped to catch the parade's end on television before kick-off, creating more excitement for fans watching at home.

The cheerleaders and the band needed to be on the field before the game began. This meant that the ABC camera crew had a lot of work ahead of them. They could film the parade before the game and showcase parts of it at halftime. During the game, they'd capture the sellout crowd by panning the stadium to enhance the second half's excitement. After the game, they'd conduct interviews with the winning team's MVP and some players, with some of these interviews airing live.

Marty Glickman dedicated his life to helping kids and worked with New York City high schools and the Police Athletic League, among others. He strongly believed in sports as a means of transcending divisions of race, class, and religion.

Marty faced the harsh reality of racism firsthand when he and his Jewish teammate, Sam Stoller, were inexplicably removed from the 400-meter relay race in the 1936 Olympics in Berlin, Germany. They were replaced by Jesse Owens and Ralph Metcalfe, who were not Jewish. It was widely seen as an American official's attempt to avoid offending German leaders at the time. The American team went on to win the relay race by fifteen yards and set a new world record.

Marty, the son of Jewish immigrants, attended James Madison High School in New York City and qualified for the 1936 Olympics at Syracuse University when he was just eighteen years old. He became the voice of the New York Giants football team during the 1950s and 1960s. This is why we were so thrilled and proud that he was covering our game. A high-profile sports celebrity and television announcer for the New York Giants was coming to our small town of Valley Stream from the big city of New York to announce our game on ABC television. WOW! How exciting!

Practice was light that day as the coaches didn't want anyone to get hurt before the big game. We started with our usual run around the quarter-mile track to warm up. Roger Olsen, also known as "the Big O" due to his 6'2" and 235-pound frame, wasn't a fan of running laps around that track. During the hot summer practices where we had to run four laps to complete a mile before starting practice, Roger would hide under the stands until the final lap and then emerge from the back to finish. We teased him about it, and he would just laugh, but no one ever reported him. I suspect the coaches might have known but never caught him in the act. He always looked too fresh and had a big smile on his face when he finished that last lap.

Our practice was a smooth run-through of plays, both running and passing, without any contact. The purpose was to ensure that everyone knew their positions and responsibilities on each play, such as blocking assignments on running plays and route patterns on passing plays. We also went over our defensive strategy against their running and passing plays.

Special teams practice followed, covering kicking and returning, with a focus on blocking and coverage assignments. We emphasized the importance of containment, ensuring that the opponents couldn't break free on the outside. Tommy Scibelli was a master at this, never letting the opposing ball-carrier escape his coverage for big gains.

After a quick and efficient practice, the coaches gave us instructions for Saturday morning. The game was set to start at 1pm, so we had to be at the field by 11:30am. Players who needed their ankles taped had to be in the locker room by 9am to ensure there were no ankle injuries. With practice finishing early, I changed into some comfortable old clothes I didn't mind getting paint on. I informed the guys that we were going to transform the '49 Buick into a moving display, showcasing North's superiority over South. It would be our very own float, parading around town in celebration after the game. I met everyone in the teacher's parking lot right after practice. I led the charge out of the gym locker room, heading to the teacher's parking lot adjacent to the shop to begin painting the Buick. Bernie had everything ready, and we were eager to get started. Soon, more of the guys from the team joined us. With enough hands on deck, we aimed to finish quickly, as we still had to prepare for the bonfire and pep rally.

Joe Corea, Tommy Scibelli, Steve Due, Richie Renda, Ken Halpern, Tony DiBenedetto, Lou Martorello, Vic Toto, Ralph

Zanchelli, Roger Olsen, Mike Oddo, Sal Pepitone, Barney Rukin, Phil Manzione, Dick Zucker, Dom Bonifacio, Bob Roselle, Don Howell, Rob Schiller, Barry Aronson, Barry Lublin, and Alan Congemi joined in. We began painting the Buick without any specific plan, each guy taking a different part of the car to paint as they pleased. What a blast! Everyone was laughing, having a ball, and joking around, suggesting all sorts of phrases to paint on the car. Some of the ideas were hilarious but likely would have gotten us suspended and my car impounded. Regardless, they were funny. A couple of the guys grabbed ladders to reach the roof, where they painted all the players' names. On one side of the front door, we painted in big letters, "S.S.A.L. CHAMPS," confidently declaring our intention to win the game and be crowned section champions. On the passenger door's other side, we painted in even larger letters:

**CALLAHAN'S COOLIES**
**RACKED BY BANK'S BOMBERS**

Callahan was the name of the South High School's line coach, while Banks was our line coach. We painted all kinds of lines and smaller details, even adding a bottle of booze with the words "nothing like a good party to keep your spirits up." We didn't spare the wheels either. Someone even included drag-racing symbols, which I found particularly amusing since this vehicle couldn't go much faster than 45 miles an hour downhill with a strong tailwind. We had so much fun with that car that when we finished, I drove it around the track to get everyone fired up before the bonfire and pep rally began.

# 15

## STORIES OF THE '49 BUICK

If anyone ever had more fun in their car, I'd love to meet them. It must have been one wild, exciting, joyous ride filled with friends and countless adventures. The 1949 Buick had been in my family for a few years before it became my first car. My father owned it initially, but it had little trade-in value, so he parked it at his cousin's house with the plan that he would eventually pass it along to my twin sister Linda or myself. As senior year of high school approached, Linda wasn't ready to drive yet so my dad made a deal with me; he'd give me the car if I paid for the insurance.

That summer before my senior year, I worked tirelessly to save up for the insurance, and it was finally mine. However, before hitting the road, I had to pass driver's education, a class I couldn't skip. Despite already having some driving experience, the pressure was on, as I needed to pass to reduce my insurance costs by $53, a sum that seemed insurmountable at the time. I'd been driving legally with a junior license since I was sixteen, which later transitioned into a full license, allowing me to drive at night with an adult present.

Owning a car in my senior year was a ticket to independence and freedom. I could now pick up my friends and take my girlfriend to various places like the beach, movies, games, and countless other adventures. My 1949 Buick, I quickly learned, was a well-built and special vehicle. The front bumper was solid steel and chrome-plated, stretching across the entire width of the car. It was designed to protect the car's front end, bending at the ends in front of the wheels. The metal body of the car was like a tank, made of thin sheets of steel that were painted to prevent rust. I also had two religious calendars hanging in the back to help protect me against serious accidents. With the heavy steel frame and God's protection, I couldn't help but think that my Buick was indestructible.

In my rush to demonstrate the car's safety, I found myself in a few fender benders. My first accident occurred when I left the Carvel stand in Franklin Square and made a wide turn, hitting a cinderblock retaining wall. Although my front bumper was unscathed, I knocked some cinderblocks off the wall and shifted others. Not wanting to report the accident, I quickly picked up the cinderblocks and placed them back on the wall, trying to make it look as if nothing had happened. Of course, I enjoyed my delicious Carvel milkshake before leaving. Fortunately, I never heard anything about that accident again from the owner of Carvel, as I was a regular customer.

My second accident, which I reported, happened when I made another wide turn and grazed an oncoming car. My father wasn't thrilled, but he remained relatively calm since it was my first reported accident. He explained that our neighbor, who sold cars and ran a repair shop, could fix the damage for a reasonable cost. I was grounded for two weeks as punishment, unable to use the car during that time, but it was a fair lesson learned.

My third accident occurred when I was leaving the student parking lot. I stopped at the exit because my view was blocked by other cars. As I inched my way out, a teacher hit me with her brand-new 1960 Renault. She hit my car so hard that her front end was severely damaged, and her bumper flew up into the air. Thankfully, her Renault was no match for the robust bumper of my Buick. Despite feeling bad for her, I was relieved that no one was hurt, and I was not enrolled in any of her classes.

There were also smaller incidents, dents here and there, and I always carried a small sledgehammer to knock them out from the inside, making sure no one would notice. Sometimes, my Buick would gently brush against another parked car, resulting in a dent for them and nothing but untouched steel for me. I would pull over, retrieve my trusty small sledgehammer, slide underneath the car, and tap out the dent. Cars were built much sturdier in the late '40s and early '50s.

My experience in removing dents came in handy one night

when I was leaving a party with my friend Artie Schnitzer. Artie had had a bit to drink but was in control as he got into his father's Oldsmobile. However, as he started to back up, we heard a dreadful crunch sound. Somehow, Artie had managed to hit a fire hydrant and damage the car's rear quarter panel. He looked horrified, and the damage was extensive. I reassured him, telling him that I was an expert at these types of repairs. Artie gave me a small hammer with part of the handle missing. With Artie as my mechanical engineer, we got under the car, and he directed me to the proper locations to knock out the dents discreetly. After several hard hits and my hand covered in blood, we managed to repair most of the damage. I advised Artie to use the same story that our friend Richie Barone had used with his dad. Richie had driven his father's new white Pontiac on errands and, upon returning, noticed that another car had scraped the passenger side, causing a scrape and a small dent. Afraid to tell his dad, Richie went home with the car but parked it with the undamaged driver's side facing the house. He then asked his father for a ride to the store, and his father entered the car on the driver's side without noticing the damage. Upon exiting the store and returning to the passenger side of the vehicle, Richie screamed, "Dad, someone hit us while we were inside the store and drove off!" His father was understandably upset but not with Richie, and the mission was accomplished.

One day, my basketball coach, Joe Shannon, needed a ride home because his car was in for repairs and wasn't ready yet. I agreed and stayed overnight, as we often did when playing basketball in the city with his youth group. We competed in various high schools across Brooklyn, even in some of the toughest neighborhoods. One of them was the Red Hook section, where the infamous Cape Man and Umbrella Man made headlines for killing two people simply because, as the Cape Man claimed, "I felt like it." It was indeed a tough and troubled neighborhood. During one of our games, I struck up a conversation with a teenager from Joe's youth group. He seemed like a nice kid. The following week, I asked where he was, and I was shocked to learn that he had been killed over a one-dollar bet during a softball game.

Attending roll call at Joe Shannon's was unlike anything I was used to. Instead of regular names, everyone had street names like Dice, Speed, Shorty, Ace, T-Bone, Ice Box, and more. These memories of Brooklyn's unique culture stayed with me throughout my life. I was getting an education in a world very different from mine, all within a few miles of my home. There's no education quite like the firsthand experience of people, environments, and conditions in different neighborhoods.

I recall the night when I drove Joe Shannon back to his Brooklyn home in my '49 Buick. Despite the winter chill, we were comfortable inside the car. What stood out to me was how relaxed and fearless Joe was. By then, we had grown close. Two summers ago, we even went to his apartment in Brooklyn to paint it alongside my old friend Bernie. We took the subway, and Joe had the paint and brushes ready for us when we arrived. He paid us for our work, which was a welcome addition to our pockets back then.

Joe's apartment was a narrow, elongated space with a hallway down the middle and rooms on either side. It was located next to the beautiful Botanical Gardens. He and his wife had four children, and I remember his youngest, whose unique name was Brooks. Joe was our basketball coach during my senior year, and he still led the youth group in Brooklyn. He even scheduled a scrimmage game between our North varsity basketball team and one of the Brooklyn youth groups. During warm-ups, we noticed that all the kids, including the 5'8" point guard, could dunk. It was an intimidating sight. Nevertheless, we played hard and were surprisingly ahead. But then, I noticed something peculiar. The opposing team's gang, known as the Buccaneers, all had umbrellas. In a strange twist, they pulled out the umbrella handles to reveal long, sharp swords. I turned to my fearless friend, Kenny Halpern, and suggested that we might not want to win this game, as I had no idea who those guys were or what they were capable of. Kenny's response, with his unshakable Marine-like resolve, was simple: "Screw them, let's win this thing." Kenny embodied the fearless determination that characterized most of the senior boys at our school. They never gave up and always played to win, regardless of the opponent or the stage. It was this spirit that led them to win championships in two major sports programs at our school.

One of the standout moments was a special outing to a New York Mets game in the city. My Buick took us everywhere, even through the busy streets of New York City. What made this game unforgettable was the behavior of Mets centerfielder Jimmy Piersall. After hitting his 100th home run, he ran the bases backward, displaying his eccentric and humorous character. He remains one of the most unique personalities in sports history.

Despite all the fun and adventure, my Buick sometimes attracted the attention of the police. I remember one instance when an officer opened my trunk and saw my tools, which I always carried for emergencies, minor repairs, or unforeseen car issues. I had learned how to fix minor fender benders and handle mechanical problems myself. These tools were old and well-used. I was taken aback when the officer asked me if I had a receipt for these tools. I couldn't help but respond with a hint of sarcasm, asking him if he had a receipt for the pants he was wearing. It quickly became apparent that he wasn't joking. He instructed me to wait in my car as he wrote up a stack of tickets, which took nearly half an hour. As I watched him in my rearview mirror, I began to worry about whether I would be arrested for the tools in my trunk.

Finally, the officer returned to my car, handed me the stack of tickets, and wished me luck. There were six traffic tickets in total, but at least I wasn't being arrested. It was clear that this was not a particularly friendly police officer. However, I had my day in court and managed to have most of the tickets dismissed. I paid the remaining fine and left the courtroom, feeling vindicated by the overaggressive police officer who lacked a sense of humor.

My time in driver's education also provided some valuable lessons, particularly on how to handle a skid in a car. Our teacher, Mr. Hutton, was a serious instructor in both shop and driver's education. He always emphasized safety as the top priority in his classes. Three key lessons he imparted have stayed with me: First, in shop class, a dull tool is an unsafe and dangerous tool. Second, don't force anything in the shop; if it's not working, there's a reason, so find the cause. Third, in driver's education, always stay calm, maintain control, and eliminate distractions. Mr. Hutton also had an unconventional belief that taking taxis was more cost-effective than owning a car in the long run. While his math may have been correct, the inconvenience and wasted time in suburban living made it a less appealing option.

I found it challenging to eliminate distractions in my '49 Buick. I was not willing to turn down the radio, as I believed the loud music helped me stay awake and alert. The people in the car with me were like my extra set of eyes, able to spot potential dangers from all sides. Eating and drinking while driving seemed entirely manageable, helping me stay alert in case of a sudden need for quick reactions. The occasional beer even helped me stay relaxed, preventing overreactions to unexpected situations, but it would always be just one so I didn't run the risk of driving while intoxicated.

One lesson from driver's education stuck with me: when skidding in your car, turn the wheel in the opposite direction, stay calm, and avoid hitting the brakes. As someone who enjoyed experimenting and seeking solutions, I decided to put this lesson to the test. I believed that personal experience was the best way to answer any questions that arose in my mind. So, I found a suitable icy hill, drove to the top, and started my experiment. I made sure there were no cars around to avoid any complications. What could possibly go wrong by following the instructions I had learned in driver's education class? As I started down the hill and tapped my brakes to induce a minor skid, I quickly found out. The car went into a skid that transformed into an "S" shape, with the front and back going in different directions. It felt like the car was spinning, first to one side of the road, then the other. At one point, I was heading down the hill backward. Despite the chaos outside, I remained calm, watching as my car came perilously close to parked vehicles on both sides of the road, even though it was a two-lane street. I shifted my body away from the impending impact, maintaining my composure, but my vehicle was spiraling out of control. Luckily there were no oncoming cars, otherwise, it might have been a different story. In the end, my daring experiment yielded a few conclusions: the religious calendars worked, never attempt this skid on an icy hill going downhill, and staying calm had nothing to do with avoiding an accident. I was left thanking my guardian angel and Lady Luck for seeing me through that dangerous experiment.

# 16

## FRIDAY NIGHT BONFIRE & PEP RALLY

Our school was buzzing with anticipation, for we were on the verge of hosting the most monumental bonfire in our history, and it was all thanks to a certain individual – Roger Olsen, the "Big O" Roger's schedule was unique; he only attended classes until 11am, a fact I was privy to because I crossed paths with him when I was heading in for my lunchtime class. Outside of school, he held a so-called part-time job at Lynbrook Lumber, though during weekends and school breaks, he'd clock in a staggering 60 hours. It wasn't uncommon for him to out-earn some of our younger teachers.

Roger's heart was set on working at the lumberyard and pursuing carpentry after graduation. He had it all planned out - a job lined up with a major construction company, enrollment at Farmingdale College for blueprint reading, and dreams of marrying his high school sweetheart, Pat Seiler, and raising a family. While Roger had his future neatly outlined, my mind was wrapped in questions about life after high school. Was it possible to retire early and savor life's pleasures, instead of waiting for four or five decades? The idea of postponing happiness until retirement felt distant, especially when I considered the frailty of old age. It was a time when the mind could play tricks with forgetfulness, and dinners were served at 4pm. The so-called golden years seemed better suited for the present.

In the meantime, Bernie had orchestrated a plan with Roger. After Roger finished his classes, he would borrow the sizable Lynbrook lumber truck and head to the supermarkets to collect empty wooden crates. Back then, products were packed in sturdy wooden crates, not the cardboard boxes we see today. Roger and Bernie were dependable; their word was their bond. As expected, it took them the entire day and two trips in the mammoth truck to complete the task. After school, the rest of us took over, organizing and stacking the crates. The result was astounding, as they reached a towering 25 feet into the sky, with a base circumference spanning a colossal 100 feet. Fortunately, this was a time when there were no restrictions on such extravagant bonfires. However, our bonfire became so renowned that it ushered in a new era of regulations and restrictions.

With football, practices concluded and my '49 Buick freshly painted, the time had finally arrived for our grand bonfire. The football field had been prepared, and the bonfire awaited its ceremonial ignition. The stage was set; the band, cheerleaders, football team, teachers, and administrators were all present. The only thing left was to light the fire.

As the bonfire roared to life, its flames illuminated the school, the surrounding fields, and the night sky adorned with stars. Its warmth embraced everyone on that chilly November night, creating a memorable atmosphere. The band played spirited marching and fight songs, galvanizing the student

The bonfire burning brightly into the night

body, cheerleaders, and football players. The cheerleaders performed their routines, providing a sneak preview of their performances for the big game. Their chant, "Two, four, six, eight, who do you appreciate? Roger, Roger, he's our man!" echoed through the night, expressing gratitude to Roger for his role in the magnificent bonfire. Then, our head coach, Mr. Miele, took center stage and delivered a heartwarming speech. He extended his thanks to the coaches, cheerleaders, teachers, students, and the band for their unwavering support and contributions, making this weekend exceptionally special.

Behind the scenes, the marching band had diligently been practicing to deliver a performance that would be etched in our memories forever. The cheerleaders, too, honed their routines, blending new moves with perfected classics for the upcoming game and the watchful eyes of television cameras. Those responsible for designing and constructing the parade floats received well-deserved congratulations for their exceptional work. Our coaches had toiled ceaselessly, crafting the game plan and ensuring that the players thoroughly understood their roles and responsibilities.

The symbol of our enemy, the South football team, and what they would look like after the game.

Our team was led by the smart, tough, and focused junior quarterback, Gary Halpern. The senior players were fortunate to have several talented juniors who could step into crucial positions, with some even starting in key roles. Looking ahead, the juniors, along with the sophomores, would go undefeated the following year, securing the division championship for 1961.

As the bonfire gradually dwindled, an iconic tradition unfolded. The Auto-shop donated an old, battered car, labeling it "South." We took turns striking the symbol of our rival school with a sledgehammer until it was reduced to a heap of scrap. Someone captured this moment in a photograph, and we affectionately dubbed it "The Battered Symbol of the Enemy." It was the perfect way to cap off the bonfire and pep rally, leaving everyone with a sense of joy and victory, even before the game had commenced.

The school bonfire pep rally concluded with smiles, laughter, and a palpable sense of camaraderie. The field slowly emptied as the band returned to the school to stow their instruments, and the cheerleaders changed into their regular attire. Teachers, administrators, custodians, and maintenance crews returned to the school, gathering their belongings, as they had an early start planned for the following day.

However, the excitement still coursed through us teenagers. We couldn't bear to let the night end just yet. The '49 Buick, decked out for the occasion, beckoned us to continue the festivities. Without hesitation, we loaded it up and set off, honking the horn to start a triumphant caravan through town. Laughter, shouting, and whoops of joy filled the air as we slowly cruised through the streets, our youthful exuberance on full display. Led by the iconic '49 Buick, our caravan embodied the essence of our excitement. Kids piled on top of each other hung out of windows, and even perched on the front fenders. The exact headcount was a mystery, but no one complained; we were all too busy relishing this unforgettable moment.

My girlfriend, Sue, sat beside me in the car, or at least I think she did. Marilyn sat atop her, while Chris occupied the shotgun seat, with Pat perched on top. That made five of us in the front, and there was still ample space given the car's width and high roof. In the back, the rest of the gang, including Bernie, Tony, Joe, Sal, Noel, Lou, Mary, Artie, Barney, Pat, Pam, and others, enjoyed the ride. I couldn't recall exactly when each person got into the car or clung to the front fenders, but I'm sure the wild ones, Steve and Vic, were among them.

Despite the spectacle, you might expect a swarm of police

officers handing out tickets or worried calls to law enforcement, but this was the '50s, and things were different. Instead
of trouble, we were met with waves and well-wishes from the
public, and the police simply smiled and let us continue our
jubilant journey through the streets around Valley Stream
North and South having a great time. In retrospect, what we
did the night before the game was nothing compared to what
the North High class of 1963 wound up doing two years later.
As the rivalry continued to grow with excitement and competition over the years, so did the pranks for both schools. One
early morning a group met at the North parking lot to play the
biggest prank in our rivalry so far. Bob Romano, Bob Renda,
Dom Bonifacio, and Ricky Rizzuto planned a mission to go to
South High School and light their wood pile ablaze so they
wouldn't be able to have a bonfire the night before the big
game. That didn't work out, so instead Ricky climbed to the
top of the Valley Stream South flagpole and hung a dummy
with a sign pinned to its chest that read, "North Beats South".
They then painted the flagpole green and painted the words,
"North beats South" several places on the school building
before leaving filled with laughter. The next morning on our
school's PA system, the principal Mr. Woods announced what
took place at South the day before and wanted to know who
was responsible. The whole school started cheering and
shouting "Yes, yes, yes!" The boys were never identified as the
responsible party, so they escaped without any punishment.

Although our wild night of fun didn't compare with theirs
and was devoid of any alcohol, it was still a lot of fun and we

returned to North High well before midnight. With Bernie and Joe living the furthest away, I decided to drop them off first since they didn't have any other ride arrangements. I bid Bernie farewell, then Joe. "See you guys bright and early, around 8:30 am for the game," I assured them. "I'll be on time. Right now, I'm dropping off Sue and heading home for some much-needed rest. Good night, guys."

After dropping everyone else off, Sue remained in the car and I drove her to her house in Valley Stream. I kissed her on the cheek, and with a smile, she thanked me for a night that had exceeded her wildest expectations. She confessed that before we started dating that year, North High School had been quite mundane for her. Despite participating in volley-ball, basketball, hockey, and even Daisy Chain, she'd never experienced this level of excitement. She credited me with transforming her high school experience and expressed her eagerness for the game the following day. She would arrive early with her sister, Linda, to cheer me on. She planned to sit with Marilyn and the girls in the stands, their eyes glued to the action on the field.

Upon reaching Sue's house, it was around 11pm, leaving me with ample time to get to bed by midnight, ensuring a solid eight hours of sleep for the upcoming game. As I bid Sue good-night, we shared a few more moments, and then I stepped out of the car. We exchanged loving words, knowing that the night had been truly memorable for both of us. I waited until she was safely inside her home, the front door clicking shut, before I drove away.

By the time I arrived back home, it was 11:40pm. I made a quick stop in the bathroom to wash up and then headed off to bed, just before the bewitching hour of midnight. As I lay there, I hoped for a swift descent into slumber, knowing that a good night's rest was vital for the game ahead.

# 17

# CROWNING OF THE HOMECOMING QUEEN

T he annual North-South game and its accompanying festivities held a special place in the hearts of North High seniors, especially for the young woman chosen as the Queen. This year, the honor had fallen upon the attractive Chris Beuttenmueller. Her selection wasn't solely based on her good looks; it was also a testament to her sparkling personality and her extensive contributions to the school. At the time, Chris served as the treasurer of the school's student council, and a member of the leader's club, and the German Honor Society. In the previous year, she had been a varsity cheerleader, the vice president of the Ladies Athletic Association, and a member of the Daisy Chain at graduation. Even as a sophomore, she had held the positions of secretary in the G.A.A. and historian for her grade.

Assisting Queen Chris as ladies-in-waiting were four other

remarkable senior girls: Barbara Goldberg, Arline Schneider, Francine Silverman, and Pat Stone. These young ladies, also admired for their involvement in various aspects of school life, had made significant contributions. Barbara had been part of the Daisy Chain, served as the vice president of Phi Beta Chi Hi-Y, and co-captained the varsity cheerleaders. Arline, on the other hand, was the president of Omega Pi Epsilon Hi-Y, headed senior social affairs, and was a member of the senior council. Franne had taken part in the Daisy Chain, been a member of Green Key, and had served as the historian of the Hi-Y council. Lastly, Pat, who was also involved in the Daisy Chain, held the position of secretary in the Student Council and was a Green Key member. Chris marked the fifth Queen of our school, following in the footsteps of Carol Amorello in 1956, Susan Goering in 1957, Carol Nielsen in 1958, and Wendy Swensen in 1959.

The traditional pageantry of the North-South game was set to begin with the bonfire on a Friday evening, featuring the burning of the South in effigy. It was during this event that Chris Beuttenmueller would be officially crowned queen, ushering in the float parade. Not to be outdone, the cheerleaders, football team, and band would all be present to celebrate these festivities.

The following day, the float parade would wind its way through the streets of Valley Stream, culminating at Fireman's Field, where the much-anticipated game would unfold. This year's parade, aptly themed as "bigger-and-better-than-ever," promised a series of unique floats, all connected by song titles. These floats included:

- Yorker Float - "Surrey with the Fringe on Top"
- Hi-Y - "Hang Down Your Head, Tom Dooley"
- Student Council - "A Pretty Girl Is Like a Melody"
- Senior Float - "Bye Bye, Blackbird"
- Junior Float - "Around the World in 80 Days"
- Sophomore Float - "Somewhere Over the Rainbow"
- Freshman Float - "Come, Josephine, in My Flying Machine"

The senior float, however, had faced its share of delays and manpower challenges, nearly jeopardizing its participation in the parade. Thanks to Marilyn's determination and ingenuity, the senior float miraculously made it to the parade just two days before the big game.

Marilyn herself provided an account of the wild rush to complete the float on time:

"When I heard about our building a senior float parade for the final football game, I called my mom to see if there was any way we could put it all together maybe for two or three weeks, and she reluctantly said yes! We had a big two-car garage that would be perfect for this project.

I promised her that she would only be inconvenienced

for two or three weeks. When my classmates heard about it, they came in droves, and the construction began! That was for the first three days... and then seven or eight people would come by the end of the first week, and it dwindled to two or three. That wasn't good. When it got down to a few days left, the float still wasn't built and my mother was perturbed that she wanted her garage back.

I knew we had to do something, so I went to school on the last Wednesday before the Football Game and told my friends Christine and Susan that I had a plan. We would all go into homeroom where they took attendance. That way we wouldn't be absent, and parents wouldn't be called. When the bell rang after attendance, we all briskly left school, went over to my house, and began stuffing the football-shaped chain link fence with tissues.

I was kind of proud! Who am I kidding, I smiled throughout the morning! It was a very good plan except for one thing. The two people I asked to come over, told at least three other people, and they told their friends... We could have held a parade right there! We were making progress! And we could have been finished, but then something happened... No, the float didn't fall... but something worse!

A teacher called down to the principal's office and inquired if the senior class had an outing that he wasn't informed of because he had a senior class, but no one was there! A foil in my plan! Suddenly three cars pulled up in front of my house and six teachers and the principal jumped out, and we all scattered every which way. It looked like a silent movie with Laurel and Hardy! I ran into my house and sat behind my kitchen door which was a half door and half windows... I heard a noise. I thought it was my heart beating, but no, it was a teacher peeking in the window. I didn't dare move. He was making a shadow on the floor... And finally, he left. They all did.

Is it possible that we got off scot-free? But when we went into homeroom the following day, our names were announced to report to the attendance office but it wasn't much of a punishment, so it was worth it! I remember Chris Beuttenmueller the most beautiful girl, on the float, waving to all the crowd. I miss those days; I miss Chris and Sue too."

# 18

# HISTORY OF THE NORTH-SOUTH GAME

The annual North-South football game, with its float parade, marching bands, and the fervor of students, parents, and the community, remained a prominent attraction year after year. This remarkable event took place just before Thanksgiving on a splendid autumn day, serving as the closing game for both North High and South High football teams. The neutral ground for this showdown was Firemen's Field, situated between North and South High Schools. Thousands from the town flocked to this festive gathering, with some passionately supporting the South and others championing the North.

Families lined the streets, exuberantly cheering as the floats and marching bands passed by. It was an awe-inspiring spectacle from days long past, now a cherished memory. For a fleeting moment, time stood still, and nothing else mattered except the grandeur of the North/South football game in the lives of those residing in this tight-knit community on Long Island, New York.

The inaugural football encounter between the two Valley Stream schools unfolded in November 1955, featuring junior varsity teams. The South Falcons emerged victorious with a score of 26-13. Both teams were in the process of cultivating the talent that would go on to produce breathtaking plays in the following two years.

In 1956, still operating at the JV level, the Spartans secured a resounding 26-7 triumph over South. Led by Dick Ryer, the North High defensive line put up a remarkable performance. A blocked punt was the only factor preventing the Spartans from maintaining an unblemished defensive record.

Varsity-level football debuted in 1957, and the Spartans, propelled by the running prowess of Chuck Gary and Tuffy Cicero, clinched a hard-fought 18-13 victory over the Falcons. The game's standout moment was an 80-yard kick-off return by South's halfback, Charlie Angwin. Unlike it had been the previous year during the blowout victory, this year's game was a heart-pounding spectacle from the first whistle until the final horn sounded.

In 1958, the Falcons mounted a comeback against an early North High lead, thanks to the impressive running of Don Greene, Mike Lenzo, and Ross Grosch. With a resolute defense, they managed to fend off the charging Spartans, led by Lou Martorello, Ross Vassallo, and Steve Gelfand. The unforgettable final play of the game will forever be etched in memory: North, vying for a tie, saw Jay White launch a long pass downfield to Bob MacKay. MacKay caught the ball on the run and charged toward the South goal line at full tilt. With fans roaring with each stride, Frank Jeffreys closed the gap and finally tackled MacKay inches from the goal line, denying North the tying touchdown. The final score: 20-13 victory for the Falcons.

In 1959, South claimed a 12-7 victory. As the closing minutes approached, North reached the South 9-yard line when time ran out, at least from the North High viewpoint. The "Coolie" defensive unit held firm, preventing North from scoring. The game's first score came early in the first quarter when Ray Worsdale recovered the ball in the end zone following a blocked punt by Ed Hughes. The winning touchdown was executed by Pete Pedone, a senior, after a 60-yard run. Lou Martorello contributed North's lone touchdown in the third quarter. If South were to secure a victory on Saturday, November 19, 1960, the coveted trophy would become permanently theirs.

# 19

## SATURDAY: THE NORTH/SOUTH GAME!

It was finally here, "Game Day." I had waited all year for this moment and all the excitement it brought. I woke up early, having had little sleep due to the anticipation from the previous night and the dreams of today that had made it difficult to fall asleep. I picked up Bernie and Joe on the way to school, and we were all exhilarated, talking about the game and thrilled that it was finally happening. Driving to school, we had wanted to be on time in the locker room to get taped up before the coaches assembled the team for final instructions.

We got our ankles taped, then put on our pads and uniforms. We dressed in our favorite colors: dark green jerseys with white pants and a dark green stripe running down the sides, complemented by white socks and black cleats. I slipped into my number 27 jersey with a smile, knowing we had never lost when wearing these colors, and today wouldn't be any different. Bernie Havern put on his All-League number 32, and another one of our captains, Joe Corea, donned his number nine jersey.

That hour went by fast, and soon the team gathered in the gym with all the equipment, where the coaches gave us a short speech and final instructions. The buses would take us to Fireman's Memorial Field in Valley Stream and park near the Fieldhouse where we would depart. The players would assemble on the field for stretching, calisthenics, and a general warm-up before we started running and passing the football. We would set up lines for catching the football and for receiving punts and kickoffs and the equipment men would bring all of our gear to our bench on the sideline. Understanding the plan for the trip, we then exited the gym, loaded up on two buses, and headed to Fireman's Field. The cheerleaders, marching band, and the floats had gone ahead to begin the float parade through Valley Stream on the way to the field.

As our bus turned onto Wheeler Avenue and then Emerson Place, we were greeted by thousands of people on both sides of the street to the field, cheering and wishing us luck. It was about two miles from the school to the field. We had to use a neutral field between North and South because of the rivalry; the crowd size was too big for the schools. It was almost noon, and the field was already full, with hundreds of people outside cheering our parade. The floats, made by the student body of North, were beautiful and a testament to their hard work. The parade was led by the homecoming float with the homecoming queen, Chris Beuttenmueller, and her attendants, featuring the theme "A pretty girl is like a melody." We slowly pulled into the field parking lot next to the fieldhouse, which housed the bathrooms that most of us would use before the game after all the excitement. The bus had to move very slowly as the crowds of people grew larger.

Now it was time to get off the bus and head to the field, where we began to stretch and warm up. Bernie led us in calisthenics, yelling out the cadence to fire up the team. The passing lines were formed, and G. Halpern and Aronson warmed up their arms with the ends and backs. Lublin, Zanchelli, Howell, Leeds, Rozelle, Heron, Martorello, Toto, K. Halpern, Mansion, Schiller, Bonifacio, and Pepitone practiced his booming punting, with center Rukin hiking the ball. Due practiced his kickoffs and extra points, with

Float parade queen Chris Beuttenmueller

Van Nostrand holding for him. Corea and Scibelli caught the punts as they were the return men. The linemen, Olsen, Havern, Nyland, Zucker, Oddo, Abbott, Principe, Guarnieri, Renda, Rodway, Friedman, Guarneri, Camera, and Congemi, practiced their blocking assignments on the side of the field.

Everyone was yelling, getting fired up for the game. So, I

looked around, standing in the middle of the field, unable to believe the size of the crowd and feeling the excitement from all the people getting ready to watch the game. I scanned the crowd for my family, my mom, dad, sister Linda, my seventh-grade brother Michael, and my grandparents. I couldn't find them in the crowd and didn't know if they were even here yet or where to look for them. I didn't have time to keep looking, so I started to look for Susan and the girls. That also was a lost cause as I gazed into a sea of faces. It was like they say, "looking for a needle in a haystack."

After warming up for about 45 minutes, the coach called us into the fieldhouse for the last meeting before the game. We used the bathroom and got a drink of water. Final instructions were given by the defensive coach and head coach John Miele, and the defense was covered by the defensive coach and line coach Phil Banks, with words of encouragement from Dick Suprina and Leo Disend. We headed out to the sidelines where ABC Television reporters were waiting for a pre-game interview with the coach. Old Glory was flying above the scoreboard as we placed our hands over our hearts during the national anthem. It was a little after 1 o'clock; I looked around, and the stadium was full of roaring spectators as chills ran up my back when the referee blew his whistle to start the game.

We kicked off to South, and the game was finally underway. I wasn't on the kickoff teams or the receiving teams. I was just used on offense during passing plays because of my size and my good hands. I didn't remember ever dropping a pass thrown to me. I always believed in myself, and if I could touch it, I knew I had to catch that football.

We were primarily a very good running team, with a big All-League line that loved to block for the running backs and knock people down in the process. The line was led by one of our captains, Bernie Havern. This fiery leader and All-Conference guard brought the best out of all his teammates with his winning spirit displayed in his actions and vocal statements.

Next to Bernie on his right was the Big "O," another All-Conference lineman who played right tackle. These two 6'3", 230-pounders anchored the right side of the line. On the left side of the line, which protected the quarterback's blind side, was another All-League decorated player, Dick Zucker, at 6'2" and 233 pounds. He, along with Rusty Congemi, held down the left side of the line. The center, Steve Due, a wrestler in the heavyweight division, made sure our quarterback received the ball on a direct snap or a long snap into his hands flawlessly and repeatedly. The ends, when they were running the ball, were Ralph Zanchelli, Barry Lublin, and Bob Rozelle. Our team did not execute many pass plays with a high level of success, so we mostly stuck to running the ball. However, I stayed ready to go into the game and always made sure to catch the ball when it was thrown my way.

*The First Quarter*

We won the coin toss and decided to kick off, knowing we had the best defense on Long Island, with four shutouts and only eighteen points allowed all year. The coach's thinking was, "Let's give them the ball and hit them hard so they know they won't be able to do anything all afternoon." The coach got his wish as North stopped South on their first possession with no gain. It was three and out for the Falcons of South High School. We didn't do much better in the tough first quarter. It was a hard-hitting, close, and tough game, as both teams were trying to find a weakness in their opponent. But, to no avail, as both defenses proved that the offenses at this point of the game were no match for their superior defenses. The clock ran down, and the first quarter ended tied at zero.

*The Second Quarter*

It became a field position game, with us having better field position for most of the first half thanks to Sal Pepitone's booming kicks, both in height and distance. Most were 60 yards and very high, so they were covered by our speedy defensive team with little or no gain. Marty Glickman even commented that he hadn't seen anything like it in a high school game before. Then, one of Sal's kicks hit the turf and began to roll, not stopping until it had traveled 73 yards downfield, pushing South deep into its territory. With the clock running down in the first half, the excitement in the stadium began to build.

All the players felt it too, as adrenaline pumped through their bodies, motivating them to give their all on each play. They never knew if the next play could be the one that led to a score. After two hard-fought quarters, the players now had their uniforms covered in dirt and grass stains. The half ended tied at zero.

We all then ran off the field to the Fieldhouse, assigned to our team. South was doing the same, with both teams staying far apart from each other. The scoreboard read: "Half-Time Score North 0 South 0."

Back in the Fieldhouse, we sat down, got some water, and listened to the coaches, who were anxious to make sure we knew what they wanted us to do. They congratulated us for fighting hard and shutting down South in the first half. They emphasized the need to continue our suffocating defense and get the offense rolling. To that end, we were going to put in more passing plays and use the halfback pass option in the second half.

This meant more action for me, as I was always in on passing plays. The coach liked my size against the smaller defensive halfbacks and safeties. I also had never dropped a pass in a game so far that year. There hadn't been many opportunities, as we were a 90% running team because of our tremendous offensive line, led by Guard Havern, tackles Olsen and Zucker, all 230 pounds. They blocked for our great backs: the Halpern brothers, Martorell, Toto, Bonifacio, and Schiller, who ran through the large holes they created.

Float parade preparations

VS North Marching Band leading
the float parade

Float parade

L to R: Albert "Rusty" Congemi, Vic Toto
(standing) and Ralph Zanchelli waiting
to get into the action

L to R: Coaches Banks,
Miele and Suprina

Me catching a pass for Valley Stream North

Names and slogans painted on my '49 Buick for the North - South game. We confidently declared our intention to win the game and be crowned section champs in advance.

*START OF 2ND HALF / 3rd Quarter*

We took the field, and South kicked off to us. On our first possession, we made a first down, and then we were stopped. We punted to them from their 35-yard line. We stopped them after they gained only 8 yards. Now, South's punter, James, had his best kick of the day, a deep booming punt that sailed over the head of Scibelli and rolled to the North 8-yard line.

On the second play from scrimmage, the Spartan ball carrier was hit hard and fumbled, with Paul Silvestri recovering for the Falcons. Three plays later, after a penalty and a loss of a yard, the Falcons found themselves on the fourteen yard line. Tony Spizzucco tore off left tackle for a touchdown, and then John Uhlar lunged through the line, just crossing the goal line for the extra point. South kicked off to the Spartans, who now trailed the Falcons 7 to 0. North ran for a first down but couldn't make much progress beyond that.

The Falcons were also stopped by the ferocious frontline of the Spartans. North knew they couldn't let South score again if they wanted to win the game. The Falcons having scored both the touchdown and the extra point meant that North needed two scores to win the game. We couldn't settle for a tie; it was like kissing your sister. It left an incomplete feeling, and there were no winners. We had to score twice, and there was still plenty of time left on the clock.

The Spartans got the ball back after the Falcons were forced to punt yet again. Now the North team was determined to score after being down seven to nothing. They began to move the ball in the closing minutes of the third quarter, with runs by halfbacks Lou Martorello, Ken Halpern, and fullback Schiller. Now, Havern had them fired up with one of his famous quick motivational speeches in the huddle. The offensive line responded, with Zucker and Olsen creating mammoth holes for the backs to run through.

The Spartans, with their season and the championship on the line, came to life. They pushed the Falcons like they were birds off the line and steamrolled toward the goal line and a tying score. They moved down the field from the 50-yard line to the 45-yard line, then the 35-yard line, and finally, a sweep around the right end to the 25-yard line as the third quarter ended, with the Spartans still trailing but on the march. They would start the last quarter on the Falcon's 25-yard line.

As the third quarter ended, the score was Falcons 7, Spartans 0.

*4th Quarter*

This was it, as the fourth quarter began with North on the South 25-yard line, desperately needing a score on this drive. The Spartans huddled up after talking to the coaching staff during the timeout between quarters. North needed a touchdown and an extra point to tie the score at the beginning of the quarter. Then they would have the last seven minutes to score again and win the game, as high school football quarters were only eight minutes in length.

This was it, the last eight minutes of football for all sixteen seniors on the team, and our leader Bernie, full of fire, let us know with a short, inspiring speech ending with "Let's take it in now, boys." The ball was now on the 25-yard line. The Spartans ran but were stopped for a one-yard loss. On the second down, North was again stopped at the line of scrimmage. Now it was third and eleven on the Falcons' 26-yard line. The coach called a halfback option pass play. Gary handed off to Lou, who passed the ball to Bob Rozelle, wide open over the middle, and carried the ball to the one-yard line. On the next play, Gary Halpern executed a quarterback sneak behind Steve Due and Bernie Havern for the touchdown. The pass play for the extra point was knocked down, leaving us trailing by just one point with 7 to 6 on the scoreboard. This meant we had to score again, and time was running out.

Both teams were dominated by the defense, and it seemed like the score of 7 to 6 in favor of the Falcons would hold. With two minutes to go in the game, the Spartans took over the ball and moved it down to the Falcons' 42-yard line. With just a minute and fifteen seconds remaining, things didn't look too good for North, as they faced a fourth down and four yards to go for a first down.

We had to make the first down, or the game would be over for us. Martorello took a handoff from quarterback Gary Halpern, rolled to his left, and threw a pass to his brother Ken Halpern in the right flat. Halpern advanced to the 19-yard line, and the Spartans were still alive.

Then, the unthinkable happened. Ken Halpern, while hitting the ground, fumbled the ball, and it was recovered by South. Stunned, the North fans fell silent while the crowd for South let out a loud uproar. Then, there was tremendous news for North when everyone found out that the referee had whistled the play dead before the fumble! To add to the excitement as the game wound down, Ken Halpern then carried the ball to the 5-yard line as the scoreboard clock ticked down to 0:00 However, the referee indicated that he had 22 seconds left on his wristwatch which was the official time, so they corrected the scoreboard, and play continued. On the next play, Martorello lost 2 yards on the right side of the line.

Then, with only fifteen seconds left in the game, coach John Miele called North's last time out with the ball on the seven yard line prior to our fourth down play. The Spartans' entire season and the seniors' last high school game came down to one, last play. It couldn't get any closer or more nerve-wracking than this; this play would determine the conference championship.

The sellout crowd was on the edge of their seats, and most spectators were standing to get a better view. All eyes were focused on the 7-yard line, and the dramatic ending of this exciting game, with only a few seconds left, had fans on both sides filled with anticipation. The Falcons' fans believed they would hold North and survive, while the Spartan fans believed that somehow this last play would bring them the championship.

The coach needed to talk to his team. While coach Miele was speaking to his players about our last play, line coach Phil Banks called Dick Zucker, a 6-foot-2-inch, 230-pound lineman, to the sidelines. During the timeout, in the shadows of the end zone with seconds to play, Banks told Dick that he had to block for the halfback out of the backfield. He explained that they would use the trick quarterback pitch-back play with Ken Halpern and then go on a rollout to the end zone to receive a pass from the pitchman, Lou Martorello. Lou would receive the pitch from quarterback Gary Halpern. For the play to be successful, tackle Dick Zucker would have to block both the opposition lineman and then sprint in front of Halpern to ensure that he was not disrupted.

This was a very difficult play to execute, as the ball would move four times: from center Steve Due to quarterback Gary Halpern to halfback Lou Martorello to the other halfback Ken Halpern in the end zone. The line had all their blocking assignments, with Dick Zucker's being the most critical, as he had to clear the way for Ken Halpern to be free.

It was a gutsy call by the coach, but he knew his players could execute it. Now the timeout was over, and the referee blew his whistle. North came to the line of scrimmage for their last play of the game. A touchdown meant a win and a championship; anything else meant we would lose everything.

So here we go; the pressure was on. Steve Due, our center, hiked the ball to QB Gary Halpern, a direct snap. Gary turned, faked the handoff to Kenny, and then pitched the ball to Lou, who was rolling out to his right. Lou pulled the ball in and got set to throw a pass to Ken over the middle in the end zone. Tackle Dick Zucker barreled across the field and leveled the linebacker who was coming in to tackle Kenny thinking he had the ball, ensuring that Kenny would be free to run into the end zone to catch the pass.

Lou saw Ken free over the middle and fired a pass to him. Ken made the catch, and for the first time, North took the lead against South with just 8 seconds left in the game. I had a great view as I ran my pattern to the left side of the end zone to clear space for Ken. I jumped in jubilation as soon as the referee raised his hands to signal a touchdown. We celebrated in the end zone, knowing how significant this moment was.

Gary then ran up the middle between Steve Due and Bernie for the extra point, making the score Spartans 13, Falcons 7. The game wasn't over yet; there were still 8 seconds on the clock, so we had to kick off to a very dangerous return team. They had beaten us in years past by returning kickoffs for touchdowns, so we were taking no chances with this kick-off. Steve kicked the ball deep to Ray Erbig, a speed demon who flew up the field before being stopped by Tommy Scibelli and Joe Corea, finally ending the game. It was a tremendous victory for the Spartans of North High School.

As the players left the field after the victory celebrations, coaches Phil Banks and John Miele came over to Dick Zucker to congratulate him on his crucial block of the linebacker that freed Ken for the touchdown. They were also excited for him and wanted to inform him that he would be nominated for the Long Island Press Scholarship Award at the May awards ceremony.

The final score of the game was North 13, South 7, and now it was time to let the celebration begin!

1960 North High Championship Football Team

L to R: Artie and I celebrating after the victory over South

Me celebrating after the victory over South with my '49 Buick

# 20

# THE CELEBRATION BEGINS

We sprinted off the field, yelling, tossing helmets in the air, and screaming, "We are the champions!" Gary Halpern found himself in the spotlight, interviewed by CBS television as one of the game's star players and the victorious Spartan team's quarterback. The packed stadium erupted with cheers, celebrating one of the most thrilling games ever witnessed by the North/South teams. A record crowd of approximately 12,000 fans both in and around the stadium had gathered to witness this unforgettable showdown.

North High quarterback Gary Halpern being interviewed by ABC News after the game

The bus ride back home was indescribable, filled with a whirlwind of emotions and tears, a culmination of all the hard work that began in August, finally realized on this crisp autumn day in November. We basked in the glory of the moment, knowing that this victory was the result of months of dedication and determination. Press clippings from local newspapers, including Newsday and the Valley Stream town newspapers, chronicled the post-game events.

The headlines and quotes from coaches and players in these local papers spoke volumes:

"Trophy Changes Hands, Spartans Nip Falcons"
"North's Final Play Earns Coach a Shower"
"Four Local Boys Named Conference "B" All-Scholastic"

From North High School: Bernie Havern (Guard), Roger Olsen (Tackle), Kenny Halpern (Halfback). From South High School: Lloyd Domenico (Guard)

"Second team Conference "B" All-Scholastic"

Steve Due (Center), Ray Erbig (End), Gary Halpern (Quarterback).

"Conference "B" All-Scholastic Honourable Mention"

From North High School: Lou Martorello, Joe Corea (Safety)

From South High School: Pete Pedone (Running Back)

Dick Zucker in the US Air Force

This was a remarkable tribute to all the players and coaches from North High School. Having seven players recognized in various categories on the Conference "B" All-Scholastic Team was a testament to the team's excellence. It was particularly noteworthy that six of these honorees were seniors out of the sixteen on the North team.

But the accolades didn't stop there. Seven seniors received awards after the game, and the celebrations would continue at the May awards ceremony. Nearly half of the senior team was honored for their outstanding contributions, both on the football field and in the classroom. One standout among them was Dick Zucker, who was nominated for the Long Island Athlete

Scholar of the Year and emerged as the deserving winner. Dick was a dedicated student-athlete who excelled both academically and on the football field. He had already been accepted to the Air Force Academy, where he would play football and train as a jet fighter pilot. Congratulations to all these accomplished individuals.

No one needed to look at the scoreboard to understand that Valley Stream North had won the game and what a game it had been. The elation on the faces of North's coach John Miele and halfback Lou Martorello said it all. North had managed to halt the previously unbeaten crosstown rival, South, on the last play from scrimmage, clinching the South Shore B Conference championship. The jubilation was palpable as we embarked on the bus ride back to North High School.

Did Martorello ever doubt that North would pull it off? "I didn't know," he admitted. "I was praying hard. The last minute felt like an eternity. I kept asking the ref how much time was left—first, it was a minute and five seconds, then 33 seconds, and finally, eighteen seconds. And then we scored."

"Two years ago, we had the ball on the 1-yard line when time ran out. Last year, we had the ball on the four, and they intercepted. This year, we couldn't lose. We were really up. This is the last game for me... and all the other seniors. We have sixteen seniors."

Coach Miele, cigar in hand as always, entered his small office. A well-wisher tossed a more expensive cigar across his desk, but before he could put it away, his green-shirted athletes swarmed him. "Just let me get my jacket off," Miele pleaded. The jacket came off, and then he and assistants Dick Suprina and Phil Banks were swept into the celebratory shower.

The shower room was large and open, with no individual stalls. There was no issue fitting everyone inside, thanks to the players' help. Laughter filled the air as everyone got drenched, their uniforms clinging to their bodies. "We probably deserved this for riding them so hard all season," laughed Miele as he wrung out his sopping shirt. Meanwhile, Lou Martorello, with glare-reducing grease paint under his eyes, resembled a gleeful 160-pound owl.

"We worked so hard," piped Martorello, "and if we didn't beat South, it would've all been in vain."
"Best defensive team on the island," proclaimed tackle Dick Zucker. "The line never blocked like that in the last two minutes."
"The best thing was not getting the extra point," added end Ray Heron. "That way, we couldn't tie. We knew we had to win."
"This was worth the whole football season," exclaimed a voice from the locker room. "Being champions."

South High School had suffered its first loss at the hands of their biggest rival, North High School. The game had drawn a record crowd, both at Firemen's Field and in front of TV screens, and both local teams had a lot on the line. A South victory would have secured them the Conference "B" crown and permanent possession of the trophy. The Falcons had held the trophy for two consecutive years. For North, this victory meant claiming the top spot in Conference "B" and holding the coveted trophy, at least until the next year. In terms of the North-South encounter, North's win had brought the series to 3-2 in favor of North. In 1956, when both schools had only sophomores and juniors, North had emerged victorious. The Spartans had claimed victory the following year, but the Falcons had taken the trophy in 1958 and 1959.

It had seemed like South's game, having shut out North for three quarters, only to be stunned by North's comeback in the fourth quarter, resulting in two touchdowns and a last-play victory. It was a bitter pill for South, not only losing the conference championship but also missing out on the opportunity to retain the trophy forever. The rules stipulated that after three consecutive victories, the school kept the trophy.

As we reveled in the locker room, it felt like only minutes had passed, though our jubilation and celebration had continued unabated. After soaking the coaches, and ourselves, in the showers, we laughed heartily as we struggled to remove our dripping wet uniforms, pads, and gear. Finally, we managed to take off our uniforms and cleats, and reporters gathered their stories and left the building.

The cheerleaders were getting ready in the girls' locker room, and we planned to meet them outside. Our mission was to escort them to the various house parties celebrating our remarkable victory.

I arrived at my car, where Sue was waiting patiently. I informed her that we had to wait for some of the guys before we could leave. She greeted me with a warm smile and a tight hug, expressing her congratulations. She remarked on the excitement of the game's final moments, and we shared a passionate kiss. The emotions of that last-minute victory had left a lasting impression on all of us.

Bernie approached us and extended an invitation to his dad's party at their house. He encouraged me to bring my parents along as well. Bernie had arranged to go home with "Big O" Roger in his Chevy, along with Sal Pepitone. I agreed to take Joe Corea and "The Gump" in my car. I assured Bernie that I would inform my parents and meet them at his house shortly. Bernie and I were raised with the belief that if we were hosting a party, everyone was welcome. No one was deliberately left out, and this inclusive spirit was part of what made our celebrations so special. We loved bringing people together and ensuring everyone had a good time.

I stopped by my house, where my parents were waiting. My sister and brother were out somewhere else. I informed my parents about the party at the Havern's and let them know that I would see them there shortly. They were thrilled for me and the team, having watched and cheered for us during the game.

Returning to the Havern's house, I found it filled to the brim with people. Guests were scattered throughout, occupying every available space, from upstairs to downstairs, in the front and back of the house. Mr. Havern had invited what felt like the entire town. It was heartwarming to see so many parents coming together and having a great time. I couldn't recall ever seeing them all together at a party before. My parents arrived, and I gave my mom a warm hug. Mr. Havern was the consummate host, always gracious, and he knew how to make a good drink. I hardly saw my parents for the rest of the night; they must have stayed at the Havern's until the early hours of the morning.

It was as if the entire neighborhood had gathered at this victory party. The Morris family from behind the Havern's home, the Cash family from up the block, the Corea family from around the corner, and the Heron family from several blocks away—they were all there. The gathering was a beautiful testament to the bonds that had formed among the families, brought together by their children's shared experiences. This game had brought their parents together for the first time, despite having known each other through their kids for years. It was a lesson in how the victory of a single football game could unite families who had watched their children grow up together.

What I didn't fully comprehend at the time was that this celebration of the championship football game and its impact on the players and their families had only just begun. The celebration would span 57 years, with the team, their wives, and their children continuing to revel in their shared triumph. We would gather at various backyard barbecues, bars, restaurants, and class reunions held at elegant venues all of which seemed to revolve around "the game, culminating with our last party in August 2017 at Vincent's Clam bar with eighteen members of the team.

This team, along with the cheerleaders, band members,

coaches, teachers, and the entire student body, had a special bond. It extended from their high school days through almost six decades after graduation. The numerous parties and reunions were a celebration of life together, first as high school students, then as grade school students, and finally as young children who had grown up in the same extraordinary era— the '50s. They were all children of "the greatest generation" and had cherished the simple joys of life. What better way to celebrate life than with family, friends, teammates, and class-mates at a party? For many of us, our classmates were an extended family.

Three cheers: *Hip, hip, hooray! Hip, hip, hooray! Hip, hip, hooray!* And the celebration would live on in our hearts forever!

# 21

# AFTER GRADUATION: SUMMER OF 1961

Belive it or not, I did graduate with the rest of my class, and on time. There was a rumor started by one of the wise guy students that the faculty had a meeting to discuss the possibility that Ray Heron would return for another year at North if he didn't pass all his classes. They made sure that possibility was eliminated regardless of whatever mark he received on his final tests. I can assure you that the rumor was false.

I breezed through all my finals in the only three courses that were mandatory for graduation: English with a final score of 79, Health with a 76, and Mechanical Drawing with a 78.

Now I was free with no plans but to have a good time and chill during the hot summer. Sue had other plans for herself. She was going to start working at the phone company on split shifts. She would go in the morning and come home, then go back in the late afternoon. Well, that's no fun. She would be making good money, around one hundred plus dollars a week. I, on the other hand, was trying to figure out how to retire.

Well, my dad had plans for me if I was now retired. He said I could work for him, and my payment would be room and meals. I would have to make some money by the end of the year to pay for my car insurance. So, I started working, painting the house. My next project was the lawn, which needed way too much attention as it was a mess. There was no power lawn mower; everything was done by hand. Then it was down to the basement to finish it for entertainment purposes. My dad wanted to turn it into a party room, so he built a bar using white birch trees that were on the lot next to our home. We painted the cinderblocks to look like red bricks. June was done, and July flew by to the beginning of August.

Dad said, "All you have to do is work during the day, and you can go out every night." This, with a little money for gas and taking my girl Sue out. The first thing we did was put up sheetrock on the ceiling then tape, spackle, and paint. Dad built a ramp to walk up the sheetrock to the height we needed to hold the sheetrock to the ceiling while we screwed it to the studs. It worked well, and we finished the job in the first two weeks of August. We had to lift the house first as it was leaning to the right. Dad had steel columns that expanded with large gears at the end that were turned with a steel handle. We put up three of them, and the house was now straight for the sheetrock to be placed. After the ceiling was finished and painted, we were just about done. The bar, brick walls, ceiling, and now just a rug to cover the cement floor, and we have our party room. Boy, did we use that space for some of the greatest parties with both family and friends!

Something went wrong between Sue and me, and we had a falling out. We broke up! I was still very much in love, and I just couldn't function at home anymore. I had to get away. Then one morning I got up early and left a note for my parents which only said, "Going south, I'll call you later when I get there." What a terrible note for a kid who was still only eighteen years old to leave. I had no understanding of how parents would react. I must have been really upset not to be thinking very well. I had 47 dollars, a full tank of gas, and a road map. I just assumed they thought I'd be heading for Grandma's house in Miami, Florida. Figuring that with my driving, what could it take, one day I thought to myself. I'd be there in no time and I planned to call them at night so they knew I was safe and so they didn't worry too much.

It was about 4:30 in the morning and first light. I started up my 1952 Oldsmobile convertible and took off for an exciting adventure with some food and water for the one-day trip. To head south, I had to go through Manhattan because the Verrazano Bridge hadn't been built yet. I thought it would take the whole day to pass through Manhattan and get to the New Jersey Turnpike, but it only took a couple of hours because there wasn't much traffic that early in the morning. At that time highways US 1 and 95 also didn't exist yet, so I took anything that said south and looked like it was heading in the right direction on my map.

This was a good thing for me because Highway 301 took me through Baltimore, MD instead of avoiding the city by passing through remote towns and countryside. Still in the mid-morning, I lost my brakes in Baltimore. I pulled into a gas station, and my Guardian Angel must've directed me there because they were so nice. They asked me where I was headed, and I replied, "Miami." The mechanic looked at me then looked at the car and shook his head like we wouldn't make it. Then looked at the brakes and said he could fix them, but after looking at me and my car, said, "I don't know what it will cost until I start working on them."

I said, "I have 47 dollars, but I will need some of that for gas to finish my trip." I proceeded to do my calculations out loud so the mechanic knew just how much money I had for the brakes. I didn't want him to start a job if I couldn't pay him because I didn't know what he would do. Maybe impound my car and leave me stranded, I thought. I had a 22-gallon gas tank which cost $4.50 to fill. At fifteen miles per gallon, I would need four more fill-ups to get to my grandma's home. That's 47 dollars, minus the eighteen dollars, which leaves 29 dollars for brakes. I asked him if that was enough to get me on my way. He smiled and said, "Don't worry, son. I'll get you going soon, and you will have money to see Grandma."

So, he went to work right away, and I went for a short walk to stretch out my legs and use the bathroom. I washed my face, which felt good in the heat. He finished the job and said that'd be thirteen dollars, and then gave me some sandwiches and drinks. I have no idea what he did, but the parts must have cost more. Then the food and drinks and directions to the highway. Wow, I said thank you very much for your kindness and generosity. Of course, I thanked God for sending me an Angel in this beautiful man who helped a lost teenager survive a long dangerous trip.

It's off we go to the highway south to Virginia, North Carolina, South Carolina, and Georgia before I hit Florida. I had lost so much time, but now I have brakes, so I can speed up on the open road. I drive through Virginia on a beautiful afternoon. The countryside with the mountains in the background is just magnificent. It would take a poet to describe this picture that my eyes are witnessing these magnificent views for the first time. Then when I hit the Carolinas, it starts to rain, but it's light, so I stick my head out the window to feel the cold water on my head. Refreshing me as I still have a long way to go. South Carolina was the 740-mile marker on my map. Now 4 in the afternoon because of lost time in Baltimore with my brakes.

The highway was straight and open through the Carolinas. Now I'm in Georgia, which is a large state, 366 miles to the Florida border. Traveling along, I see these old shacks on the roadside, but what is strange to me is many have new cars parked outside of them. Some even have Cadillacs in front of those run-down homes. Coming up on my right, I see a chain gang and the Sheriff's deputies with loaded rifles standing guard. I had never seen a chain gang up close and personal, only in the movies. It was a sad sight but a reminder that I better not do anything wrong in Georgia. Or I could be standing there with those guys on the chain gang. I wanted to speed up past the gang, but my brain kicked in and said do the speed limit only, please!

I kept my composure, refrained from speeding, and was almost out of Georgia when my car just stopped. I pulled over on the shoulder of the road to see what was wrong. I put the car in park and tried to start it, but nothing happened. I opened the hood to see if I could find the problem. It's now 8:30pm in Georgia and getting dark. I don't want to be here, but I can't find the problem. So, I'm thinking if it's not visible, it must be internal. Maybe if I just let it sit for a while to cool off, it will start again.

I waited maybe 45 minutes, which seemed like a lifetime as the sun sunk and the blackness of night covered everything. There were no streetlights, and no lights coming from anywhere except cars passing by. No one was going to stop for a stranger, and I was not leaving the car to flag a stranger down. Only the police would pull over for a car parked on the side of a major highway at night. Well, luckily for me, the police didn't come because I had little money left and as I later found out, I could have been locked up as a vagrant. After another prayer, the car started, so I was right; there was a defective part internally, and when reaching a certain high temperature, the engine cut out. Wow, these last 550 miles were going to be very interesting, I thought to myself as I continued on my journey.

At last, I saw a beautiful sign that read, "Welcome to Florida." It was very late at night with 400 miles to go. If traveling

50 miles per hour, the trip would take eight more hours. But I could cut that time by driving faster and taking a shortcut, bringing the travel time down to less than six hours. To save time, I decided to take Highway 27 which would pass through Everglades swamps and a Seminole Reservation. Florida's 27 was listed as a highway but was actually a two-lane road, one in each direction, with no lights and no shoulders. It passed through the Everglades, and the road narrowed as it graded down into the marshes that were filled with every bug imaginable and all kinds of dangerous wildlife like alligators, snakes, and panthers. Additionally, the Seminoles had not signed a peace treaty with the United States Government, so back then crossing their land in the middle of the night added to the feeling of danger already building in my young, naïve, late-teenage mind. However, as I got on Highway 27 heading to Grandma's in Southwest Miami, I convinced myself that neither the alligators, snakes, panthers nor Seminoles would be a problem because I'd be in my car going 90 miles per hour.

I started down 27, and as I looked down the road, I couldn't see anything except my headlights that were illuminating the road in front of my car. Surrounded by the darkness of night, I sped up to reduce my travel time to Miami and the safety of grandma's. My front windshield was being bombarded with hundreds of bugs splattering all over it, making it difficult to see clearly. I thought if I turned on my windshield wipers, they would probably make a bigger mess, and make it impossible for me to see the road at all. Having no windshield wiper cleaner fluid, I decided against trying the wipers. Besides, I could still see enough and the roadway was empty of any traffic. Now going 90 mph and sailing along, I heard a bang and my car started to wobble. Oh no, it was a flat tire! I pulled over on the side of the road, and because there wasn't a shoulder, my car was parked on an angle leading into the swamp. I checked the trunk for a spare tire, but it was also flat. It wouldn't have made a difference because the flat was on the side of the car that was leaning into the swamp so there was no way I could have jacked up the car to change the tire under these conditions.

Now I was stranded in the middle of the Everglades at around midnight with no other company than the sounds of the animals and bugs. I've never heard sounds like these before in any jungle movie I've ever seen. They were so loud and different; I just started to laugh, thinking what a way to go, swallowed up by the crocodiles in the swamps. I saw headlights in the distance coming my way, so I decided to waive for help. As the car came closer, the driver saw me and was afraid. He stepped on the gas to pass me by. Then another and another; all the cars did the same thing when they saw me. They stepped on the gas and went as quickly as they could to pass me. At the time, I couldn't understand why someone wouldn't stop to help. Later, the police told me why nobody stopped.

I saw another car coming toward me, but this one was different; it was slowing down as it came close to me. Then some red lights illuminated form the top of car, it was the police! I'll never forget the first words the policeman spoke to me in his southern drawl, "Well, boy, you're lucky! If the gators didn't git ya', the snakes would've!" So, that's why no one would stop for me. It would just have been too dangerous for them to get out of their car and try to help me fix my flat tire with poor visibility, wildlife lurking in the swamps, and cars passing close by at high speeds along Highway 27 in the middle of the night.

The officer then asked me if I had any money to get the car towed back to a repair shop to be fixed. I said, "No, sir, I have no money left." He then asked me where I was headed and if I had any family here in Florida. He knew I was from New York from my license plates, license, and my New York accent. I said yes, I was going to Miami to be with my grandma, aunt, uncles, and cousins. He said great; otherwise, I would've had to lock you up as a vagrant. He said take what you need from your car, and I will take you to the nearest gas station. I got my stuff, which wasn't much, and hopped into the police car. The officer said, "If the car isn't towed right away, there will be nothing left when you come back." I said, I understand how that works as the same thing happened on some highways like the Cross Bronx Expressway back home in New York.

He dropped me off at a big station where tractor-trailers stop and told the station manager about my car situation. I told him that I'd be back the following day to pick up my car and pay for it. The manager said that they wouldn't be able to repair my car that night, but that they could get me a ride to Miami. I thanked them very much and asked who would drive me to Miami which was still about 200 miles away. He said,

"Go over to that big rig over there, tell the driver I sent you over."

On the way over, I couldn't help but notice the boys sitting outside under the lights with no shirts on, just talking. It was a very hot night, but with all those bugs flying around them, it didn't make any sense to me. They never moved or swatted at the bugs or paid any attention to them at all. I wondered how they would look in the morning after all those bites.

I headed over to see the driver standing next to his tractor-trailer, checking the tires and the lights. He said, "Hop aboard, son, where are you headed?" I said, "Southwest Miami, sir; can you drop me off somewhere around there?" He said, "I'm headed that way, sure thing, kid." And we were off for Miami at last!

What the station manager didn't tell me was that this driver was looking for someone, anyone, to ride with him because he had been driving for 7 days non-stop. He couldn't keep his eyes open all the time and needed someone to watch so he didn't fall asleep during the trip. I deduced this brilliant reasoning at only eighteen years old. He told me, and I'll never forget his words to me when we started to pick up speed on the highway. "Talk to me, boy! Keep me up; I've been on the road for seven days, and these NoDoz pills aren't working as well anymore." Wow, I'm in trouble now, I thought to myself!

Now I was wide awake, talking, and watching the driver's eyes so he didn't close them and fall asleep. Well, he stayed awake for our entire trip to Miami and dropped me somewhere off the highway, but nowhere near my grandma's house in the southwest part of the city. I wished him luck and thanked him for the ride. He thanked me for keeping him up and wished me good luck as well. I prayed that God would watch over him because he needed God now more than I did.

God had done such a great job of watching over me during my brief eighteen years of life up until that point, and I still needed God to continue watching out over me. The Guardian Angel that God assigned to me should get a medal as I've counted more times than I have fingers that he saved me from an early grave. Here we go again.

During that time, there was a popular TV series called "The Fugitive" running as one of the top shows. The mysterious killer of a doctor's wife was a one-armed man that the police kept hunting. Why in the world does this come up now, you ask? Now, at eighteen years old, I'm completely lost, standing out on the street at 4am, 24 hours after I left home with nothing but a few dollars and some clothes in a bag. I started to hitchhike, hoping someone would know which way was best to get to the address that I had memorized in my head. Finally, a gentleman pulls up in a small car and says, "Where are you going?" I said, "Southwest Miami; are you going that way?" He says, "Get in, and we'll find your address." I get in, and it's a stick-shift vehicle with the gearbox on the floor and the stick coming straight up to him on his right side.

I had never seen one that high up. Usually, the stick was much lower and had to be reached with the right hand while holding the steering wheel with the left hand. Upon looking closer, I realized he only had one arm, so he needed his right hand up next to the steering wheel to steer after he shifted. He used the stub of his left arm to hold the steering wheel steady as he leaned forward. Holy crap! I thought to myself, could this be the one-armed man they were looking for on the TV series? Come on, Ray, that's all make-believe; it's a TV series! I started getting a little nervous and thinking what in the world are the odds of this happening? With this kind of luck, if I escape this predicament, maybe I should go to Las Vegas and gamble next! He then started to ask me all kinds of questions. "Where are you coming from? Where is your car? Why are you alone on this long trip?" Normal questions you would ask an eighteen-year-old teenager who only looked about fourteen, standing in the middle of the road at 4am.

He then said he had to stop at home before he could take me to my location. I started thinking that wasn't good with all that's happened so far on my journey. Sure enough, he invited me into the house while he said he needed to get a local map. Then he asked me if I would like some milk and cookies which made me nervous at the thought they could be drugged or poisoned. I moved next to the front door wanting to escape if needed while replying no thank you to the snack. He said, "Are you sure? You must be hungry." I again politely declined saying that I was fine and that I would be home in a little while. He then found the map and said, "Ok, let's go. It shouldn't be too hard to locate."

It turned out that God sent me another angel in the gentleman who picked up a total stranger without any fear in the middle of the night even though he only had one arm to defend himself if the stranger turned against him. Wow, I thought as he drove me to Grandma's house with the map. He stopped in front of Grandma's house on 9865 SW 49$^{th}$ St and wished me luck. I got out, and as he drove away, I waved to him and said, "Thank you very much, you're a real lifesaver."

Finally, I arrived at my Grandma Anne Mackey's house in Miami! It seemed like my parents had called her because when I knocked on her door early that morning, she was already waiting for me. We shared a hug, and she quickly whipped up something for me to eat. Afterward, she prepared a bed for me, insisting that my Uncle David would help me retrieve my car. I kissed Grandma and told her how much I missed her. She used to live in Queens, but her son David had purchased this house

L to R: Linda, myself and our Grandma Mackey circa 1945

for her in Southwest Miami. It was nestled in a lovely neighborhood close to her daughter and six grandchildren. Grandma had grown quite content with the move, especially after a year of adjusting to her new surroundings.

Later that day, David accompanied me to retrieve my car, which had been repaired after the flat tire incident. However, my uncle informed me that all the tires were in poor condition.

There was very little tread left on any of them. David decided to follow me back, just in case one of the tires decided to go flat. He emphasized, "Don't speed." Fortunately, we made it home without any issues, and I called my parents to let them know I had arrived safely. I skipped mentioning all the challenges I had faced on the journey and simply said it was a good trip.

My other uncle, Dick, mentioned an intriguing opportunity for me to work as a hand on a sailing ship that traded goods in the Florida islands if I decided to stay. I told him I would consider it. During my visit, I also caught up with cousins I hadn't seen in a while. They had all moved down here from Brooklyn in the early '50s, and our family had visited them in 1958.

Little did I know that my dad was planning to fly down and take me back home at the end of the week. In hindsight, it was a fortunate decision because the sailing ship I had contemplated joining ended up sinking. Meanwhile, the tires on my car were in terrible shape, and I didn't have the money to replace them. My last week had provided plenty of adventure to last a lifetime, and I was ready to return home. My visit with my Florida family had been wonderful, and my anxiety about the breakup with Sue had significantly diminished.

When my dad arrived, we were both overjoyed to see each other and greeted with a big hug. He looked at the tires and suggested we replace them all with new ones. We did, and the car was running smoothly for our trip back to New York. Dad enjoyed his visit with the family, and my Godmother Ellie was relieved that Dad would be driving back up north with me. She had been quite anxious when my mom called to inform them of my trip down here. Thankfully, everything fell into place.

On our journey back up North, Dad suggested, "You drive, and I'll get some rest in the back." It was a very different trip compared to the one down, free of any drama. The one thing that stood out was a memorable steak dinner we enjoyed in a small town in northern Georgia. It was both affordable and incredibly delicious, reflecting the area's cattle territory. We returned home without any hiccups, and Mom was overjoyed to see us. We hugged tightly, and I kissed her. When she looked into my eyes, she admonished me, saying, "Don't ever do that again," as if she knew how close I had come to not returning home. Mothers possess a sixth sense when it comes to their children. That marked the end of the excitement for my family during that summer, and the rest of the season was pleasantly quiet.

# 22

---

# MY RETIREMENT BEGINS

The end of my summer marked the beginning of my retirement. For the first time since I was five years old, I wasn't going to school. My thoughts often ventured into uncharted territory, pondering how I could retire and still cover my expenses. If I truly wanted to make the most of my youth and retire early, I needed to redefine retirement. Here was the blueprint had in mind:

1. Instead of being jobless, find one that pays enough to get by with minimal responsibilities, short hours, mindless tasks, and the flexibility to take days off as needed.
2. Avoid getting engaged or married.
3. Live at home until I save enough to move into an apartment.

Following these plans, I would be able to do whatever I pleased and go wherever I pleased, whenever I pleased, with whomever I pleased, for as long as I pleased. It was the perfect formula for my retirement! So, I embarked on a quest to find that perfect job. I landed a position as a taxi driver in Malverne. The owner offered me a daytime gig from Monday to Friday, with no nighttime or weekend shifts, plus the added perk of taking the cab home after work. It was perfect for my retirement plan! My parents had granted me the freedom to stay at home until I figured out what I wanted to do with my life. At just nineteen years old, I knew it would take some time. As for Sue and me, we had no chance of getting engaged; we weren't even dating anymore.

And so, at the age of 19, my retirement officially began. I zipped around town in my taxi, picking up fares during the day and using the car to go out at night. It was a beautiful arrangement because the Malverne police recognized me as the taxi driver, sparing me from minor traffic infractions. Whether I was working or enjoying the cab for personal outings, they didn't know. And I was getting paid for all of it. Dreams do come true.

One night, I was out with Tommy Scibelli, who was upset because his girlfriend had just moved to Ohio. We were drinking in the taxi, and on our way home, he asked me to stop by a roadside sign. Tommy ripped it down and flung it back at a taxi. This became a regular occurrence along Franklin Ave. in Franklin Square. At one point, a police car noticed Tommy walking beside the cab and pulled over to inquire about our late-night escapade. I told the officer that Tommy had had too much to drink and had called a taxi to pick him up. I was trying to get him into the cab and take him home. The officer sternly instructed Tommy to get in the cab and head home. Tommy hopped in, and we drove off. Thankfully, the cop didn't inspect the inside of the cab, where a pile of signs lay strewn on the floor.

My best tip came from Butch Hoffman's mom, whom I chauffeured to the beauty salon once a week. She always tipped me more than the fare. I adored Butch's mom; she was unfailingly kind. She was also the first person to introduce me to English muffins, which I had never encountered before. They were delicious toasted with sweet butter and jelly. Everything was going according to plan until the following year when I got back together with Sue.

Although I wasn't making much money as a taxi driver, I was having a blast. Now, I needed to boost my income while maintaining the job criteria for retirement. I found the perfect opportunity at Mercy Hospital, working in the X-ray department as an orderly under the supervision of Sister Mary Constance. The hospital was overseen by the benevolent nuns, led by the Mother Superior, whom I once met in an elevator. We had a pleasant conversation on our way to the third floor, which housed the X-ray facilities. The job was from 8am to 4pm, with an eight-minute commute via the parkway, only a few exits from my home, getting on the Southern State at exit seventeen and driving only two exits before getting off at exit nineteen and right into the hospital parking lot.

My most fulfilling moments at the hospital were spent with the kids on the second-floor pediatrics section during slow periods. There was also a small chapel on the same floor where I would pray for those who needed it most. It was the most rewarding job I had ever held. There was no pressure; the only requirement was to care for all the patients with love, kindness, and compassion. I cherished my time there.

After a year, I left the hospital and embarked on another trip to Florida to visit the other half of my family. Why not? I was retired, free from restrictions or demanding responsibilities. This time, my parents were in the know and had ample funds, fresh tires, and a different car. There were no issues during the journey down or back. I had a fantastic time with my cousins in Florida and cherished the moments spent with my grandmother.

Upon returning home in 1963, it was time to secure a mindless job to support my activities. I began my search for that ideal retirement job, just as Tommy Scibelli was looking for a job to earn money. He wasn't considering retirement yet. I found a position in the shipping department at Oxford Filing Supply Company in Garden City. The hours were from 8 to 4, with no nights or weekends, and it was only a fifteen-minute drive from home. It offered the highest pay I had received thus far, and I was hired. However, they didn't hire Tommy. The mistake we made was saying we were friends; businesses didn't usually hire friends.

This job fits perfectly into my plans. I started working there and discovered they had an industrial fast-pitch softball team that competed with other businesses. I felt like I was in heaven; it couldn't get any better in the workforce. But it did because they also had a bowling league. It seemed like the ideal place for me.

Over the next ten years, I worked at this company while playing fast-pitch softball, bowling with coworkers, participating in a slow-pitch softball league with my oldest friend, Bernie, engaging in a two-man scratch bowling league, and bowling side games for money at nighttime with my childhood friend Sal Pepitone, playing on an eight-man touch football team, and drag racing my Corvette on both tracks and streets. I even won a trophy in the quarter-mile drag race at Islip Speedway. Could I have managed all of this by waiting until the age of 65 to retire?

At this time, I was back together with Sue once again. Our relationship had its ups and downs, with periods of being together and apart from 1960 until our final breakup in March of 1965. Despite the turbulence, we had our fair share of good times and even some rather interesting ones.

One notable memory was when President Kennedy was assassinated. In a somewhat impulsive move, Sue, her sister Linda, and her boyfriend decided to jump into my car and head to D.C. to pay their respects. I probably said something like, "It's a piece of cake, just 226 miles. An average person would take about four hours, but I can do better." And so, off we went, with Linda and her boyfriend sharing some affectionate moments in the back seat for most of the journey. It must have been quite romantic because they eventually got married.

As we were driving, the radio delivered a shocking news-flash: Jack Ruby had just shot and killed Oswald in the basement of the Dallas police headquarters. This happened just two days after President Kennedy's assassination. We couldn't believe what we were hearing, but we didn't turn back. We continued to D.C. to view the President.

Upon arriving in D.C., we encountered heavy traffic, and National Guard soldiers were scattered throughout the city, all heavily armed. The soldiers halted us from getting anywhere near the White House or the Capitol buildings. They inquired about our intentions, and I informed them. However, they promptly informed us that it wasn't happening that day and politely asked us to turn around and head back home. I noticed them searching other cars, presumably because they appeared suspicious. Strangely, they didn't find anything suspicious about two teenagers in the back seat and a young couple in the front seat.

What I had completely forgotten about was the loaded 30/30 rifle in the trunk of my car. If they had decided to search my vehicle under those conditions, I would likely have ended up in jail. The girl's father would have had to come to their rescue, and I doubt the family would have ever spoken to me again. I never mentioned the rifle to Sue or Linda, as it would only have caused trouble for me. We turned around and drove back home without any further incidents.

Another memorable incident occurred during a night out

at a club called The Sands with some high school friends. An exotic dancer was performing on the dance floor, attempting to entertain the crowd. However, as I looked around, not many people seemed to be paying attention to her.

After a few drinks, I decided to help her out and capture everyone's attention with some dance moves of my own. I jumped onto the dance floor, making all kinds of wild moves, and it worked. The crowd went wild, and I even received a standing ovation. Unfortunately, the poor young lady trying to make a living didn't get the attention she deserved. After my performance, I looked up to see a fight erupting on the mezzanine. Roger Angrisani had thrown a punch at someone, and chaos ensued. My act may not have been as much of a distraction as I had hoped, or perhaps everyone was too intoxicated to notice. I attempted to go upstairs to intervene, but I was blocked, and by the time I got there, the fight had already ended.

During those wonderful ten years of retirement, there were countless games, parties, and adventures. While I can't possibly list them all here, I'll share one memorable summer experience when the guys returned home from college. We decided to venture up to Loon Lake in upstate New York.

We set out in a couple of cars, with Bernie Havern, Roger Olsen, Tony DiBenedetto, Artie Schnitzer, Tommy Scibelli, Steve Due, and Lou Martorello, to stay in a cabin by the lake. We all arrived together around lunchtime on the first day, except for Lou Martorello, who arrived later that evening in a small convertible bug.

Bernie had made all the arrangements for our stay. It was a lovely cottage right on the lake, and there was a college nearby. We had a couple of canoes at our disposal, as well as some lawn furniture to relax outside. We wasted no time jumping into the lake, with some of us daring enough to venture into the canoes. Roger swam like a fish, looking completely at home in the water, while some of us did not share his aquatic talents. We had a fantastic time, filled with laughter, mischief, and nostalgia. It was our first vacation together since high school, and we were making up for lost time. Notably, Lou was married at the time, and his wife had to stay home. She showed remarkable understanding and patience.

However, our great mistake was allowing Artie to be the bartender for the day. He whipped up his infamous punch, you know, the one where he empties an entire bottle of vodka and adds just a thimble of juice with a bit of ice. After the guys finished that bowl of punch, all hell broke loose. To make matters worse, none of us had eaten much, exacerbating our intoxicated state.

Steve, known as "Mr. Tranquility," kicked off the afternoon with a bang by sinking both canoes in the lake. But Steve wasn't finished yet. While Bernie and Tommy wrestled in the cabin, essentially tearing holes in the walls as they tossed each other around the room, Artie sat comfortably at the kitchen table, staring at the now-empty punch bowl, attempting to figure out where all the punch had gone.

Steve continued his escapades outside, cleaning off the furniture by throwing it all into the lake. Then, the people staying in the neighboring cabin pulled in, took one look at our chaotic scene, and promptly left.

Once we managed to pull Bernie away from Tommy and avert a potential homicide, things finally calmed down. We took a break, cleaned up, and headed into town. Another friend from high school, Lou, was supposed to meet us at Loon Lake. He spotted us walking in town and pulled over. We all went out for dinner, as it was around six o'clock and none of us had eaten since earlier in the day. After dinner, we treated ourselves to some ice cream and then hopped back into our cars for the short drive back to the cabin. Lou was in his convertible with the top down on a beautiful evening.

Now, you might think that after the ice cream cone incident, the guys would have finished their cones, but you'd be mistaken. Instead, they decided to use those ice cream cones as ammunition and fired them at Lou's convertible. As they pelted the car, I started to pick up speed while Lou desperately tried to raise the convertible top, attempting this daring feat at 60 miles an hour to avoid being bombarded with frozen treats.

Unfortunately for Lou, he couldn't get the top up, and it looked like the wind might rip it off. He had no choice but to lower it again as our speed continued to climb. In the darkness, someone came up with the brilliant idea to lose Lou.

We found ourselves on mountain roads with twists and turns, no streetlights, and only the headlights of the car behind us visible. How do you lose the car tailing you? Well, apparently, in our infinite wisdom, we decided to turn off our headlights. Yes, you read that correctly. We were cruising at high speeds on dark, winding roads, trying to shake our friend. This was the only road leading to the cabin, so he would've found it anyway, but adding some suspense to the trip made it interesting. We may not have been the brightest crayons in the box, but we sure knew how to have a good time.

Back at the cabin, we met up with Lou, and we all headed inside for a night of card games, jokes, and boisterous laughter, much to the chagrin of any nearby wildlife. After a long day filled with adventure and a fair share of drinks, we slept soundly that night.

The next morning, Tony took charge of the kitchen, whipping up bacon and eggs, and brewing coffee for the guys. One of Tony's great talents was that he had a knack for cooking up just about anything, which is one of the reasons why Bernie always insisted on bringing him along. Surveying the damage from the previous day's antics, Bernie asked the inevitable question, "What are we going to do about all this?" My response was simple: Steve would fish out the canoes and outdoor furniture from the lake, and we would all pitch in to help. Bernie had another question, "What about the holes in the wall?" I casually replied, "No problem, just move the pictures to cover all the holes." I pointed out that there was even one hole a foot off the floor, but a picture could easily mask that as well. I thought it would make for a great conversation piece. As for what happened when Bernie made the final payment or if there were any additional charges, he never mentioned it, but that was the last time we visited that place.

On the second day of our trip, we ventured into the lake,

retrieved the canoes and lawn furniture, and placed them back on the beach in front of the cabin. Tony and Artie tackled the kitchen cleanup, while Bernie and Tommy covered the holes in the wall with strategically placed pictures. Roger and Ray took care of the canoes, and Steve and Lou handled the outdoor furniture. With everything cleaned up and we changed after our swim, it was time to head into town.

We ended up at a local bar and grill for food and drinks. However, Bernie and Roger, it turns out, weren't great drinkers. Soon enough, I heard two loud voices exclaiming, "Does anyone here want to take us on?" I looked up and saw them both standing back-to-back, each over six feet three inches with a combined weight of over 500 pounds. Laughter erupted from our group as we playfully challenged the locals.

We managed to have dinner without any further outbursts, but we wisely decided not to let Bernie and Roger drive back to the cabin. We spent the night talking under the beautiful summer sky on the shores of the small lake in upstate New York. The next morning, it was time to leave and head back home. It was a weekend none of us would ever forget, and we all shared a sense of fondness for the experience. During my retirement years, there were many more gatherings, barbecues, games, and events, including a couple of wild trips to West Point football games and Mets baseball games.

Now, we fast forward to 1964, and I have managed to save enough money to buy my very first Chevy Corvette. It was a 1961 model with two tops and was specially set up for racing. Under the hood, it packed a 283 HP engine with fuel injection and 327 heads. The gear ratio was optimized for quarter-mile drag racing, featuring a 256 first gear and a 4.56 rear end. I took it to the Islip Speedway track, where I won a trophy for first place. There were also numerous street races, none of which I remember losing. I had the seats rolled and pleated in leather for an additional $60. I eventually sold it in 1967.

Then came my 1968 metallic blue convertible Corvette. Not only could that 'Vette could fly, it had the bonus of four-wheel disc brakes so it could stop on a dime. One night, I decided to put its braking system to the test. I took it on the Parkway to Jones Beach and hit a whopping 135 miles an hour to see how those brakes would respond. With just a tap of the brakes, the car slowed down immediately. It was the most responsive braking system I had ever experienced.

By 1969 my retirement days were going just as I had hoped and I was thriving. I moved out of my parents' home and bid them farewell with heartfelt thanks for giving me the space to live life on my terms. I found a charming three-room apartment in Long Beach, just a block away from the beach. It was located on the first floor of a house and even had a patio in the backyard, all for the reasonable rent of $150 a month. Here I was, driving a new Corvette convertible, living near the beach a 27-year-old with a sports car by the ocean. This, I thought to myself, is how retirement should be!

As for my romantic life, Sue and I had parted ways for good in 1965. I was still actively engaged in sports and didn't have any intention of settling down with a steady girlfriend, but I still enjoyed the company of the young ladies. I met some at work through our coed bowling league, where we'd hit the lanes around 7:30pm and inevitably end up in the bowling alley's bar, chatting away until nearly midnight.

One memorable night, after a few too many drinks, I put my bag with the bowling ball down to chat with one of the young women. After saying our goodbyes, I hopped into my 'Vette and backed right over my bowling ball. I was puzzled, thinking how that could have happened because I didn't see anything behind me when I backed up. Upon getting out of the car, I noticed the ball and realized I might have indulged in one drink too many that night. Fortunately, the ball and bag were both made very well so there was no damage to either of them or my car.

Speaking of ladies, I met a couple of noteworthy young ladies at work. Mary was very nice, but when I asked her out to a nightclub, her mother promptly intervened, deeming her too young for such adventures. Then there was Phyllis, with whom I enjoyed bowling; we had a great time hanging out after our games. We even attended a wedding in Queens together, which made for a memorable evening. I thoroughly enjoyed our time together.

But I eventually found the perfect girl for Saturday night dates and special occasions like weddings, bar mitzvahs, and birthdays. Her name was Maureen, and we went on a date almost every Saturday night and for any special event. We never dated during the week or on Friday nights. On Fridays, she did her own thing, and during the week, we rarely saw each other except at bowling or company gatherings. Our arrangement was unspoken but mutually understood. We always had a date when needed, saving us from the last-minute scramble to find one. I'd pick her up at her house, but I never went inside, as she preferred to avoid her parents' barrage of questions like, "Is this the one?" or "Are you serious about this boy?" or "What does he do?" This arrangement went on for about a year before we simply stopped seeing each other.

What a truly magnificent time it was in the history of New York sports when I moved into my apartment in the fall of 1969. Everything in my sports world seemed to take on a magical quality. First, the Mets secured the pennant and went on to face the formidable Baltimore Orioles in the World Series. I remember my dad asking me, "What do you think, son?" My reply was confident: I bet on the Mets winning in a four-game sweep. Well, I was almost right; they did win in a four-game sweep after losing the first game. The New York Mets were crowned World Series Champions in 1969!

Then, in the winter of 1970, the New York Jets, led by quarterback Joe Willie Namath, secured the American Football League title. They faced off against the Baltimore Colts, led by Johnny Unitas of the National Football League, for the world championship. Joe boldly guaranteed a win, despite Las Vegas odds favoring them as eighteen-point underdogs. Joe Willie flashed a grin and quipped, "The one-eyed monster doesn't lie," referring to the projector he used to watch game films. Inspired by his confidence, I placed a bet on the Jets. It seemed Joe had spotted something in those films that he could exploit during the game, and indeed, he did. The Jets pulled off the biggest upset in football history, becoming the World Champions of the NFL!

As spring arrived, the New York Knicks were making their way through the playoffs, inching closer to the finals. I vividly recall listening to those games on the radio in my new apartment, thinking that this was simply unbelievable. The magical journey continued as the 1970 New York Knicks faced off against the LA Lakers for the world championship. In the fifth game, held at Madison Square Garden and with the series tied at 2-2, their star center Willis Reed suffered an injury. Despite this setback, the Knicks somehow found a way to win the game. They then traveled back to L.A., where the Lakers emerged victorious. This brought the series back to New York, tied at three games each. It was a do-or-die situation, and with Reed still injured, could they possibly pull it off? To everyone's astonishment, Willis Reed made a dramatic comeback, and Clyde Frazier played the game of his life. The Knicks secured the victory, winning 4-3, and were crowned World Champions in 1970. It marked the culmination of one of the greatest New York sports stories of all time, with three New York teams securing championship titles!

However, amidst all this sports glory, life dealt some heartbreaking blows. On December 27, 1969, I lost my childhood friend to a booby-trap bomb in the jungles of Vietnam. Tommy, my friend, had chosen to enlist in the army, a decision prompted by his father's sacrifice on the beaches of Normandy in 1944. Tragically, Tommy's father gave his life in World War II when Tommy was just one year old, and his brother Bobby was still in his mother's womb. His mother never remarried and raised the boys with the help of her father, creating a close-knit family.

During that time, Tommy's wife, Lorraine, called me seeking advice about Tommy's upcoming R&R in Hawaii for two weeks. She expressed concerns about the distance and expense. I told her, "Go and be with him, cherish your time together in the beautiful Hawaiian Islands. When he returns home, you'll always have those incredible memories. What a wonderful vacation you two will have and deserve." I believed that regardless of the outcome, it was the right decision. If she didn't go and something happened to Tommy, she might never forgive herself. But by going, they could create beautiful memories in paradise to hold onto even if the worst should occur.

Then, in November, 1970 took a tragic turn for our family. On election day, my father, only 52 years old, suffered a heart attack and passed away. I was devastated because I never had the chance to bid him a proper farewell or express how much I loved him. The day before, he hadn't been feeling well, and my mother called for an ambulance. Unfortunately, I was still at work, or I would have taken him to the hospital myself. My boss, Terry, a kind and understanding man, assured me that everything would be alright and that my dad was in good hands at the hospital. I rushed to the hospital to see what was happening, as my father had always disliked hospitals.

I couldn't help but recall a previous incident when I had driven him to the hospital. I was eighteen years old at the time, and he was in excruciating pain. He had asked me to drive him because my mom was out, and he would never consider calling an ambulance. So, I drove him there, and they rushed him to the emergency room while I waited anxiously outside. He spent quite some time inside, and when he finally emerged, he was still in pain but insisted on going home. I asked him what had happened inside, and he explained that they wanted to perform exploratory surgery to locate some kidney stones. He said that's when he decided he'd had enough and left the hospital. Despite the pain, he never underwent the procedure. I drove him home, and he passed the kidney stone eventually.

This time, things were different. When I walked into his hospital room, I found him hooked up to an IV and asked how he was feeling. He smiled and assured me that he would be going home the next day. I inquired about what had happened, and my mother explained that his blood pressure had spiked dangerously high. The first thing they did was measure his blood pressure, and it had registered a shocking 200 over 190. They quickly managed to bring it down and started him on medication, advising us to pick him up the next day. We left the hospital, thinking that everything was under control, as my father had even managed to make light of the situation and had us laughing about it. However, the next day, when my mother went to pick him up, she discovered that he had passed away alone during the night because no one had called us. It was an unimaginable shock for our family, and it took a long time to reconcile with the doctors' inaccurate diagnosis and the hospital's complete lack of compassion for our loss.

In the aftermath of my father's passing, I moved back in with my mother to ensure she wouldn't be alone and to provide support wherever it was needed. I decided to keep my apartment in Long Beach, which I visited on Saturdays for walks along the beach. I continued to work, and my employer granted me time off for the funeral and to help take care of our family's needs. My mother, a remarkable woman, was still working at Sperry Gyroscope as an executive secretary for Mr. Sperry himself. I felt immense pride in her accomplishments, as she had taught herself to type at over 80 words per minute and was skilled in shorthand. My brother, Michael, was serving in the army, stationed in Washington, D.C., working in the military police. He came home to be with us during that challenging time, and together with my sister, Linda, we bid our final farewell to our beloved father.

## 23

---

# MY RETIREMENT ENDS

After enjoying twelve years of early retirement, in 1973 everyone started trying to get me to settle down. All of my friends were married with children by that time, so they wanted me to get married and start a family so I could be as happy as they were. Or maybe they were just envious to see me as a young single guy driving a hot new Camaro, living at the beach, and enjoying my retirement. My most recent retirement transaction had been selling my Corvette convertible and special ordering a new Camaro Rally Sport with Super Sport additions. It was a rare, powerful car perfect for showing off near the beach.

I was set up on blind dates, fix-me-up dates, and dates that I met in bars or parties. Thinking back, I realized that I had gone out with about fifteen different young ladies in my life up until that point, but still hadn't found the right one. There was

Sue, Mary, Maureen, Phyllis, Barbara, Sophie, Roslyn, Jane, Carol, Janet, Josephine, and a few others whose names I couldn't remember. My friends too had realized this and were on a mission to get me hitched, but I was in no rush. My old friend Joe Corea's wife Mary Jeanne was especially keen on finding me the perfect match for me. Mary Jeanne thought that I was rich because I drove a fancy Corvette convertible and lived on the beach. But she couldn't have been more wrong.

I just quit working for Oxford Filing Supply in Garden City and, wasn't looking for another job because I had saved enough money to cover all my expenses for a while. I was just enjoying my retired single life. As many retired folks do, I figured I'd dabble in a night class at Nassau Community College. I would try just one three-credit course to see if I would like it, learn something worthwhile, and keep my retired mind sharp. In addition to taking a class, I was also coaching and running our eight-man two-hand touch bar league football team to keep busy. Our team's sponsor was McQuade's Pub in Rockville Centre where we would go every Sunday after our games. Some of our games started as early as 9am, then it was off to the bar where we drank, ate, and watched football and baseball for the rest of the day. It was so much fun to hang out with my friends all day and watch games on TV together. There was so much kidding around, laughing, and betting on every game. But many of the bets only consisted of who was buying the next drink, big money was never part of our bets.

We were all close friends and we all simply enjoyed spending the day together.

Though this was a two-hand touch bar league when someone carrying the football got "touched", the defensive player made sure the referee saw the contact clearly by making sure the ball carrier hit the turf. There were some tough guys and exceptional football players in this so-called touch league. We played against Rollie Stichweh, who quarterbacked the Army team against Navy quarterback Roger Staubach in the 1964 Army/Navy game. Behind Stichweh, Army defeated heavily favored Navy led by the 1963 Heisman Trophy winner and celebrated rival quarterback Staubach, by a score of 11 to 8. After being named the best college football player in the nation in 1963, Staubach then went on to an illustrious eleven-year NFL career leading the Dallas Cowboys to two Super Bowl victories and three additional Super Bowl appearances. Just nine years later, we were privileged to play on the same field with Stichweh. This was the league, one-time outstanding high school or college players now in their late 20s or early 30s maintaining their love for the game after their days of tackle football had ended by playing rough touch football on Sunday mornings. Except now, most of the guys, except single guys in early retirement like me, had to go to work the next day to support their families.

On a Saturday night one weekend, which happened to be October 26, 1973, we had a get-together to celebrate friendship and excitement for our upcoming game the following day, a sort of adult pep rally you could say. Unbeknownst to me,

Mary Jeanne had invited her friend Lois, and told her before the party started that I was rich, had a place at the beach, drove a sportscar, was single, and was only 30 years old. God bless Mary Jeanne, she never stopped trying to set me up! Lois came to the party with her friend Barbara, who was Mary Jeanne's cousin. I knew Barbara because Mary Jeanne tried to fix me up with her a few years ago, but I had declined that attempt because Barbara was too young for me at the time. Remembering what had happened back then, Mary Jeanne lied about my age to Lois (I was actually 31 years old) and told me that Lois was 24 though she was only 23. So, Lois and I both believed that only a six-year age difference existed between us when we were actually eight and a half years apart. But at that moment, I didn't see age, I just saw a beautiful young lady with long flowing brown hair sitting across from me.

The first thing Lois noticed that night was that we were wearing the same color shoes. Joe's living room was full of people having talking, laughing and having a good time, so it the environment did not provide ample opportunities for Lois and I to get acquainted. But Barbara and Lois said they would be coming to the game the next morning, so I'd have more time to get to know her after the game at the bar. Lois and Barbara said that it was getting late, so we said good night and they left. I found out much later that they were just dumping us and going out for some drinks at McQuade's, a neighborhood bar and grill. Mary Jeanne came over to me and said, "Well, what do you think?" with a big smile. Joe piped in, "If I wasn't married, I'd ask her out right away." "She is very nice, I'll talk to her tomorrow after the game, " I replied.

Early the next morning, which was a Sunday, Lois was right there on time to watch the whole game. I noticed that she was very enthusiastically cheering on our team to victory. I remember thinking to myself how great it was that she was a real sports fan, just like I was! Then it's off to the bar where we spent some time chatting. She was enjoying the games on TV, which I found refreshing in a young lady. Wow, I thought she loved sports. I discovered upon further conversation that she was a real Yankee fan who also loved the Jets. We had a great time, but I didn't ask her out until three weeks later and a couple of calls from Mary Jeanne urging me to call her. I don't know why I waited so long. Maybe I waited because I knew she was the one and I was nervous about committing.

I finally called and made our first date together and then everything changed. She gave me her address and the time to pick her up. I drove over to New Hyde Park to take her out for a casual bowling night. She said she liked to bowl, and I was a very good bowler so I thought it would be a fun way to spend our first date together.

I pulled up in front of the house and rang the bell. Much to my surprise, a young lady with short blonde hair opened the door and greeted me with a friendly hello. I wondered to myself whether this person was Lois, or perhaps a sister, because her hair looked so different than it had when we first met just a few weeks earlier. But then as she swung open the clear glass storm door to invite me inside, I saw her big beautiful brown eyes, her wide, glowing smile, and realized that it was Lois, but that she was wearing a wig as she liked to do when going out sometimes. She was so cheerful and seemed excited about our bowling date. She talked the whole time while I listened, which I thought was a good combination because I was never talkative when dating, but Lois loved to tell stories. Being Italian, she was very animated in conversation using her hands, and expressive body language like her beautiful facial expressions. We went to the bowling alley on Hempstead Turnpike in Elmont a big, beautiful establishment that had a bar and open fireplace in the lounge area where damaged bowling pins were used firewood for extra ambiance. Well, Lois didn't bowl that well, and I didn't want to show off and embarrass her on our first date. Let's just say we had a good time and leave the scores out of it, just like I do nowadays when I play golf on a beautiful day but don't shoot very well. At those times, I stop keeping track of the score and just enjoy the day, the people I'm with, and the scenery.

Lois and I went into the lounge to sit near the fireplace and have a drink. We both loved it there and often returned to enjoy the warmth of the fireplace, talk and get to know each other better. After our first date, as we were getting out of the car, Lois said she was sorry for talking so much. I said it was okay because I wasn't very talkative and thanked her for carrying the conversation thereby preventing too much awkward silence from ruining our date. She smiled, and we kissed good night. As I left, I thought to myself how foolish it was to have waited three weeks to ask her out on our first date, and knew I could not wait very long to take her out again!

Two months later, during our first Christmas together as a couple, we both agreed that we were already in love. Realizing deep in my heart that we'd be spending the rest of our lives together, I knew my early retirement had come to an end and that an exciting new chapter in my life was beginning. I realized that I had to find a job, anything to start earning some income until I could find a career to support a family.

Me, start a family? Wow! I couldn't believe it was going to happen. On that Valentine's Day, I knew that other traditional, fleeting, Valentine's gifts like flowers or candy just wouldn't suffice. I had to get her something more special, something that represented my love and commitment to our relationship. So, I decided to get her a Holy Bible with the following inscription, "Presented to Lois Ann Margaret Bianco by Raymond Philip Heron II with much love - February 14, 1974, St. Valentine's Day." Together, we planned to make this our future family Bible and keep it for our children to read someday. She loved it, I was glad to have given her the perfect gift that would last forever like my love for her would.

Shortly afterward, I found a job as an airport security guard, patrolling empty tarmacs in a Jeep on the lookout for vandalism during an airline strike. At that time, Lois was already saving money for her future by working as a full-time clerical worker at Metropolitan Life Insurance on weekdays and as an A&S Department Store fitting room attendant a few evenings per week and Saturdays. When things were slow at work, she would write me sweet little notes or love letters, and I would also write to her during my security job because there was a lot of downtime. I was never able to express love in my letters as eloquently as she could, and my letters were never as well written as hers were, so I never really understood if my meaning was coming across how I wanted. Nevertheless, her notes and letters meant the world to me, so I kept them all. Over the years, when things weren't going as well as I thought they should, I would just pull out a letter, read it, remember how much she loved me, and re-discover why I should never take that love for granted. As we grew older, our expression of love for each other grew in its own way. Our love is now deeper and more committed but expressed differently, so I love to reminisce by reading those letters that remind me of how we felt about each other at the beginning of our relationship. One letter that stands out was the one she wrote me on March 13, 1974, in which she explained that even when we weren't physically in each other's presence, she still felt that our strong and special bond always kept us spiritually united. She explained her love as a type of energy that was magnified when I was there to share it with her, and that was all the proof we could ever need that we were meant to be together forever.

Now realizing that my early retirement was certainly over, I knew I would need a higher-paying job to support a family on Long Island. So, I left my airport security job to become a Receiving Manager at Fortunoff Department Store in April of that year. Having fallen in love and secured a full-time job with a good salary and benefits, I felt the time was right to get married.

Eight short months after I met Lois, I proposed to her on the Long Beach boardwalk. It wasn't much of a surprise because she had picked out the engagement ring where she worked, and we applied her department store employee discount towards the purchase. I don't know how much we saved, but the ring only cost $600. To give context about how much the value of a dollar has changed over the years, the ring is now worth over $3,500.

Next, I gave up my apartment in Long Beach and moved back home with Mom and brother, who had just completed his Army service, to save up for a bigger apartment or a home in which to raise a family. Lois and I got married the following year in the little church where I made my sacraments growing up, Our Lady of Lourdes (OLL) in Malverne. Choosing our wedding location was an easy decision. We both loved how OLL looked, and Lois wasn't very fond of her church's aesthetics because it had been converted from a school gymasium.

A few days before the wedding, my best man Bernie Havern broke his leg sliding into third base during a softball game he was playing with his team of comrades from the Nassau County Police Department. He called me from the emergency room and told me that he was very sorry, but he wouldn't be able to make the wedding because he needed an operation on his leg. But this was my friend since we were six years old, and I needed him to be there celebrating my wedding with me. I told Bernie if he couldn't make it, the wedding wouldn't happen, so he needed to decline the operation and get out of his hospital bed. If any issues arose later, I assured him he could get his leg fixed after the wedding. So he agreed, convinced the doctors to put him in a cast, and they sent him on his way. As it turned out, I was right. He never wound up needing an operation and he was able to play ball for the rest of his life without any further difficulties. After all, they didn't call me "Dr. Quack" for nothing. Despite his full leg cast, Bernie happily attended the wedding. Our friend Phil Manzione, who Bernie sometimes worked side jobs for driving limousines, sent us a Rolls Royce limousine to use for the day so Bernie could get into the vehicle without bending his leg. He really toughed it out for me; he was truly my best man. Michael was also in the wedding party, but I felt closer to Bernie probably because my brother was five years younger than me, and we had differing interests. When I was playing on the football and baseball championship teams as a high school senior, Mike was only in seventh grade. As we grew after high school, I remained dedicated to sports and the beach while Michael gravitated towards working on cars and electronics.

On our wedding day, May 4, 1975, Bernie and I stood beside the altar in front of the church at 4pm waiting for the ceremony to begin. Lois was late to most of the occasions we attended together as a couple over the last year, so I was happy to see her standing in the back of the church waiting for the music to start. She was there alone, waiting to begin her long walk down the aisle towards Bernie and I unaccompanied by anyone else. Her father, who she loved very much, passed away on July 4, 1970. Lois always imagined her father walking her down the aisle on her wedding day, so nobody could take his place. A very emotional bride-to-be appeared to be walking down the aisle alone, but she wasn't. In her mind and heart, her dad walked beside her up the aisle. I also always imagined how proud my father would be on my wedding day, and knew that he too was with us in spirit. At the moment when Lois reached the altar, her mother stepped into the aisle and gave her daughter to me. As I looked at the joy in my beautiful bride's eyes, I felt peace and calmness come over me. I knew then we would be joined together as one forever. I will always remember the words of Matthew 19:6 uttered by Father Tim, "So they are no longer two, but one flesh. Therefore what God has joined together, let no one separate." We both loved Fr. Tim, a gentle, kind, visiting priest who was also a teacher where he lived in upstate New York. At that time, he only came down to say weekend Mass at OLL occasionally, but he gladly agreed to marry us. With Fr. Tim presiding, it was a perfect wedding ceremony. What a joyous, fulfilling, and loving wedding it was!

Wow, that was fast! In November of 1973, I was single and retired; now in May of 1975, my retirement was over, and I was suddenly a married man. In only eighteen short months my life had completely changed, and I had officially joined the "rat race". Well, looking back I guess I knew what I was doing. If I had not taken that twelve-year retirement before getting married, I might have wound up divorced like so many people who had rushed into marriage at a younger age. I knew someone who married, had two children, divorced, and then remarried before I finally got married in the first place. I thought it was a shame for that beautiful person and her family, but I also thought to myself that I might have wound up in the same situation if I had gotten married shortly after high school. I guess my English professor was correct; my internal clock finally rang at the right time for me.

Lois and I on our wedding day, May 4, 1975

## 24

## CATCHING UP!

Happily married, working a secure full-time job, and residing in an apartment on the second floor of my mother-in-law's house, it was time for Lois and I to catch up with our finances. Because Lois was working two jobs and her mother charged us a graciously low monthly rent, we were able to secure some extra income to put towards the down payment on a home where we could spend our lives together raising a family. However, having taken a one-week honeymoon at a resort in upstate NY, Lois thought that we deserved a proper vacation before moving on to the next chapter of our lives. Her idea was for us to take a trip to Italy and Switzerland where many of her relatives lived. So, I mustered up the courage to ask my boss for ten days off in August, and being from Europe himself, he understood and granted me the time off.

Lois, being the efficient planner that she was, took care of all the arrangements including plane tickets, passports, and other details. In August, she introduced me to two of God's beautiful earthly creations, the Northern Italian mountainside region and the awe-inspiring natural beauty of Switzerland. Our journey began in Rome, Italy, and took us northward to her aunt's house in Switzerland, with stops along the way to meet her relatives in Italy.

Lois's mother Bruna hailed from northern Italy and had met her father, John, during World War II. While John was serving in the US Army, he was stationed in Varese, a city in northwest Lombardy. There, he met Bruna in the auto repair garage where she worked as an office clerk when he and his troops took over the shop to repair their military vehicles. They fell in love, and after the war at the age of 27, John returned to Italy to marry his beautiful bride who was eighteen years old at that time.

Back then in Europe, it was normal for women to marry and start families at much younger ages than the average age at which women marry and start families these days. It was also typical for younger Italian women to marry men older than themselves who were believed to be more settled down in life, more mature, and better prepared to raise a family compared to men closer to their age still in their late teens or early twenties. So, Bruna took a big but calculated risk, leaving behind her country, her family, and her friends to travel across the Atlantic Ocean by ship with her new husband John to make a new life together in the USA. The happy couple first rented an apartment in South Ozone Park, Queens then moved to an apartment in the Bronx before finally settling into a New Hyde Park, Long Island home where their daughters Carmen and Lois spent most of their childhood. Over the years, Bruna learned to speak English by listening to Yankee games on AM radio stations, then worked as a crossing guard and as a butcher in the local A&P grocery store. John, after his military service, made a career as a court officer in the Bronx and enjoyed deer hunting trips on their property upstate. I am sure that many people would uncover similar stories if they were to examine their family history. And I am sure that they too, like my family and I, would all be very thankful to their ancestors for going to the lengths they did to raise a family which eventually led to the current generation we are today.

Reflecting on the improbable circumstances that brought John and Bruna together and hearing so much about Lois's family overseas, I started to get excited about the idea of visiting Europe. Our discipled financial decisions put us in a position to afford the trip, so I mustered up the courage to ask my boss for ten days off in August. Being from Europe himself, my boss understood how much meeting my wife's family and experiencing different cultures would benefit me, so he approved my vacation request. Lois, being the efficient planner that she was, took care of all the arrangements including plane tickets, passports, and other details. Our trip began in Rome and took us northward through two of God's beautiful earthly creations. In northwest Italy, we stopped in a spectacular mountain region to meet her relatives, then headed to the awe-inspiring natural beauty of the Swiss Alps where her aunt and some other relatives lived.

Our journey took us to many stunning places. St. Peter's Basilica's magnificent paintings and Michelangelo's La Pietá sculpture in Rome left an indelible mark on my memory. Lois then took me to the Trevi Fountain, famous for the movie 'Three Coins in a Fountain,' where we threw in coins of our own. Legend has it that if you toss a coin into the fountain, you'll return to Rome someday. We did return to Italy two more times, though not necessarily to Rome itself.

Our adventure continued on a train journey north to Milan, where we began meeting Lois's extended family. A family member picked us up and drove us to a quaint, cobblestone-paved town high up in the mountains called Tapigliano where it seemed everyone was related. The town had an ancient well that had served for centuries as a storage place for milk and butter on hot summer days. The crystal-clear, cold water from the well was refreshingly delicious. The hospitality of the people and the delicious food made our stay memorable.

Later, Lois's cousin Silvio drove us across the border into Switzerland through winding mountain roads to Lois's aunt's home in Sion where we received a warm welcome. The breathtaking view from their yard across a valley to a mountain crowned by a castle on the opposite side, felt like a scene from a movie. Lois's Uncle Albert owned a marble quarry and as a result had marble floors in his home. Behind the house were vineyards leased to farmers, who paid the family for the right to harvest grapes. Their spacious home boasted an indoor-outdoor swimming pool. One evening, Uncle Albert took me for a swim, followed by a special drink to ensure a peaceful night's sleep – chamomile tea and cognac, heated to perfection. It indeed led to the best night's sleep I could remember.

Uncle Albert also showed us around town, highlighting the works he had created. Then, he took us high up into the mountains to their chalet in Evolène. The sight of snow-capped mountains in August, the aroma of freshly baked bread in the morning air, and the view that greeted us were unlike anything else in the world. We then had coffee in a small village that was so high in altitude that we could see clouds in our view below. Then suddenly we saw a plane fly across our vista of the valley below which added to the sense of elevation. It was an experience that left me in awe.

One day, Lois's cousin treated us to a picnic on the mountainside, complete with barbecued sausages and vegetables. As I sat in the hot August sun, gazing at the snow-capped peaks and valleys, the play of sunlight on the landscape painted a picture of magnificent beauty, a creation of our divine Creator. No human painting could ever fully capture such splendor.

Our vacation was a remarkable journey, but what made it truly unforgettable was the warm embrace of the people we met. The works of art, both man-made and created by nature, left a lasting impact on us. Conversing with and observing the people who lived in these places was a learning experience and a reminder that regardless of backgrounds, people all share the same basic needs for food, water, shelter, clothes, and a means to support our families. If only governments around the world could grasp this concept and stop trying to exert control by force, perhaps many types of wars would end, especially those based on the economy, geographic borders, and religious / philosophical differences.

Returning home marked a return to the daily grind. I worked from 9am to 6pm, with two late nights until 10pm each week. Two other evenings I attended night classes, which meant I was keeping busy for over twelve hours, four days per week. Lois also worked the same evenings that I did, so we had only one night to spend together during the week. But we were both motivated to secure our families' future, and we had no qualms about putting in the effort.

In a memorable Christmas announcement in 1975, Lois shared the wonderful news with our family, we were expecting a baby in June. She had kept the secret, skillfully concealing her pregnancy until Christmas to surprise everyone. Our first child, John, arrived on Lois's father's birthday, June 4th, of the following year. We had chosen the name John Joseph Bianco Heron, a tribute to Lois's

| Lois, John and I, 1976

family. Lois's mother lovingly cared for John, even having a crib in her bedroom since we often arrived home after he was asleep.

Then my college journey took an interesting turn when I enrolled in an abnormal psychology class in the fall. I reasoned that as a new father, I would need to be well-prepared to navigate the challenges that would come about if my son inherited any of my quirks. Balancing night classes with a demanding full-time job and raising a family was no easy feat. I set clear ground rules with my professors, urging them to provide all course requirements on the first day. I had no time for surprises or meaningless exercises. Understanding their expectations from day one allowed me to efficiently manage my limited time. I diligently highlighted crucial sections in their textbooks, and any required reports were completed ahead of schedule. My transcript reflected my success, boasting a 3.5 GPA.

I vividly remember a pivotal moment when Lois proclaimed that our second child was due in June. Now, we would need a bigger place to live. The task of finding a suitable home fell to me, with a long list of requirements that not only had to meet Lois's criteria but also her mother's extensive checklist. The list included being within three miles of her mother's house, a large kitchen, a double sink in the kitchen, a slop sink in the basement, copper plumbing, a spacious back-yard, four bedrooms, two bathrooms, and a good school district, all within a budget of $60,000 or less. In February, I began my search for a home that would satisfy the wish list my wife and mother-in-law had made. Winter presented its chal-lenges, with snow and ice making house hunting a chilly

adventure. I scoured newspapers for listings, inspecting properties whenever one piqued my interest.

My beautiful daughter
Nicole and I, circa 1979

Months passed, and by June,
Lois's cousin Titienne had arrived
from Switzerland for the birth of
our second child, to whom she
would be the Godmother. Yet,
despite finding homes that met
the requirements, Lois couldn't
decide and the birth was immi-
nent. However, fate intervened on
Father's Day, just a week before
Lois's due date. I stumbled upon a
house that appeared promising
and implored Lois to inspect it
immediately. We rushed to see the property, and it indeed met
everyone's expectations. I seized the opportunity and without
anyone else knowing I made a deal with the owner, securing
the home with a handshake. On June 26, 1978, Lois gave birth
to a beautiful baby girl, Nicole Marie Heron. The very next
night, she inquired about the house we had seen a week
earlier. I replied, "You own it now." Tears welled up in her eyes
as she asked how that could be. I revealed that I had arranged
the purchase, leaving her surprised.

We moved into our new home on October 26, 1978. It was a
magical day, marking exactly five years since I first met Lois at
Joe and Mary Jeanne's house party. Continentally, many years
prior on October 26th, Lois and her family moved from their

apartment in the Bronx to their permanent home in New Hyde Park, and that date was also her dog Poppy's birthday. Poppy held a special place in our hearts, so we celebrated his birthday annually, complete with a party hat, a seat at the table, and a cupcake that he wouldn't touch until we finished singing "Happy Birthday." He had a remarkable rapport with our children as they grew. My place in the family was made clear when Lois and I went to the hospital, ready to give birth to Nicole. On the wall next to Lois in the hospital room, I noticed that some pictures were hung in a vertical line, one above the other. First was John, then Poppy, and then finally, me. Yes, even the dog came before me! It was a humorous illustration of my standing in the family hierarchy. Another story that highlighted my place in the family occurred when I returned home one frigid night after a late class. I walked into the house, and the aroma of hot chicken soup filled the air. Eagerly, I reached for the stirring spoon, only to have my hand gently slapped away by my mother-in-law. "That's for Poppy," she informed me. It was abundantly clear where I stood.

| Our new home circa 1978

# 25

# A GROWING FAMILY AND HOME

F inally, we got the babies home and settled them into their new bedrooms. Our son John had a spacious room on the second floor, and we decided to add an upstairs bedroom for our daughter extending the roof over the expanded kitchen. This brought the total count of bedrooms upstairs to three, along with a full bath. Our home now resembled a colonial cape, with all the bedrooms located on the upper floor. On the first floor, there was a generous eat-in kitchen, a comfortable living room, a formal dining room and a full bathroom. Instead of using the other two main floor rooms as bedrooms, we made one into a cozy den where we would watch TV and the other into a children's playroom. The basement had seen some transformations too. We adorned the walls with knotty pine wood and added a standing cast-iron wood-burning stove later in 1978 which provided plenty of heat for the basement and entire first floor. On days when we really loaded the fireplace with wood, its warmth could even be felt all the way up on the second floor. The other side of the basement housed a half bath, a laundry room, and an exercise / weight room which I thought was essential.

After settling into our new home, we invited all of our family and friends to a housewarming the following summer of 1979. By then, most of my friends had already married and started families which meant an amazing turnout for our party. By nightfall, the house and backyard were buzzing with more than 65 guests, all there to celebrate the significant milestone of home ownership with us. Taking it all in with friends and family that day, what I had accomplished in a relatively short amount of time really sunk in. At 36 years old, I had become a homeowner, a husband, a father of two, held a well-paying job, was enrolled in a management training program at work, and attended college classes at night. I was catching up, and I had no qualms about putting my life into high gear. This period marked a time of unparalleled happiness in married life, the sheer joy of fatherhood, and the exciting journey of raising children. I was living my childhood again through my own children's eyes and hoped to guide them away from the mistakes I had made in my own life. It was truly an awesome experience!

Thankfully, we had established our roots in the perfect house because a heartwarming surprise was on its way to our home just in time for Christmas in 1979. Our little bundle of joy, Keith Michael Heron, made his entrance to the world on

December 17<sup>th</sup>, and Lois brought him home just in time to spend his first Christmas with our family. Still being so tiny, Lois sat him in a high chair that belonged to one of Nicole's dolls and placed him under the Christmas tree. What a wonderful Christmas present he was for all of us; excitement filled the air!

Keith's first Christmas, 1979

Being a big kid at heart, I eagerly started building and making improvements for our children to fully enjoy their home. We hung two swings in the apple tree, set up a monkey bar set, installed a sandbox, permanent poles for a volleyball net, and using our imagination and existing structures like the volleyball posts as foul poles, we even created a wiffleball park. We expanded the driveway to accommodate a new basketball court with an adjustable hoop, ranging from six to ten feet in height. The driveway was even painted to resemble a basketball court, complete with a foul line for shooting free throws.

My wife and I had an agreement when it came to raising our children. She would focus on their educational development, while I would oversee their physical growth. This arrangement seemed perfect, considering my educational background. Lois, on the other hand, excelled academically, particularly in English and languages. In fact, she could complete crossword puzzles in record time, solve word jumbles in less than a minute and could speak English, Italian, French and Spanish. In my quest to ensure that our children grew up strong and physically fit, I devised a plan for them from a very young age. My goal was to make games and sports enjoyable, and I provided all the necessary equipment for their success. Our home became a wonderland of sports with various setups in the garage, the front and back yards, the basement, and even on the street.

L to R: John, Nicole and Keith on the loose for some outdoor fun in front of our home, circa 1983

The garage stored their balls, bats, gloves, roller skates, skateboards, hockey sticks, volleyball nets, shuffleboard, bocce, croquet, horseshoes, games, and bicycles. I even set up a work-bench in one corner for repairs, complete with a compressor for inflating balls. Although it was technically a garage and a half, all of the sports equipment we had stored inside left just enough room for our smaller car. Our big light blue Chevy

Caprice Classic station wagon with wood panel door trim and later our dark grey Ford Econoline 150 van would be parked on the driveway or out in the street when the kids wanted to play basketball on the driveway. As the kids grew older, I adapted both the outdoor and indoor spaces to accommodate their changing interests. Old enough to be trusted with a little more freedom, we would allow the kids to ride their bikes to the town pool complex and spend the day there with friends, many times unaccompanied by adults. When not at the pool, the kids played in the street with neighborhood kids or visited friends across the street. It reminded me of my childhood playing outside all day, albeit without the modern luxuries they had.

This unstructured playtime was an essential component of their physical development, contributing to their mental well-being, but I also provided some structure to nurture their physical abilities. At the tender age of three, we enrolled the children in gymnastics classes led by Russian instructors who taught them how to maintain coordination, build strength, and exhibit controlled movements during athletic activities. They continued with gymnastics for years, with Nicole making significant progress. However, the boys didn't show as much interest, and I never forced them to participate in activities they didn't enjoy.

At four years old, I signed them up for soccer, providing them with an opportunity to run and chase the ball across an open field. This early exposure helped build their leg strength and lung capacity. Their first soccer coach, hailing from Italy, taught them the fundamentals of the game. They made new friends and learned valuable teamwork skills. Next on the agenda was the softball for Nicole, and Little League for the boys. Nicole, a natural lefty, and the boys, natural righties, displayed different preferences. I didn't insist on teaching them to switch-hit until they were older, and even then, it didn't quite click for them. However, I took it upon myself to teach them all how to hit, and they all became proficient hitters.

Our schedule was packed with sports throughout the year including soccer in the fall, baseball in the spring, gymnastics a few days a week, and swimming during the summer. Basketball, another sport with great potential for physical development, was added to the mix when I enrolled them in the Police Boys Club (PBC) program which later became the Police Athletic League (PAL). I had the privilege of knowing the man who ran the program, Hank Cluess, a former player for St. John's University and the New York Nets professional basketball team. His coaching expertise was invaluable.

As time marched on, they played in various leagues and sports, including PBC, PAL, Catholic Youth Organization (CYO), travel soccer, and high school sport programs at Chaminade and Sacred Heart. Keith was the only one who ventured into football playing until he was thirteen years old. As a result of their athletic experiences, they grew up happy, healthy, and socially proficient, forging new friendships wherever they played. My mission was a resounding success, and now, my grandchildren are following in the same footsteps.

Meanwhile throughout this time, Lois held up her end of the bargain and had a knack for managing the children effectively. After school, they would get some fresh air and play outdoors, followed by a healthy snack. An hour later, it was time for homework, which was closely supervised. Dinner was served promptly, and any remaining homework was diligently completed. We bought one of the first type of VCR television recorders for the family, a device that would have a significant impact on our screen time. On Saturdays, instead of allowing the children to watch cartoons during the day, we brought them to their sporting events or encouraged them to go outside and ride bikes or play with their friends. Then after dinner, we would watch some of their favorite Saturday morning cartoons together as a family.

As they got older, we introduced them to some structured, educational games and activities. One of these games was Memory, and I vividly remember my daughter, Nicole, at just four years old, beating me consistently. She would playfully urge me, saying, "Come on, Daddy, don't let me win. Play to win, Dad!" I'd respond with a smile, "I'm trying my best, sweetheart." Nicole was an such an exceptional student that she needed more challenges to reach her full potential which she found in the LEAP program. Nicole graduated first in her eighth-grade class and moved on to Sacred Heart Academy, where she excelled in advanced classes and even earned twelve college credits before high school graduation. Her academic journey continued, resulting in a Master's Degree in Business Administration (MBA) and a Ph.D. in the field of accounting.

Today, she serves as a published professor at a prestigious higher education institution specializing in entrepreneurship, Babson College located in Massachusetts. She was also honored as the best teacher in her field at Suffolk University in Boston where she taught before recently accepting a professorship at Babson.

John, too, was an excellent student with a unique writing talent. He entered an essay contest at Chaminade High School, competing against some of the brightest students in the country. He asked our family for a topic, so my mother-in-law suggested that he write about Danny Thomas, given his work with St. Jude Hospital. John's essay not only won the contest but also garnered a heartfelt response from Danny Thomas himself, just before his passing. John continued to excel academically, graduating near the top of his class at Chaminade with a non-weighted average of 96. Weighted averages became a topic of discussion for John when he realized the disparities between Chaminade and other schools. At Chaminade, a grade simply reflected performance, with no additional weighting involved. John couldn't fathom how someone could achieve a perfect 100% average, as he saw posted in the halls of Chaminade. John, now a math teacher at Oceanside Middle School and a sought-after tutor for his ability to help children understand complicated subjects, continued to shine academically, achieving a 4.0 GPA in his first year of college. He credited the good brothers at Chaminade for providing him with a solid academic foundation, much of which he had already learned in high school.

Our youngest, Keith, shared some of my traits, particularly when it came to taking shortcuts and doing the bare minimum to achieve success. Like me, he had a knack for finding the easiest route. However, he quickly realized the value of hard work and dedication as he progressed through school. I remember looking at his report card in seventh grade, advising him to stop fooling around, and telling him that he was capable of making the honor roll. He took my advice to heart and proudly walked down the aisle during eighth-grade graduation wearing the distinctive honor roll cords. Just as I eventually thanked my father for his academic push, years later after high school, Keith recognized the value of the brothers' demanding educational standards and he thanked me for sending him to Chaminade. Despite his initial resistance, he graduated with honor roll distinctions, just like his siblings. His educational journey led him to earn a Bachelor's Degree in psychology, a Master's Degree in School Counseling, and a fulfilling career as the athletic director at the Fashion Institute of Technology in New York City. He had achieved my dream job, overseeing a college-level sports program.

I couldn't be prouder of all my children for their dedication to their education and the paths they had forged for themselves. The foundation for their successful educational journeys had been laid by Lois during their early years. Through their achievements, I learned the importance of education for attaining success and happiness in life. The road they were on, with their completed degrees, promised a smoother journey than the challenging one I had traveled.

As our children thrived and our family grew, our home also underwent significant changes. After adding a bedroom and a basketball court with an expanded driveway, I decided to build a shed to free up space in the garage. The landscaping saw a revamp, with old shrubbery replaced and the lawn replanted. We updated two bathrooms and the kitchen, and the hardwood floors received a fresh finish. We also transformed half of the basement into an entertainment room, complete with a bar. Additionally, we built a family room adjacent to the kitchen, featuring cathedral ceilings and a gas fireplace. We upgraded the electrical service, installed solar panels on the roof, replaced all existing windows, added two large bay windows in the front and an eight-foot picture window in the kitchen. Our home had seen a complete transformation, becoming one of the best investments we had ever made. The results spoke for themselves as the value of our home skyrocketed. What was once a $54,500 investment in 1978 was now valued at an astounding $750,000. It was truly unbelievable, proving that sometimes the most unexpected investments could yield the greatest returns.

Our home, 2024

My family circa 1984 L to R: Myself and John (top)
Lois (middle) Nicole and Keith (bottom)

My family in 2019 L to R: Myself, Nicole, Lois and John (standing)
Keith (sitting)

# 26

# OLDER YEARS: LIFE'S LESSONS

A s I begin my eighth decade of life, I find myself in great shape thanks to taking good care of myself. My health underwent a dramatic change in 1965 when I was 22 years old, as I had my tonsils and adenoids removed. In my younger years, I had never understood why I couldn't swallow vegetables or run for an extended period without being out of breath until I had this operation. Ironically, my dog was very healthy, as he consumed most of my vegetables for me under the kitchen table.

In my youth, we didn't have a family doctor, and I only saw the school doctor once every two years. It was the school doctor who administered the polio vaccine to us in grade school. During one of these visits, the doctor noticed the enlargement of both my tonsils and adenoids, which I had been unaware of. He suggested to my parents that they should have them removed. However, my parents thought everything was fine because I wasn't sick and didn't complain about any discomfort. Little did we know that my adenoids were so large that they completely blocked the passage of air through my nose, forcing me to breathe solely through my mouth.

In 1965, at the age of 22, I began experiencing frequent sore throats and infections, prompting the doctor to recommend the removal of my tonsils and adenoids. I underwent the procedure and was sent home the same day, although the thought of enjoying the post-surgery ice cream was far from my mind, as the pain in my throat made even swallowing air a painful endeavor. During this time, my girlfriend, Sue, visited me in the hospital to check on me. After returning home, she visited me once but then she didn't call or visit again, and I was left perplexed by her sudden absence. When we were together, everything seemed to be going well. I assumed she was waiting for my call, but I was in no condition to make it as my health deteriorated rapidly.

With only one phone in the house, located in the kitchen, I found myself bedridden with a fever, vomiting, and an inability to keep anything down. At one point, my mother contemplated calling the doctor for assistance, but I felt so awful, like I was on the verge of death, that I told her to forget about the doctor and call a priest because I believed my time had come. During this period, I went from weighing 170 pounds to a mere 117 pounds, despite being six feet two inches tall. I was nothing but skin and bones. However, to my relief, the doctor did come and with the help of new medications, was able to combat the infection and reduce my fever. Just to clarify, this was in the 1960s, when doctors still made house calls by visiting the sick in their own homes.

Determined not to let myself slip into a poor state of health ever again, I decided to rebuild my strength. I made a promise to myself to never look or feel that sick again as long as I lived. Drawing inspiration from my father, who had been a weightlifter in his youth, I turned to weightlifting as a means of building both strength and muscle. In my basement, I had an assortment of weights, although I lacked the modern machines available today. All I could rely upon was old-school hard work. I began with light weights and gradually progressed to heavier ones, all while adhering to a high-protein, high-calorie diet.

For the first time in my life, I experienced the ability to breathe fully and engage in running without losing my breath. I couldn't help but wonder how different my high school experience might have been had I undergone this procedure earlier. Eating and swallowing became easier with each passing day. As I continued to increase the weights I lifted, my arms and chest grew. I started with a ten-pound dumbbell bar, gradually progressing to 50 pounds for arm curls and reverse curls. Eventually, I was lifting a 180-pound bar for both arm curls and was benching 325 pounds, further increasing my weight as I added raw eggs to my milkshakes for extra protein. By my 24th birthday in August of 1966, I had undergone a remarkable transformation. In just eighteen months, I had gone from my lowest point, weighing only 117 pounds at six feet two inches to a robust 210 pounds. My weight gain consisted of nearly 100 pounds of muscle. My father declared this to be the perfect build, with a 16" neck, 16" arms, 16" calf muscles, a 44" chest, and a 32" waist. From that point forward, I committed to a lifestyle of healthy eating and regular exercise.

During that same year, I unexpectedly crossed paths with Sue. She did a double take when she saw me, as my appearance had changed so dramatically. We exchanged pleasantries, but neither of us delved into the unanswered questions of why she hadn't called or why I hadn't called her during my illness. It seemed that we both believed our affection for each other had waned during our eighteen-month separation. We moved forward in different directions in our lives but remained friends. Today, I continue to prioritize exercise, although I have downsized over the years. I now weigh 185 pounds and stand six feet one inch tall with a 33" waist, proudly retaining all my original parts.

I'm still quite busy even though I'm supposed to be retired and relaxing in a rocking chair somewhere, but that's just not me. My view of life is very different now than it was during my youthful early retirement days. Instead of wanting as little responsibility as possible, I thrive by staying busy to keep my mind sharp and body in shape. I continue to work, doing something I love that also keeps me young, driving a school bus every day. But I do more than just drive the children. I greet them by name, ask how they are doing, and take an interest in their college choices, career aspirations, and sometimes even their problems, lending a listening ear and trying to offer some advice when possible. I also decorate my bus for holidays, and at times I distribute handouts and handwritten holiday cards to every child with encouraging words of support.

One of my grandsons and I in front of my 39' school bus

I enjoy teaching the children on my bus about life skills that they might not learn in school, like perseverance and motivation. I hang signs in my bus with positive sayings and frequently change the signs to keep the themes and quotes fresh. The following are some of my favorite sayings. I occasionally change the display, rotate other signs in and out, and add new ones to the mix to keep things interesting throughout the school year. I do not know the author of most of these sayings, but it is important to note that I did not create any of these quotes myself. These hit home with me, so I like to share them with the children on my bus:

"There is no elevator to success, you have to take the stairs."
"Learn something new every day."
"If you want something you never had, you'll have to do something you've never done."
"Difficult roads lead to beautiful destinations."
"The best view comes after the hardest climb."
"Having money in your pocket is good but having God in your heart is perfect."
"Remember, anyone can love when the sun is shining. In the storm is where you learn who truly cares for you."
"Be fearless in your pursuit of what sets your soul on fire."
"Home is not a place, but a feeling."
"Smile."

But of my 22-sign collection, my favorite remains on permanent display, hung over the door as a constant reminder for the children to see every day as they leave the bus. The placement and message of the sign are like one that might be hung near a locker room exit for a sports team to see as they storm out to take the field or court for battle: "Never, ever, give up!"

The following are two of my favorite handouts that I've always enjoyed giving to the children over the nineteen years I've been privileged to be a school bus driver. The first is an excerpt from a children's book written by Nancy Tillman, The

Spirit of Christmas. The second is a true story of a simple gesture of friendship that took place on a cold winter day in New York, and what friendship means to me.

*Handout One – An excerpt from The Spirit of Christmas by Nancy Tillman:*

"The spirit of Christmas. It's all about giving of
yourself. It's a warm hug, a gentle pat on the
back, the tucking in at night, a reaching out
to a stranger. It's a smile for a neighbor,
forgiveness for past grievance, it's the
spreading of peace, and the leaving of joy
and its wake.
The spirit of Christmas is alive wherever you go,
as long as you bring it with you.
For the spirit of Christmas is love. It's born in
the soul and it lives in the heart. It grows
when you give it away."

Underneath the poem on the same page, I added:

"Regardless of your beliefs, I encourage you to
live and spread the spirit of Christmas, as
Nancy so perfectly described, as much as
possible every day of your life. Doing so will
bring you peace, love, fulfillment, and
happiness throughout your life."

*Handout Two – A true story of a simple gesture of friendship, and what friendship means to me:*

"When I went out to pick up my school bus at 5:55am one winter morning, I didn't know whether I was in Alaska or the North Pole. In the dark, frigid cold, the wind was whipping through me, and I thought this couldn't be Franklin Square on Long Island, New York. It could only be a dream where I was carried off to the Arctic North. Then the icy winds slapped me in the face to wake me with the reality that we were in negative zero wind chill temperatures as I wrestled to open my frozen car door and check the temperature gauge which read twelve degrees. But honestly, it felt more like twelve below! Welcome to a winter morning on Long Island.

When I pulled into the bus yard and looked around, I broke out in a smile that almost cracked my frozen face. I was expecting to spend the next two hours shivering cold, driving an ice box on my morning run because it took almost 90 minutes for the bus to warm up to an acceptable internal temperature. However, that morning would be different because one true friend had started my bus much earlier when he arrived, so when I got inside, I already felt some heat defrosting my bones! What a warm gesture of friendship that was, on such a brutally cold morning. Sometimes it's the smallest of gestures that can make the biggest difference in someone else's day. In turn, if that does something unexpectedly nice for someone else and that chain continues, like a ripple effect in a pond one small gesture of friendship can wind up having a much larger positive impact on the world itself.

Thinking back to when I was your age, I am very thankful for the many lifelong friendships I made while I was in a school just like yours. I still remember how it felt to enter middle school in a much larger building serving grades seven through twelve and sharing the hallways, the schoolyard, and the lunchroom with much older kids. Also, half of my seventh-grade class came from a different elementary school, so my friends and I no longer knew everyone in our classes. It felt like stepping into an exciting new world. As it would turn out, the most important life lessons I learned from school didn't come from textbooks but came from spending time with classmates and friends during activities outside the classroom. Playing on sports teams where I learned teamwork, sharing, sacrifice, trust, discipline and never giving up was a great place for me to make new, trustworthy, friends. I suggest that you too take time during school to get to know other students in sports, music, arts, or any kind of club as they are all great opportunities to make new friends.

When you think about friendship, keep in mind that a good friend is a special kind of friend; one who is more like a close family member that you can trust in any situation, and one with whom you feel comfortable enough to tell about your deepest thoughts and feelings. The following blurb I once read online which compares friendship throughout a lifetime to a big, long party, sums it up best:

*Life is kind of like a party, you invite a lot of people, some leave early, some stay all night, some laugh with you, some laugh at you, and some show up late. But in the end, after the fun, few stay to help you clean up the mess. And most of the time, they aren't even the ones who made the mess. These people are your true friends in life.*

Today, over 60 years after graduating high school, I am still friends with many of my classmates with whom I enjoyed going to school when I was your age. Over the years, we had many reunions celebrating our high school days and many of us still meet at a restaurant once a year around the holidays to catch up. In between larger gatherings, those of us who still live near each other continue to get together for dinner or maybe to watch a big game on TV from time to time. Some classmates have moved away and live in different states, but the distance doesn't matter. We still manage to keep in touch via emails, phone calls, or text messages. Whenever we get together it's a very special time with lots of laughs, smiles, and hugs.

If you're very lucky like me, you'll form some true friendships now that you will keep forever like I did. But also remember that the number of friends isn't nearly as important as the quality of the friendships you make, so be sure to choose friends wisely. Spend time with others who will be positive influences in your life and distance yourself from others who try to lead you down a path your conscience tells you isn't the right way to go. Having only one or two close friends to whom you can talk about your true and

deepest feelings is more valuable than
having ten friends to whom you wouldn't
dare admit what you're really thinking at
any given moment. I hope that you have as
much fun, learn as much outside the classroom, and make as many lasting, true
friendships as I did and that you enjoy your
journey through high school!"

I find it quite ironic that I used to look for any excuse to skip school and that I used to have a reputation for being a wild driver as a teenager. I would have never believed that someday I would be responsible for safely transporting kids to school every day and encouraging them to make the most of their education along the way. However, that's exactly what I do now, and as a result of my diligence and caring, I was recognized as "Employee of the Month" by the school bus company a few years back. It might seem like I underwent a drastic transformation since my carefree high school days, but I've always had a love for children and driving. I just drive a lot more safely now and also with a purpose to brighten the day of the children on my bus.

St. Catherine's CYO 8th Grade Team, 1989 Top row far left: Myself Bottom row far left: My son, John

Another way I've worked to help children is by coaching and running youth sports programs. When my children were very young, I enrolled in classes and earned New York State certification in five different sports, First Aid, CPR, and child abuse recognition. As my children got a little older and more skilled in their sports, I felt they needed a bigger challenge. So in 1989, I organized an initiative to resurrect the Catholic Youth Organization (CYO) basketball program at our local parish, St Catherine's of Sienna in Franklin Square, NY, that had been dormant for many years. Deserving of special recognition for offering their time and talent to help St. Catherine's CYO throughout the formative years were good friends like Tony Gunther, Tom and Mary Heineman, Tim Hughes, Mike Karcher, Mike Krasnoff, Tony and Eileen LoPiano, Billy O'Connor and Gene Sullivan just to name a few. We started with just one eighth-grade boys team, but the program quickly grew to include teams for boys and girls from grades three through twelve. During the early 90's, we took the program to another level when we began hosting our annual Winter Classic Tournament each February break, extending invitations to some of the most competitive teams from Long Island, Queens and Brooklyn. CYO basketball at St. Catherine's continued to run successfully for over 30 years until the COVID-19 pandemic of 2020. Despite the recent decline, I am very proud of the program in which I coached my own sons, Nicole was a member of the cheerleading squad, and up to 200 other children of the parish and their families benefited from being involved with our teams each year. Just as it can be said about an intense game of basketball, our St. Catherine's of Sienna basketball program had a "good run."

Table with benches, bar with barstools and a birdhouse I built out of reclaimed wood during the pandemic of 2020

In addition to dealing a heavy blow to the CYO program, the COVID-19 outbreak also disrupted local schools, causing them to shut down and teach students virtually via online meeting platforms like *Zoom* from mid-March 2020 through the rest of the school year. To keep myself occupied during those challenging times when I barely left my home for about six months, I also took to making furniture out of old shipping pallets. I would collect the pallets from local stores and then break them down to use for building materials and fuel for my wood-burning stove. From the reclaimed wood, I created a variety of pieces: outdoor flower planters, tables, and benches for my picnic area, a bar with barstools for my patio, a bird-feeder, a workstation for my grandson, benches for my son's patio, and even an outdoor shower which I particularly enjoy in the summer.

These projects served as the best remedy for me, and they made me feel especially fulfilled knowing that I created all of these pieces out of something that might have been bound for the trash. It's remarkable what you can fashion from items that people discard.

I also enjoyed sending and forwarding positive or humorous emails throughout the week to as many people as possible. In the first couple of months of the pandemic, I shared 50 such messages with individuals across the country. I hope that they, in turn, passed on the positivity and brought some much-needed energy and cheer into the lives of many who were feeling isolated during those trying times.

But most importantly, I finally got a chance to write this

book centered around a very special period of my high school years and the friendships I formed. I had thought about, and talked about writing this book for about ten years until, unexpectedly, the pandemic finally pushed me into a room with ample time to document the life stories I wanted to share. Having so much downtime at home essentially eliminated that notorious thief called procrastination, leaving me, and so many others who had been putting off working on a big personal project, without excuses to delay any longer.

Although the pandemic is over, and I've accomplished so much during that time, including writing this book, I'm still going to keep busy in my personal life outside of work. Looking ahead to my next project, I plan to construct a set of stack tables, each personalized with my name, date, and a brief message, for each of my children. This way, whenever they sit down to have a snack using these special tables, they'll feel my presence with them in spirit. It will serve as a reminder that I love and support them in everything they do, even after I am gone.

But more importatly than physical items, I've passed on my life lessons to my children which have become the foundation for their success and happiness. Seeing my children embrace what I've taught them and use those lessons to make the world a better place for the people they encounter each day is something the young man in my yearbook picture could have never imagined. Some people continue learning much later in life, while others seem to learn very little after leaving school. I firmly believe that each new day is a blessing, and the least I can do is learn from it and give something back because tomorrow is not promised. The seven most significant lessons that life has taught me, and that I have taught to my children, are as follows:

My first life lesson relates to God, love, and religion: *All things are possible with God.* Faith is so important because it helps you understand the true meaning of unconditional love and forgiveness. I'm profoundly grateful that my mom instilled in me a strong faith and taught me to pray and trust in God, our loving Father. She made me aware that His spirit resides in all of us, and we are all His children.

Can you imagine, not the song that John Lennon wrote many years ago which broke down the barriers dividing humanity, but can you instead imagine if the whole world followed the first two commandments of God? These commandments have the power to overcome all the barriers that mankind has erected. "Thou shall love the Lord thy God with all thy heart, and with all thy soul, and with all thy mind." This is the first and greatest commandment, and the second is similar, "Thou shall love thy neighbor as thyself."

All Judeo-Christian religious doctrine and influence stem from these two central commandments. So simple, and yet they have never been fully embraced in the world. They've been rejected since the dawn of time, from the days of Cain and Abel to the present day, when nations amass military power at the expense of millions who suffer and starve in the streets worldwide. Have you ever wondered why it's so difficult for the world to live in peace?

We raised our children on the foundation of God's commandments and His boundless love for us. We encouraged them that, during challenging times on their journey through life, they could trust in God, knowing that everything would eventually work out for the best. Sometimes following God's plan did not bring about what they initially wanted, but in later years they'd come to realize that it always led to the best outcome. Remember that God always knows what's best for you, especially when in doubt or in times when you think know better. Straying off the path God planned for you may seem tempting at times, but it is never in your best interest in the long run. Always staying on that path, or at least as close to it as possible, also means never having to work too hard to find the way back which can become increasingly difficult and humbling the further away you stray.

Another example of God knowing best relates to that English professor mentioned in chapter eleven who told my class that biological clocks ticking within us tell us when the time is right to get married. But there's more to it than just a biological clock. True love is something that two people share not just when they are moving along on the same timetable, but when they hear God's voice calling them to each other. And it will happen in God's time, not in your time. So, you might have to remain faithfully patient. You might have to try hard to mute the ticking of the biological clock growing louder within you as you get older in order to open your ears and your heart to what God truly wants for you! After all, the most important decision you can make in your life is who to marry because it will change the rest of your life, for better or worse. When you truly find the right one, you will know it. You may wind up going out with many people, some of whom might seem like the right one but aren't, before you find the one that is truly right for you.

When two people get married with a love for God, they do so in a sacred place like a church or temple, with friends and family gathered as witnesses. They make a solemn vow before God and their loved ones, pledging to love each other through sickness and health, through richer and poorer, until death do them part, seeking God's guidance and strength. How can two people stay married for a lifetime, weathering the storms of life's temptations, distractions, challenges, failures, and demands, year after year? It's because of God. That's why, on your wedding day, it's not just the union of two people but the creation of a triumphant triangle: you, your life partner, and God. Nothing in this world can ever break this bond, as it is written, "what therefore God has joined together let no man put asunder."

My second life lesson is: *Maintain lasting friendships.* Valuing and nurturing meaningful friendships is one of the keys to happiness in life and one of the easiest ways to learn new things. French essayist Anais Nin once wrote, "Each friend represents a world in us, a world possibly not born until they arrive."

God has blessed me with countless friendships during my lengthy journey through life. My children find it hard to believe that I still have friends I've known since childhood, with our friendships spanning over 70 years. People often find it hard to believe that after 60 years since our graduation, the class of Valley Stream North 1961 still reunites to celebrate. Many others have difficulty grasping how this could be possible because they didn't experience the same kind of enduring friendship that lasts a lifetime as so many of my classmates have enjoyed together over the years.

The concept of friendship was introduced to me at a tender age by my dear and oldest friend, Bernie Havern when we were just six years old. He taught me that our family could always grow larger by adding friends. Bernie wasn't just a friend; he became my brother, and was always there for me. He opened my eyes to the idea of making as many friends as possible, so my family would continuously expand, with each new friend making it bigger. I formed friendships in grade school and high school that endure to this day. As an adult, I made many more friends through work, sports programs, and my wife's friends, who are as wonderful as she is.

My third life lesson is: *Never, ever, give up.* Persevering in the face of challenges, especially when it comes to believing in yourself is a major key to success. This valuable piece of wisdom is very useful to remember when faced with life's challenges that can sometimes knock you down. It's tempting to throw in the towel, but when you persist, you grow stronger, and future challenges become less daunting. An early foundation built on God, family, and friendships that support your beliefs is crucial. These pillars surround you with love, friendship, and the knowledge that they will stand by your side, no matter what. Surrounding yourself with positive influences, people with a bright outlook on life serve as a formidable shield against the negative forces and the constant barrage of information from today's social media. Always believe in yourself and know that with determination, you can turn your dreams into reality. I was truly blessed to have all these elements in my life, making it easy for me to persevere in myself and my dreams.

A story I like to tell the children on my school bus about not giving up is the story of Thomas Edison and how he failed 2,774 times before finally inventing the light bulb. I often tell the children that if they're having a rough day, they should not think of themselves as a failure. Instead, when they feel discouraged about not making a sports team, getting dumped by their girlfriend, or failing a test, I tell them to think about how many times Thomas Edison failed before he was successful every time they turn on a light switch. Thomas Edison believed in himself and believed he could do it when others thought he was crazy. It was that mindset that made him successful so I encourage the children to remember that they can be successful if they believe in themselves and keep trying too.

My fourth life lesson is: *Take one day at a time.* Learning to live in the present moment and trusting God's plan for you takes patience and courage, but once mastered can give you the boost you need to persevere and never give up! This outlook has been central to my life while trying to live each day to the fullest, learn from yesterday, and not worry about tomorrow. Today is the only day you can control and by living it fully you are preparing for tomorrow without even realizing it. By being a good person and focusing on the present moment, you will likely find that what you need and what you're looking for align with what God has already planned for you. You will likely find that things come to you naturally without needing to worry or spend too much time thinking about them in advance. And I think you'd agree that life is much easier to live that way.

My fifth life lesson is: *Get a good, complete, education.* The significance of a full education and embracing learning both inside and outside the classroom can not be underestimated. My realization of the value of a good education was essential for my children's development and their success in life. I made sure that all my children received the best education I could provide. The educational process begins at home, even before school starts. Parents must be actively involved in every aspect of their children's education, from the early years before school begins through their grammar school years. These early years lay the foundation for the rest of their lives and determine how much they will learn throughout their lifetime.

Education isn't limited to the classroom; it encompasses physical development and social activities as well. My wife and I agreed that she would be responsible for their formal education in school, while I would oversee their physical development and activities. We believed this was the best approach since I had a sports background and a less-than-stellar academic record. Lois, on the other hand, was an excellent student who always followed the rules of a good education. To prepare for fatherhood, the first college course I took was abnormal psychology. I figured that if I had a son who was anything like me, I needed to stay one step ahead in my thinking.

Our children's education began from the moment they were born and entered our home. We provided them with mobile toys in the crib, read stories to them, sang to them, and surrounded them with love. Lois taught them to read before they even started kindergarten, and at the age of three, we enrolled them in a gymnastics program run by a Russian couple in our town. By the time they were four, they joined an intramural soccer program, allowing them to run around and build strength in their legs and lungs.

I'm not advocating for children to become professional athletes or star players in high school or college. Instead, I believe that every child should have the chance to play outside and engage in intramural sports. This allows them to enjoy the outdoors, make new friends, stay active, develop communication skills, and learn how to get along with others their age. These are just some of the benefits that involvement in sports can bring to every child's life.

In my experience, intramural soccer was ideal for young children because it involved everyone in the game and kept them constantly active. I never forced my kids to play any particular sport; I simply encouraged them to explore their interests. My older son decided he no longer wanted to play baseball because he found it boring, so I supported his decision to switch to soccer, where there was more action, and he got to travel to new places. My younger son, on the other hand, didn't enjoy soccer's constant running, so he opted to play football instead. The key lesson I learned was that every child is unique, and their choices should be driven by what's best for them, not what you want for them.

Lois excelled in her role and discipline regarding the children's education. After their long day at school, she allowed them to play outside for a while after a fruit snack. Then, they would come inside, complete their homework, wash up, have dinner, prepare for bed, and enjoy 30 minutes of a show that we had recorded on Saturdays, accompanied by cookies and milk. Kid's shows were typically aired on Saturdays during their early years, and we never allowed them to spend a beautiful day sitting in front of the television.

Additionally, I discovered a new technology that proved helpful in raising my children. I was one of the first to purchase a tape recorder, recording five half-hour shows on Saturdays, which I would then play for the kids in half-hour segments before bedtime. My mother-in-law also purchased an Apple IIe computer with a printer for them before they reached the age of ten. They quickly mastered it and utilized it for schoolwork, excelling in the classroom.

Lois's routine and commitment to the children's education yielded tremendous success. All of them developed a love for reading, which significantly eased their academic endeavors. They all graduated from grade school with honors, with Nicole, my daughter, earning the top spot in her class. She was also part of the LEAP program for exceptional children. In seventh grade, she participated in the Long Island spelling bee, finishing in the top ten out of 180 schools that entered. Her elimination was only due to a mispronunciation by the moderator; she could spell any word if pronounced correctly. They all went on to graduate from high school with honors. John even won an essay contest at Chaminade High School against some of the brightest students in the country. His essay was about Danny Thomas and St. Jude's Children's Hospital, which Mr. Thomas read and sent John a note of congratulations before his passing.

Continuing their educational journey, they all attended college and once again graduated with honors. Nicole received a Fulbright scholarship and spent a year studying in Finland, becoming fluent in Finnish. She earned multiple undergraduate degrees, a Master's, and a Ph.D. in accounting.

John graduated from Hofstra University with an MBA and a degree in mathematics education. In his first year at Hofstra, he achieved a 4.0 GPA, claiming he had already covered much of the coursework during his time at Chaminade High School. I joked that I should thank the good brothers at Chaminade and ask Hofstra for a refund.

Keith, my youngest, graduated from Chaminade but chose to attend Nassau Community College to avoid accruing debt. He then attended Queens College, where he graduated with honors and a psychology degree. He then pursued a Master of Science in Education in School Counseling at CW Post.

My sixth life lesson is: *Learn something new each day*. When you stop learning, you stop growing. Remember, you can continue to learn after your days of classroom education are over by learning from others. The most important lessons I've learned in life didn't come from professors in classrooms with their advanced degrees like MBAs or Ph.D.'s Instead, they were learned from life itself, from the diverse people and situations I encountered, often vastly different from what I had imagined. In my view, a complete education encompasses four key components:

- Book Learning: Traditional classroom education.
- Team Experience: Participation in any team, whether in sports or the arts.
- Social Engagement: Interacting with peers in different settings, and discussing thoughts, ideas, and beliefs.
- The Arts: Involvement in music, dance, painting, playing musical instruments, joining bands or choruses, acting in plays, participating in orchestras, exploring poetry, and delving into literature. Pursuing personal interests and understanding the arts' impact on humanity is essential.

These four elements together make up a formula for life-long learning. Gestalt theory emphasizes that the whole is greater than the sum of its parts. In this context, the whole is the totality of one's learning experiences and these four parts constitute the components that make up that whole.

My seventh and final life lesson is: *Give back.* There's no better feeling in the world than giving time and talents to help others! The abundance of something you have is sometimes exactly what someone else needs. And what you are good at doing is sometimes exactly what another person could use some help with. The opposite is also true. Sometimes the abundance of what someone else has is exactly what you need. And what someone else is good at doing is sometimes exactly what you could use some help with. If everyone realized this and embraced the importance of sharing their time, talents, and possessions with others, it seems that the solution to most of life's problems would never be far away. Unfortunately, I have seen the generous society in which I grew up during the '50s become filled with selfishness, greed, and disregard for others. So just as importantly as Lois and I stressed education to our children, we also made equally sure that they were raised to be considerate and caring.

Giving back has always come naturally to me because I view helping others as a way of thanking God for the many blessings He continuously gives to my family and myself. I try to give to others as often as possible each day, especially by using my friendly personality and gift of humor to put a smile on someone else's face when it looks like they need it. But my favorite way of giving back on a greater scale is jumping in the cold ocean water every Super Bowl Sunday as part of the big Make-A-Wish annual fundraiser in Long Beach.

My family and I at the Long Beach Polar Bears
Super Bowl Splash in February of 2020

Make-A-Wish is an organization that grants wishes to children who are living with life-threatening diseases. Many years ago, a little boy named Paulie Bradley was one of those children. He loved the beach and wished to go to Puerto Rico and play on the beach. Unfortunately, he did not live long enough for his wish to be granted so a few members of his family then started the Long Beach Polar Bears Super Bowl Splash in his memory. Today, Paulie's spirit is especially alive every Super Bowl Sunday when the ever-growing community of family, friends, and supporters join together to help make children's dreams come true through their support of the Make-A-Wish Metro New York chapter.

I started going to the Long Beach Polar Bears Super Bowl Splash by myself in 2008 before my son Keith worked up the courage to join me in 2011. Since then, my son John and my grandchildren have also recently joined the annual tradition, and my daughter Nicole attends to cheer us on when she is in town. At first, I did the plunge just for fun. I would send some pictures and videos to my family, classmates, and friends just to show them what I was doing. But then over the years as the event grew into the huge spectacle, it is today, and my group of participants grew into a team of Herons, I started asking for others to sponsor Team Heron in our plunge by donating to Make-A-Wish. Looking back at what we have accomplished, I am overjoyed with the results and am very proud that three generations of Herons are now working to help others. And I take comfort in knowing that after I'm gone, they will carry on the tradition by continuing to help the children of Make-A-Wish and their families who so desperately need encouragement and joy in their lives.

Over the last seven years, Team Heron of the Long Beach Polar Bears has raised over $5,000 for Make-A-Wish. This year Team Heron, thanks in large part to the Valley Stream North Class of 1961, raised over $1,000 and I also came up with the idea of collecting motivational cards and notes to go along with our donations which I hope will motivate the children to persevere

One of the many encouraging cards collected for the children of Make-A-Wish in 2024

through their challenging times. The annual fundraiser started by the Bradley family overall has collected over $9,000,000 since its inception in 2001 and over $850,000 was raised last year in 2023 alone. I encourage you to come down to

Long Beach to cheer us on and donate to Make-A-Wish every Super Bowl Sunday.

To close this chapter, I will share a poem written by a Shawnee Chief named Tecumseh in the late 1700s. The poem demonstrates respect, goodwill towards others, and thanking God for simple pleasures like food and the joy of being alive each day. Life way back in Tecumseh's day had something in common with life back in the '50s, simplicity. I can personally attest to the beauty of life's simple pleasures because I had a very happy upbringing while growing up with little more than the basics. We didn't have televisions to bombard us with advertisements for the latest toys, no magazines arriving at our doorstep filled with enticing products for sale, and certainly no cellphones, internet, or email. I enjoyed a happy childhood by playing with friends in the streets, spending quality time with family at home, or enjoying the beach, all of which were entirely free. We didn't need fancy toys or gadgets to amuse ourselves. Like Tecumseh, we didn't depend on possessions or technology to make us happy. Looking back, I am also amazed to realize how much fun we had without organized youth sports programs. We created our own rules, relished the competition, and experienced no pressure.

Drive-in movies were a special treat where the entire family would pile into the car for a single admission fee. As I grew older, my early years instilled in me the understanding that accumulating wealth, driving a new car, or owning the latest TV weren't important. Instead, I was content with having a roof over my head, food on the table, clothes on my back, and a car to get around. I never felt compelled to keep up with the Joneses or impress anyone. I was a young man who found joy in life's simple pleasures, without having, or wishing I had, any extravagant luxuries.

The themes in Tecumseh's poem relate perfectly to the message I'd like readers to consider after reading this book: That a life focused primarily on faith, family, and friends, although simple, is very rewarding and fulfilling.

*Live Your Life by Chief Tecumseh:*

"So live your life that the fear of death can never enter your heart.

Trouble no one about their religion; respect others in their view, and demand that they respect yours. Love your life, perfect your life, beautify all things in your life. Seek to make your life long and its purpose in the service of your people.

When you arise in the morning give thanks for the food and for the joy of living. If you see no reason for giving thanks, the fault lies only in yourself. Abuse no one and no thing, for abuse turns the wise ones to fools and robs the spirit of its vision."

Begin each day with a smile and surround yourself with positive people. Life is too short to tolerate negativity in your daily life.

# 27

# REGRETS

T hroughout the years, spanning class reunions, meetings, luncheons, phone calls, texts, emails, writings, and get-togethers, I've had the privilege of getting to know many of my classmates better. It has also been enlightening to get acquainted with some other classmates who I didn't know well or at all during high school. Enjoying these new connections and friendships over the years has made me realize that one of my most significant regrets is not knowing even more of my classmates during our time together at North.

I would have loved to spend more time with Barry Seedman before his father arranged for his transfer to another school. Barry was an intriguing character whose father was a police chief in New York City. Back in high school, Barry was into the betting on horses so perhaps he would have tipped me off to a winner at the racetrack, or maybe not. Either way, being closer friends with Barry would have been far from dull.

Even though we weren't very close during our time at North, I learned a lot from George Minkoff by observing his daily actions which demonstrated that no obstacle is insurmountable. This remarkable individual contracted polio at the tender age of six, leaving him physically challenged. Yet, he never lost his sense of humor, his determination, or his ability to live life to the fullest. He went on to become a husband, father, business owner, and even a published author. Had we been closer friends, I would have benefited from his infectious sense of humor, and I would have learned many more valuable life lessons about determination and ambition from him.

As the years passed, I had the opportunity to get to know Dick Zucker better, and I wish I could have hung out with him more during high school. A graduate of the Air Force Academy and a jet fighter pilot, Dick was a quiet, humble man and a true American hero. While he didn't frequently join my friends and I in our wild high school escapades, when he did, we made sure to keep him entertained and laughing.

Chris Beuttenmueller is another classmate with whom I would have enjoyed spending more time. Boundless positive energy radiated from her presence, and I wish I had basked in it more often.

I regret not having been acquainted with others like Steve Hachtman who I never encountered in school. It turns out that Steve is a terrific guy which I can attest to after getting to know him a little better after graduation. I'm also not sure where

Marilyn Grispin spent her time in school, but on the rare occasions when our paths crossed back then, it always seemed to end poorly. Over the years, I've come to know her as a sharp and humorous individual, and I wish we could have been friends in school, as we are now, many years later.

I achieved a lot of success in sports which was my main focus during high school, so I don't have many regrets related to my athletic endeavors. However, I do lament declining two college basketball scholarship offers as suggested by my coach Mr. Shannon. One offer was from Loyola University of Chicago, but I can't recall the name of the other institution. Like Loyola, the second institution was also far from home, but I didn't want to move away. Accepting a scholarship would have also ruined my early retirement plans, so I declined both offers and officially retired.

As I reflect, in addition to my devotion to sports, I also wish I would have taken advantage of more of the wonderful opportunities we had at North like clubs or the arts to round out my educational experience. I regret not having explored other extracurricular activities, expanded my knowledge base, or taken in a wider range of classmates' unique perspectives and experiences. For example, back then, I knew very little about art, music, or theater but I think I might have enjoyed playing a musical instrument or participating in a play. Having done so would have been a stark departure from my usual routine and would have helped me become more well-rounded by spending time with classmates like Peter Sperber and Steven Dorso. Undoubtedly, Steven would have shared some of his passion for the arts, exposed me to his talents, and broadened my horizons during our time at North. Peter, who was a quiet individual, an honor student, and an active participant in the school's band, marching band, and orchestra, is yet another classmate I didn't encounter in high school but have had the opportunity to know better during our reunions. Given the diversity of our school's offerings and our differing interests, it isn't surprising that our paths never crossed back then but looking back I regret not meeting him earlier in life. Peter is a fascinating person, and his wife, Barbara, is remarkably outgoing so they make a perfect couple and I enjoy catching up with them.

In addition to my unexplored interest in the arts, I also had a penchant for engaging in thoughtful debates and a curiosity about personal finance. Though I didn't possess the cognitive ability to win an intellectual argument against any of the honor students who made up the majority of the debate club, I think I would have thoroughly enjoyed listening to their viewpoints on a wide range of subjects had I joined them from time to time. Susan Friedman was one of those students with whom I suspect I would have engaged in some very stimulating conversations had we spent time together in high school because our views on life were vastly different. She remains one of the smartest people I know, having spent many years in education and having earned several degrees, including a Ph.D. I also now realize that a financial club, which I don't recall existing or whether I possessed the knowledge to request one, would have greatly piqued my interest. I yearned to find out about the intricacies of the stock market, managing a checkbook, and comprehending interest rates and their fluctuations. These were valuable skills that I only acquired much later in life, often the hard way after making mistakes. Back in those days, credit cards were not yet in use; everything had to be paid for immediately with cash or a check. Layaway, a system in which a store would reserve an item with a deadline for full payment at a later date, was the closest thing available to the credit cards we have today. The very first charge card was introduced by the Diners' Club in 1950 and Bank of America followed with the first consumer credit card in 1958. However, it wasn't until the '70s that credit cards became popular with the masses.

Back then, I gravitated towards other more outgoing classmates because the only thing I wanted to do was joke around and have fun all the time. However, I should not have overlooked some of my more serious classmates and should have embraced the academic challenges of high school by dedicating some time to studying. But at the time, I didn't fully grasp the significance of that third-floor library, where classmates I barely knew spent hours every day. If I could turn back time, I would have explored the library, where the honor students congregated, more thoroughly. There, I might have gotten to know some of the smarter students from whom I could have learned a lot; classmates like Dennis Kibler, who back then was a genius with a great sense of humor. His prowess in mathematics could have been a tremendous asset to me in math class.

I wish I had taken the opportunity to spend more time with Dan Prener, who was undoubtedly the smartest person in our class. We shared a desk in Mrs. Gold's advanced Geometry class, on the occasions when I did attend. Instead of fooling around by altering some of his answers to the proofs he presented on the blackboard, I should have asked him to explain his approach. Dan went on to work at IBM, working to develop technology that has reshaped our world. Most notably, Dan contributed to the creation of what we know today as "The Cloud," a revolutionary data storage solution that holds an incredible amount of information and allows users to access their data on any device with an internet connection, from anywhere in the world, in mere seconds. A conversation with Barbara Benson Kaplan, another of the smartest and most driven people in our class, would also have been illuminating. Barbara's philosophy was simple: with hard work and determination, anything was possible; no barriers could hold her back.

Miriam Pisk, who frequented the library and never crossed paths with me in high school, is another person I regret not knowing back then. It would have been interesting to get to know her better and hear about her Jewish relatives in Germany during and after World War II. And I would have shared stories with her about my grandmother who was raised by German sisters in an orphanage and occasionally spoke a little German to me when I was young. Talking about personal histories with others is often more compelling and complete than any book can describe, and I am sure we would have formed our bond of friendship much earlier in life had we known each other during our days at North.

In retrospect, I now realize why my father advocated for me to pursue more challenging subjects in high school, even if it meant changing my study habits radically. I eventually heeded his advice, but not until later in life after high school when I successfully applied the lessons he taught me in the business world when taking college classes, and while raising my children. I can only imagine where life would have taken me had I taken academics, and life, more seriously during my high school years.

Many North High classmates, like John Belluardo, went on to become very successful and I wish I had gotten to know them earlier in life too. John started his own innovative technology company while others became successful educators, writers, rocket scientists, pioneers in computer programming, city planners, and leaders in various fields. Had we been closer friends before he transferred to Sewanhaka High School and delved into the world of auto mechanics, John might have offered some invaluable assistance with my '49 Buick. But all kidding aside, it would have been interesting to learn about what motivated students like John back in high school and then watch them develop their success over the years that followed.

Looking back, I am thankful that most of my high school regrets are related to wishing I had done more and not regretting specific things that I wish I would not have done. But regret for one embarrassing act still endures inside me to this day, throwing a baseball through the windshield of a brand-new convertible that belonged to Sue Fisher's father. It happened when I was stationed in left field, and Sue and her friend pulled up behind the baseball field's backstop at the end of the street. They were excited and waving, with Sue at the wheel of her father's brand-new convertible. I had a strong arm and thought I could impress them by throwing the baseball over the backstop, clearing the car, and acknowledging their presence. But it turned out to be a foolish move, as the ball fell short, shattering the windshield. The disappointment and frustration on her face mirrored my own. During my high school days, I pulled my fair share of pranks and tricks, but my intent was never to humiliate or harm anyone so that incident was entirely out of character for me, and I remain ashamed of it.

Afterward, I walked off the field consumed by guilt as Sue drove away equally upset. I thought I'd be dismissed from the baseball team because everyone would assume I had done it on purpose. I went home and immediately confessed to my father, ensuring he heard the story directly from me before Mr. Fisher came to visit. When Mr. Fisher did arrive, he was understandably upset and expressed his displeasure. Fortunately, his insurance covered the damage, and I was allowed to remain on the baseball team. However, I suspect that Sue wasn't too fond of me after that unfortunate episode, and I deeply regret having marred her otherwise beautiful day.

Outside of what I regret from my days at North, my other life regrets are minimal. I've been blessed to lead a happy and fortunate life since those youthful carefree days of early retirement came to an end. I've consistently held jobs and thankfully I have never been left unemployed after coming out of my early retirement when I needed income to raise a family. I've owned two successful businesses, one of which continues to provide income even after its sale twenty years ago. All my success and good fortune allowed my family and I to enjoy a vacation home in the Poconos for fifteen years while my children were young giving them a chance to explore the mountains and the outdoors. Today, my wife and I share a comfortable life: we live in a nice home, enjoy good health, have food on the table, money in the bank, and two cars in the driveway. I still work at a job I love driving a school bus and interacting with kids. I'm not interested in the latest gadgets or cars; my newest vehicle is a 2014 Honda CRV. I've taken steps to be environmentally conscious, including installing solar roof panels to supply our electricity, using a rain barrel to collect water for our plants, and heating our house in the winter with a cast iron wood-burning stove.

My family and I owe a lot of the comfort we enjoy today to the hard work and dedication my wife Lois has shown to us throughout the past 48 years. One of life's most critical decisions is marriage, and I was fortunate to marry the right person thanks in part to caring friends who never stopped looking out for me. My wife is strong, intelligent, and an outstanding mother to our three children. As a stay-at-home mom who gave up the opportunity to pursue a career, she ensured they received everything they needed for success in life beginning with a foundation of faith in God and a quality education. She originally wanted to be a teacher, but instead of educating hundreds of students, she focused her efforts on just three, our children, and making sure they did their best in school. She taught all of them how to read before they entered kindergarten, and she always guided them through their homework assignments when needed during their school-age years. Lois also taught them to be respectful, caring, and most importantly she taught them the difference between right and wrong.

As our children grew, it was important to me that they would receive a top-notch education and not have an opportunity to get away with slacking off in school like I did. So, my wife and I made the financial sacrifice to send our children to the best schools in our area, schools in which they would be pushed to succeed, schools in which excellence would be demanded and there would be no easy way out because failure meant expulsion. The boys went to Chaminade High School in Mineola and Nicole attended Sacred Heart Academy in Hempstead. Studying at these schools provided our children with a comprehensive academic education which prepared them for success in college. More importantly, these were Catholic institutions that further enforced the religious values our children were raised with at home, thereby preparing them for the rest of their adult lives after graduating.

All three excelled academically, progressed to college, earned multiple degrees, and now have successful careers in education. I look upon my children's careers, particularly my youngest son's position as a college athletic director, with pride and a bit of regret wishing that perhaps I too would have worked in education. High school teachers generally only work 180 days per year, and though the workload varies, college employees typically enjoy a generous amount of time off around holidays and in the summertime. I feel fulfilled that my children work in fields they are passionate about and smile when I think to myself, because of how often they have time off from work, that they are already enjoying an early retirement of their own. I always yearned for a job like that, one that I'd love with perks like a lot of vacation time so I wonder what I might have done differently had I taken academics seriously and earned a college degree. I am thankful that my wife and I raised our children with a strong work ethic and that their hard work earlier in life, especially in school, has paid off for them as they now enjoy relatively easygoing lives. I am also very pleased that my wife and I instilled a strong moral compass in our children and that they have grown up to be amazing human beings of whom we are very proud.

Thanks be to God and my oldest child John, Lois and I now have four wonderful grandchildren, two boys, and two girls, who are relishing life, excelling in school, and engaging in various arts and sports. At a young age, they have already achieved something that I could not when I was in school, a balance between education and leisure time activities. My wife now devotes herself to our grandchildren, showering them with love and affection the same way she did with our children many years ago; it's a joy to watch them together.

It's amazing how many people can be positively affected when someone recognizes a way in which they fell short and decides to correct it. Recognizing my shortcomings as a student later in life has had a positive impact on two generations of my family and the many students they teach, coach, and motivate to achieve their potential. I'm so very proud of my children and grandchildren who strive to be all they can be every day. Today's youth will be tomorrow's leaders, so let's support them and inspire them to face life's toughest with courage and strength!

I'm grateful to have learned crucial life lessons from my family, friends, classmates, high school experiences, early retirement and then snapping back into reality when it was time to start a family. The friendships I forged and the wisdom I gained during my formative high school years have been life-changing and profoundly rewarding. I remain thankful for my journey at North, for the countless people who were part of that special era known as the '50s, and how it all led me to wind up sharing a wonderful life with great friends, and a beautiful, growing family, many years later. Though I regret that many of the lessons I learned did not become apparent until my early retirement ended and I grew as an adult, the collection of all those things had indeed equipped me to be successful in the business world and in raising a family.

I hope that all young people, especially my grandchildren, will one day realize the value of the people they are encountering and the life lessons they are learning now, even the ones that don't seem to make sense yet. And I challenge them to always remember that the people they trust and the wisdom they share will all prove useful at some unknown point in the future when the time is right. After all, the people I knew and the lessons they helped me learn proved to be the foundation I needed for future success, and were the only things that remained consistent as I grew in a world that changed so much over the years.

# YEARBOOK QUOTES

In the realm of yearbook quotes, where well-wishes and positivity often reign, my yearbook seemed to take a different turn. As I journeyed through North High School, I found myself seeing the world through a different lens and acting upon those unique perspectives. Here, I present a glimpse into the array of sentiments shared by students and teachers alike, capturing the moments that defined our time together.

While I won't attribute names to every quote, my intention in this chapter is to highlight the joy, laughter, excitement, and fulfillment that I had the privilege of sharing with my class-mates. To the students, teachers, and coaches who were a part of this journey, I extend my sincere gratitude for making my high school years remarkably unforgettable and for the years that followed. Our football team's triumph and the enduring camaraderie of our 55-year reunions stand as a testament to the bonds we formed and the memories we created together.

A special acknowledgment goes to Miriam Pisk Miller, who tirelessly kept us connected through meticulous record-keeping of addresses, phone numbers, and email addresses. Miriam's dedication spanned years and bridged distances as our class scattered across states. Her efforts, executed in the age of computers, ensured that our ties remained unbroken.

Through the pages of my yearbook, the following comments from classmates, teammates, and teachers offer a glimpse into their feelings about our shared experiences. I've pared down the quotes to avoid tedium or self-indulgence, aiming to capture the essence of their sentiments. These words paint a vivid picture of the journey, the friendships, and the experiences that have shaped me. Added to the end of some of the quotes are my reflections and responses, after all these years looking back on each:

Mr. Snow (Chemistry teacher): "May you turn all $CH_3$ $5OOH$ into $C_2H_3OX$" I never understood what this meant. Now you know why I didn't last in Chemistry class. He was an excellent teacher who always kept us alert.

Mr. Fleming (Mechanical Drawing teacher): "We didn't learn too much! But it's been fun. God be with you." With the marks I had, I would sure need God's help to become successful after high school, and boy was I blessed to have it! Mr. Fleming was a great teacher and I learned more from him than he realized, the knowledge just took years to surface.

Mr. Pohl (Physical Education teacher): "Lots of Luck." He

was a terrific, no-nonsense teacher who wanted to teach. But I, being a good athlete was uninterested in Phys Ed class, hence his comment.

Joe Corea: "We've had real great times together, especially with that '49 Buick." Joe loved to get picked up in that Buick.

Roger Angrisani: "Remember the wild parties before freshman football games." I asked him years later if he remembered any of those parties, but he said, "No, but they must have been really good for me to write that in your yearbook!"

Richie Barone: "These last four years we had together in North have been the best in my life. I hope our friendship lasts a long time after North." Richie loved going out with us, he was always full of laughs.

Gary Berger: "It's been great fun having class with you." I don't know why he would say that since I wasn't there that often. I guess when I was there, it was fun.

Chris Beuttenmueller: "I've known you well since the ninth grade when we had all those crazy parties. Now as seniors, we've repeated these good times ten times over." Chris was always full of life and fun to be with, I miss her.

Barbara Cohen: "You're a really great guy and I hope that we can be friends always. You deserve the best of everything." This was my eighth-grade girlfriend and yes, we are still friends today. I love her like my sister.

Ilene Danziger: "Keep smiling!" I loved to smile every day.

Tony DiBenedetto: "Always remember our good times."

There were so many that it is hard to remember even half of them, much less all of them.

Gary Halpern: "The safest driver in North High's parking lot. Throwing a baseball into Sue Fisher's windshield." The windshield was an accident and the few fender benders in the student parking lot were not unusual. Ok maybe a little unusual.

Steve Due: "I'll never forget the night you pushed Tommy and I up the stairs after the party over at Dom's house." Yes, the boys did have too much to drink at that party.

Tony Esposito: "Whatever you do in the future, it will probably include some kind of laughs or riot. You're one of the funniest, and craziest guys I know. You're driving skills will be printed in the next driver's Ed. Book." Tony was a fraternity brother remarking on my driving experience.

Pam Fernandes: "You've driven us to many great and funny times, especially the memorable day before the North-South game. Thank you for being so patient with us girls and best of luck although after driving around with you your luck shines through." Yes, I enjoyed driving anyone who wasn't afraid to get in my car. The girls were always the most fun.

Patricia Stone: "I'll never forget the day you rode around the track with your painted-up Bomb (49 Buick) the day before the North-South game. Thanks for giving me a ride whenever I needed one." Yes, that painted '49 Buick was a big hit outside the school.

Salvatore Talamo: "If you want to keep laughing, think of

our English class. Yes, this was the class where the teacher read to us." We were beyond help.

Gerald Toto: "Best of luck to a great athlete."

Joseph Toto: "Lots of luck to a fine athlete. Keep up the good work Ray and I hope to see you in the majors." These were the Toto twins whom I always had a good time with. I miss those guys.

Richie Renda: "It's been an interesting experience being on the baseball team with you. I had a couple of good laughs during the season." Yes, and we not only had a good time, but we won the league championship too.

Jeff Friedlander: "Great sense of humor." He liked my jokes.

Barbara Goldberg: "Dear Ray, the boy who definitely deserves the Driver's Ed. award. Keep up that hilarious sense of humor." Barbara had a good sense of humor and liked to laugh.

Steve Hachtman: "I'll never forget your car and your sense of humor." Steve is a terrific guy.

Bernie Havern: "May you be just a little more successful in life than you've been in your studies. We had so many laughs, adventures, and excitement it would be impossible to try and remember them all. I'll always remember you and the rest of the gang as long as I live. I just hope we can stick together after graduation and continue to have plenty of laughs." Bernie was my oldest friend since we were six years old, and we remained good friends enjoying lots more adventures, parties, and good times until he passed in 2013. He is in my prayers. I couldn't have asked for a better friend. He was always there for me and everyone else in his life when someone needed him. I loved him like he was my brother.

Jay Heller: "Ray with the real outlook on life." Jay was one of the rare ones who actually understood my outlook on life.

Kenny Halpern: "Stop your drinking." Ken was my old friend ever since we met as ten-year-olds in a fistfight. He was just looking out for me then as he continued to do during the rest of my life. We went on to play football and basketball together and I couldn't have asked for a better teammate to be by my side. He was as tough, as fearless, and as hard-nosed a player as I had ever seen.

William Jakubowski: "To a guy who doesn't make me feel so tame." I don't remember Bill being that wild.

Ira Katz: "You will get your ticket sooner or later and when you do it will be a whopper. Take it easy and you will live longer." Yes, Ira, I did get some tickets but not while in high school. He would be happy to know that I'm well and driving a school bus every day safely.

Sheila Kaplan: "Just stay happy and keep smiling and every success will be yours." I remember Sheila being a very happy, pretty young lady who always wore a smile that brightened up everyone around her. It sure did brighten up my day.

Barbara Knies: "I have enjoyed your company all through high school." I always tried to keep others smiling.

Don Lawrence: "Don't forget the great times we had in English IV." I think the teachers were still reading to us. We must have been on the lost track.

Ken Lettow: "The guy who is always fun to have around."

This says it all. I got an "A" in fun but that subject wasn't on our report cards which was unfortunate for me.

George Manz: "I hope you get through mechanical drawing." George had no faith in me but of course, I passed mechanical drawing because we had a fabulous teacher.

Lou Martorello: "We had great times in the past. I hope we can get together in the future." We did get together many times throughout our lifetime after high school.

Roberta (Bobbie) Natalie: "I hope someday you will look back at the fun we had together and remember, of course, Going Up"! I thought I said, "Going down," because we were on the top floor of her house when I made that famous comment, but then again, I never know what comes flying out of my mouth when I am under pressure. Roberta was my tenth-grade girlfriend and we remained close for the rest of our lives. She married my fraternity brother, Richie Barone who passed away last year. I call or visit Roberta from time to time, and I'm still able to make her laugh.

Maureen Porzio: "To one of the happiest guys I know." What a doll. I miss her smiling face.

Sal Pepitone: "I will never forget when you were driving my car to a party in Brooklyn at 110mph. You know Ray, I don't scare easily but that night he scared the crap out of me." That was another of Sal's famous exaggerations... the car couldn't really go that fast!

Artie Schnitzer: "Whenever I laugh in the future, I'll always remember you, for you are the only one who has had me rolling in the sides every time we went out. All the wild times in your '49 Buick were just the greatest. I think you are one of the funniest guys I've ever met. If I live forever, I will not be able to repay you for the good times we had." I called Artie and said he could repay me with a few million since he was doing well in the business world. His reply was, "You weren't that funny!"

Alex Sansone: "If you accomplish things as fast and as good as in mechanical drawing, you're in trouble. Lots of luck because you need it." Another comedian.

Sharon Weinroth: "Without you in health class, it would have been extremely boring. Keep making jokes and keep everyone laughing." This is why I had to take this class twice in order to pass, but everyone had a good time.

Barnett Rukin: "We have been on the football teams together since the seventh grade. I will miss your ranks and jokes." I love this guy. He went through a lot when he lost his dad as a senior and had to help his mom run the family business. He went on to college and graduated with an accounting degree. Now has his own business.

Bonnie Richter: "I hope that the future looks as gay and cheerful to you as it always has been through high school. Just remember one thing in life drinking and driving don't mix, you're too nice to fool around." She was a beautiful example of my classmates who were caring and always wanted the best for each other. Another exaggeration, as I never drove drunk as best as I can remember.

Dorothy Rosen: "Our years at North have been fun, especially our English class." Oh what a class, I think they were still reading to us!

Jody Sauer: "Always remember the good times we had together. Like the third grade. Love, and luck." Jody was my first girlfriend at eight years old.

Tommy Scibelli: "You've done just about anything a guy could ask for. I'll always remember the wild times. I'll remember you when the referee blows his whistle, the umpire says play ball, see a '49 Buick, see a deck of cards, have an upset stomach, hear the bells of the shuffleboard, the bartender asks what it will be, guys." Oh how I miss Tommy who gave his life on the battlefield 12,000 miles from home at only 25 years young. I'm so lucky that I knew him growing up and so proud that he called me his friend.

Dick Zucker: "We haven't been as close as friends should be. But whenever I did get to go out with you and the boys, you certainly kept me laughing." Dick, unlike me, was a serious student and a really good person. It took a bunch of us to get him laughing.

Peter Duva: "With your stomach, you'll probably become a chef." I was never a chef, but do like to cook mostly on the barbeque outside.

James (Noel) Fox: "Good luck to you, fellow Omega man, even though you don't come to the meetings." That's true. I didn't make too many fraternity meetings because of my very busy schedule. Noel is a really generous and caring person.

Ronald Freistat: "I wish you all the luck in the world." Ron and I went from seventh through twelfth grade together, and we had a great time knowing each other all those years.

Mary Graham: "Don't forget those delightful health classes. I'm sorry for all the ranks." Another good, fun person to be around who recently lost a battle with cancer. I miss those ranks now Mary.

Marilyn Grispin: "Which basketball scholarship will you accept?" I actually turned down a scholarship from Loyola of Chicago that my coach Joe Shannon said I could have. I wish Marilyn and I were on better terms in high school, but we are good friends now.

Barry Lublin: "If there is an outstanding feature that will remind me of you, it's your rabbit fur-lined gloves. You used to say, "I could lick anyone in these gloves." I can't believe Barry still remembered my famous quote when we were growing up in grade school. I didn't have them on when I fought Kenny Halpern which was a big mistake on my part.

Bob Van Dina (Mr. America 1966): "To Ray, the guy that doesn't weigh." You should have seen the build on Bobby. He sure looked like he was ready for the competition.

As I reflect on my yearbook and all of these wonderful entries, I'm reminded that the 1950s were marked by a greater freedom of expression. Interacting with others was often done in person, through handwritten notes, or the grapevine of student communication. Phone use and other modern devices were scarce, so interactions were more genuine and personal back then.

As these snippets of quotes from my yearbook reflect, high

school was a tapestry of friendships, laughter, and shared moments that continue to resonate. Each sentiment, captured in ink on paper, encapsulates a unique connection and a shared journey that has shaped us all. The journey we embarked upon together, shaped by youthful exuberance, shared experiences, and the bond of camaraderie, has traversed the years and remains an enduring chapter of our lives. These yearbook quotes, like cherished memories, continue to bring a smile to my face and remind me of the incredible tapestry of friendships that have stood the test of time.

# WHAT HAPPENED TO THE CLASS

As I write this book about my life with a focus on my high school years, friendships, and classmates, I thought it important to include what happened to some of those who I remained close to and stayed in touch with through emails, texts, and phone calls. Over the years I've learned more about some of the friends who moved out of state to places like Texas, California, Arizona, Ohio, and Florida, at our reunions.

THOMAS SCIBELLI: Tragically, Thomas was killed in action in the jungles of Vietnam on December 27, 1969. He left behind his beautiful wife Lorraine, mother, and brother. His father had been killed 25 years earlier in WWII during the invasion of Normandy. "There is no greater love than to give your life for others." I still check in with Lorraine from time to time, and she's doing well, and taking care of her aging mother who at the time of this writing is almost 100 years old.

ARTIE SCHNITZER: After graduating from Union, a small college in upstate New York, Artie married his lovely wife Lynn and had two wonderful children. He sold his house and took a management position in a California company, eventually traveling the world as the company grew. Artie, a very smart, strong, and confident person, became very successful. He's now retired and living with his wife splitting time between their homes in Austin, Texas, and New York City.

BERNIE HAVERN: Bernie married his high school sweetheart, Joan Dini, and had four wonderful children. They all married, and he now has ten grandchildren. Bernie joined the Nassau County Police Department, where he was voted Policeman of the Year and rose to the rank of detective. After retiring, he became the owner of a trophy shop with two other police officers. Bernie also joined Molloy College and built their baseball program from intramural into one of the most respected Division II baseball programs in the NCAA. He passed away on April 13, 2013, from prostate cancer.

TONY DI BENEDETTO: Tony married his high school sweetheart, Pat Dini (Joan Dini's sister), after serving in the military. He was in action in the jungles of Vietnam and witnessed the horrors of war. He had two boys who married, and he now has five grandchildren. Tony worked as a brick and mason expert in his own business, a skill his uncle taught him since he was fourteen years old. He also worked for Nassau County. Tony is now retired and living in Malverne with his wife Pat.

JOE COREA: Joe married and had two girls and two grandchildren. His wife, Mary Jeanne passed away from cancer in

2016. Joe became a Math teacher, then head of the Math department, and served as the head football and baseball coach. He won over 500 baseball games and many championships. The baseball field at Calhoun High School was named after him. Joe was fully retired, enjoying golf, and living in Massapequa, New York up until he passed away recently.

RICHIE BARONE: Richie married his high school sweetheart, Roberta (Bobbie) Natalie, and had three daughters and seven grandkids. Richie ventured into the air-conditioning and heating business, started his own company, and achieved significant success. He had a big, beautiful home built out East. Their story is like a fairy tale of two high school sweethearts who loved each other for a lifetime. Richie passed away in 2020 from heart disease.

LOU MARTORELLO: Lou married his high school sweetheart, Pat Everly, after graduating from college. He worked for Mr. Getty of Getty Oil and later ventured into security systems, becoming part owner of a very successful company he helped build. Not to be outdone, Pat started her own sign business, which she has since sold. They had three children and two grandkids, and recently retired to a beautiful new five-bedroom home in Memphis, Tennessee, enjoying their retired life.

Ken Halpern: Ken attended college, where he met and became friends with President Joe Biden at Delaware University where they played together on the football team. Ken married, had two boys, and now has three grandchildren. He joined a law firm after working as a prosecutor for Nassau

County right out of college, eventually establishing a successful career in his private law practice. Ken is still working and lives in Suffolk County, New York, with his wife Mishele.

GARY HALPERN: Kenny's younger brother, one year behind us in school. He went on to graduate from Harvard and become a doctor of Radiology.

ROGER ANGRISANI: Roger married his high school dream girl, Diane Musacchio, and they had three children and two grandchildren. He entered the construction industry, becoming a shop steward in the union and eventually retiring. Roger moved to Florida, where he now resides in a beautiful home and enjoys working at the church, while Diane sings in the choir.

JOHN BELLUARDO: John retired as a business owner (BASS, Inc.) and is a WWII vintage aircraft owner, owning a Luscombe 8A. He had the opportunity to work with Paul Allen and Bill Gates before they founded Microsoft. John designed the communication extensions to the "Basic" programming language, later adopted by both Microsoft and IBM. He wrote the book "How I Reversed Heart Disease: A Pilot's Story" in 2015. John lives in Dayton, Ohio, with his wife Barbara, and they have two children.

CHRIS BEUTTENMUELLER: Chris married and had two daughters, two stepdaughters, and eight grandchildren. She worked for the Department of Defense for 30 years before retiring in 2007 and is active in various community clubs and activities like the women's club and the Red Hat. She embodied her high school philosophy of "Enjoy life and have fun," making it her family's way of life. Chris passed away in 2021 from heart disease.

JAMES (NOEL) FOX: Noel worked for IBM for 33 years, rising to the position of Vice President, before starting his own field service business. He spent two years researching its possibilities in Japan. Noel married his high school sweetheart, Mary Graham, in 1996 after each had already started their own family. Together as a married couple, they lived with four children and eventually, they had seven grandchildren. Noel is in full retirement, while Mary passed away a couple of years ago due to cancer. He now resides in Naples, Florida.

DICK ZUCKER: Dick graduated from the Air Force Academy as a jet fighter pilot and served in Vietnam, flying many low-level helicopter missions in addition to fighter jet duties. He later became the Vice President of Beldon Enterprises and Chairman of the Board at USAA Mutual Funds. Dick is now retired and enjoys playing golf in San Antonio, Texas.

ED SIMMS & BARBARA COHEN: Ed and Barbara met in the ninth grade and started dating. They married in 1966, over 50 years ago. They have two daughters and five grandchildren. Ed retired from the New York City Police Department, while Barbara retired from teaching. They moved out west with their two daughters and still live in Henderson, Nevada. They are now fully retired and enjoy their time with their grandchildren.

MARILYN GRISPIN PEREZ: Now fully retired and living in California, Marilyn and her husband have two children and one grandchild named Brooklyn. They have been married for 51 years. Marilyn retired from the Federal Aviation Administration, where she served as the Administration Officer for the New York TRACON (an air traffic control facility).

BARRY SEEDMAN: Barry served four years in the US Air Force and went on to become an officer in the Merchant Marine, sailing on luxury liners and freighters as a purser/pharmacist mate. This experience sparked his keen interest in healing, eventually leading to a doctorate and a career as a therapist. Barry spent the last 30 years conducting motivational workshops and seminars worldwide, specializing in hypnosis. He is now retired and lives in Las Vegas with his wife Nan and their dog. They have three children and five grandchildren, enjoying the fruits of their labor and their growing family.

SAL PEPITONE: Sal served as a police officer in New York City and held the rank of Lt. Colonel in the US Army Reserves' Military Police. He sold and developed franchised business systems, primarily in the Northeast area and throughout the USA. This allowed him to travel and visit many towns and cities, which was a wonderful experience. Sal has been married to his beautiful wife Carol for over 50 years and has two daughters and five grandchildren.

ROGER OLSEN: Roger married his high school sweetheart, Pat Seiler, and they had two children and four grandchildren. He joined one of the largest construction companies globally and worked his way up to becoming the top carpenter foreman with 180 carpenters under his supervision. Over the years, they built JFK Airport and numerous bridges, along with repairing the Twin Towers among other high-profile projects. Roger was also a professional fisherman, fishing off the shores of Long Island, the Bahamas, and Alaska, where he introduced new fishing methods to the locals. He and his cousin Steve were very successful in buying rundown houses, rebuilding them, and selling them for a profit. Sadly, Roger passed away just after celebrating his 75th birthday due to cancer, following his wife Pat's passing the year before.

MIRIAM PISK MILLER: Miriam married and had two children and two grandchildren. She began her career as a computer programmer and later became a tour guide at the Noah Webster House, the birthplace of the Father of our Country's language. She co-founded the Valley Stream North High Alumni Association and played a pivotal role in keeping our class connected over the years. Her tireless efforts to update mailing lists, emails, and phone numbers were instrumental in ensuring our continued reunions over the last 30 years. Miriam's dedication to being a great detective has greatly benefited our class and kept us connected.

MARK SALITA: Mark retired from Northrop Grumman after 32 years in the Solid-Propellant Rocket business. He authored a book titled "Basic Analytical and Numerical Methods for Propulsion and Aerodynamic Analysis of Solid-Propellant Rocket," published in 2011, and distributed to the US rocket industry. He also lectured in Haifa on the Israeli rocket industry. Mark married his beautiful wife Alice and has two children. He was still playing ice hockey 50 years after high school with several former NHL players in the group.

DENNIS KIBLER: Dennis married his beautiful wife Christine and had two wonderful children. After earning a degree in Mathematics, he retrained himself and became a computer scientist at the University of California, Irvine. He went on to do research in artificial intelligence, machine learning, and Bioinformatics, while also teaching during his retirement years. He aspires to write tutorial programs in mathematics and science but finds it more challenging than expected.

DORIS WEINBERG APTEKAR: Doris earned her Ph.D. after attending Boston University, Queens College for school psychology, and Fordham University. She is a psychologist in private practice with a home office and consults for NYC. Throughout her 22 years of education, she served as a teacher, Special Ed. Teacher, adjunct instructor at Queens College, and a school psychologist. Doris is married to Sy and has five children and eight grandchildren, with more to come. Her philosophy is that accomplishment, achievement, and goals have no boundaries except for those we impose on ourselves. She encourages us to never be afraid, reach for the stars, and do something every day that's more difficult than we imagined.

SUSAN FRIEDMAN: Susan spent four years at Cornell University, leading to a fellowship at UC Berkeley, where she earned an M.A. in political science and Chinese. She was then awarded a fellowship to UMass, Amherst, where she received her PhD in political philosophy. Susan went on to teach women's studies and political theory at various universities, including Wilmington College, University without Walls in Ohio, and the University of Milwaukee. She was actively involved in the Women's Movement and raised funds for the Native American Movement. Susan also worked as an office manager at Venture Capital firms. She is now retired and lives in New York City, where she enjoys painting.

BARBARA BENSON KAPLAN: Barbara is happily married to her husband Jerry, who is a doctor. They are now retired and own a townhouse in West Dover, Vermont. Barbara served as the Executive Director of the Philadelphia City Planning Commission for seventeen years. She has been actively involved in charity work on a volunteer basis for 'The Development Workshop,' a group dedicated to benefiting communities through development, which includes developers, planners, architects, real estate professionals, economists, engineers, and more. Barbara has also served on several boards, including the Preservation Alliance, Neighborhood Gardens Association, and the Center for Literacy. Her commitment to giving back to the communities where she lives is another example of our class's dedication to making a difference.

GEORGE MINKOFF: George graduated at the top of his class from college. He married and had two sons. George is a published author and the owner of a rare bookstore business. Hollywood has acquired the rights to one of his publications, and we eagerly anticipate seeing it on the big screen.

MICHAEL GRIFFITH: Michael went on to star on the track team at the University of Virginia, becoming a state champion. He later graduated from law school and became an international attorney, specializing in representing Americans arrested overseas. His first case, "Midnight Express," became a famous book and movie.

STEVE HACHTMAN: Steve graduated from college with a degree in psychology. He married Brenda, a nurse, whom he met while treating serious drug abuse patients in New York. They went on to have three sons, four granddaughters, one grandson, and two step-grandsons. Steve has traveled around the U.S. and is now retired, enjoying life in the warm South.

STEVEN DORSO: After graduating from college with a specialization in art, Steven married his wife Eileen, and had two daughters and four grandchildren. He worked for the Capitol Record Club as a senior art director and creative director in Westchester, New York. He later formed his creative design agency in Manhattan, specializing in direct marketing. He and his wife have a vacation/retirement home in Peru, Vermont. This is not a mistake, there is a town called Peru in the state of Vermont.

RONALD GORDON: After graduating from college and surviving the jungles of Vietnam, Ronald became a fundraiser. He later established his own successful fundraising business. Ronald's passion for history led him to graduate school, where he taught social studies in the New York City school system for ten years. Ron gives back to the community by teaching home-bound students and volunteering for charities, such as the Make-A-Wish Foundation.

PETER SPERBER: Peter embarked on a 35-year career in mental health with NY State, having served as a supervising social worker, director of social work, and treatment team leader. He also served on the board of the local synagogue and became its president.

PAT STONE: After college, Pat married and had two children and one granddaughter. She worked as a teacher for 40 years in various places, including Syracuse, San Francisco, Berkeley, and Pacifica, California where she served as AFT (American Federation of Teachers) president. Her final teaching position was in Inverness, Florida, where she was the chief negotiator for the teachers' union in Citrus County.

BARNETT RUKIN: Barnett went to college, became a certified accountant, and established his own accounting business. He is still working and resides in New Jersey.

These are just 32 of my remarkable classmates, along with 8 spouses, from the graduating class of 1961. Just as I didn't understand the importance of academics back then, I also didn't realize how valuable these lifelong friendships would become to us all. I was so fortunate to be surrounded by some of the smartest, strongest boys and girls in the world! Years later looking back, I am amazed by how many of my classmates excelled in various fields. Many of them ventured to different countries and states to learn, grow, teach, and spread their North High class of 1961 experiences with the world. They made their mark in teaching, coaching, writing, computers, technology, law enforcement, education, and law. Their drive to be the best they could be is evident in the companies they built, the books they wrote to help others, the lives they lived, and how much they gave back.

More importantly than their successes, I am even more impressed with the fact that my classmates were, and still are, caring, good, and intelligent people who give back to society in a multitude of ways. I'm filled with awe for so many of them who went on to better the world, and in some cases, made the world a better place to live for everybody. Their children continue this tradition today, just as their parents did years ago. Their grandchildren are the future of our beautiful country, and if they follow in the footsteps of their grandparents, I do not doubt that America will continue to grow, prosper, and remain strong for many years to come because of people like my classmates and the families they have raised.

# ACKNOWLEDGMENTS

No creation is the work of one person. So many have contributed to this work in ways great and small that it would be impossible to identify them all. I would like to extend a special thank you to Lou Martorello, Marilyn Grispin Perez, Jo Rauch, and Barry Seedman for their written contributions to my book, and to Miriam Pisk Miller for furnishing me with all the connections to my fellow classmates. The following classmates and schoolmates from other classes at North contributed their stories, comments, or photographs so they also deserve to be acknowledged by name. Their memories of their friendships and the tremendous education they received from the many special North High teachers are a big part of this story:

Christine Beuttenmueller, Richie and Bobbie Barone, Anthony Canzoneri, Bob Cash, Joe Corea, Tony DiBenedetto, Steve Due, James Noel Fox, Ben Franquiz, Mary Fox Graham, Ken Halpern, Bernie and Joan Havern, my sister Linda, my brother Michael, Barry Lublin, George Minkoff, Mike Oddo, Roger Olsen, Sal Pepitone, Richard Renda, Artie Schnitzer,

Tommy Scibelli, Barbara Cohen Simms, Ralph Zanchelli, Dick Zucker.

My apologies to anyone I may have forgotten to mention, but I did my best to name everyone who helped contribute to the story over the long period of time it took me to collect all of the information I needed to write this book.

After gathering the content, it was my wonderful family who helped me put it all together.

My son John continued to encourage me over the years to get the job done. My daughter Nicole was invaluable in helping with the layout and intricacies of Microsoft Word, and for making me believe I could accomplish this massive technological undertaking on my own. I appreciate the time she spent helping me with this project and her motivation throughout.

I originally thought that finding the time to write this book would be the hardest part, but thankfully my family and I all maintained good health throughout the COVID-19 pandemic so I was able to use some of the downtime I had while staying close to home during the summer of 2020 to finally put pen to paper, or should I say finger to keyboard. That is until my youngest son Keith showed me how I could use my computer to convert speech into text. Over the next three weeks, he called me every night to ask for a progress update and I proudly told him how many new words and pages I had written earlier that day. At the end of those three weeks, thanks to using voice-to-text technology, I had composed over 200 pages, 30 chapters, and over 80,000 words. I couldn't believe that in only three weeks, my first draft was complete! I really appreciated his daily push and support! Then in September of 2020, I went back to work at the bus company and resumed other normal activities like going to stores and visiting others again which kept me very busy, so it wasn't until March of 2021 that I sought help with editing my writing.

But as much as being able to dictate the words instead of having to type every letter was a big help in getting the book written, it would make editing the finished product a much greater challenge. Coupled with my notoriously subpar linguistic and grammatical skills, having to sort through a long stream of ideas that flowed out almost like I was talking with a friend resulted in an editorial nightmare. So, I can't thank my wife Lois enough for the countless hours she spent editing my writing, correcting my grammar and sentence structure, and organizing my ideas. After setting aside blocks of time to meet here and there, it took Lois and I almost a whole year just to discuss the first seven chapters and for her to take notes on what needed to be fixed. We both then grew tired of what seemed like an impossible task and eventually set the book aside until, another year later, my son Keith picked up where we had left off. Even with Lois' notes as a guide, it took him almost four months to make the edits Lois suggested and reorganize the thoughts in each of the first seven chapters. At that point, three years had passed since I wrote the book, but only seven chapters were completed so we realized that more help would be needed to finish the project.

I had heard about Chat GPT and suggested that Keith give it a try, but he was skeptical. I then consulted my Goddaughter

Jeannie Robertson who works in IT to get her opinion. She explained how the software worked and encouraged us to try it. So starting fresh with chapter eight, Keith took my suggestion along with his cousin Jeannie's encouragement and turned to AI technology for help. Many trial and error attempts at using Chat GPT to edit sections of the book included some funny plot twists the computer program fabricated which had to be removed. Over time, Keith finally learned the website's intricacies and dialed in on how to take better advantage of the technology to yield better and better results. Two months later, we were happy with how Chat GPT edited the rest of the book for grammar and sentence structure. Although I generally believe that a simpler life with less technology is better, I encourage those who doubt modern technology to keep an open mind, think outside the box, and give it a try at times like this when it can help make life easier.

But as was true in this case, technology isn't always perfect; many parts of the book still needed a lot of work. Keith then spent the next four months organizing, consolidating, and rearranging the order in which my ideas were presented in certain parts of the book to produce the final product that transitioned smoothly from one idea to the next. He wound up rewriting some of the paragraphs and chapters entirely so that my meaning and sentiment were conveyed more clearly. Basically, Keith gave structure to all of my thoughts and ideas, gave life to the otherwise ordinary sentences and paragraphs I had written, and turned my rudimentary book into an eloquent story that was more coherent and easier to follow. My son

Keith then inserted the photos I wanted to include, helped determine the best placement for each picture, and helped create the wording for each caption. I think you might agree that seeing the pictures throughout the book brings the story to life!

Next, Keith worked with the staff at Spines which required an additional seven months of back-and-forth correspondence, fine-tuning, editing, providing additional details, and discussing design and business aspects of the book before it was finally published. Without Keith, the book probably would have never been finished. And even if somehow the book had come to fruition without his help, the quality of the finished product would probably have paled in comparison to the work that it has become; a work of which I am so proud, and a work for which I am so thankful. Keith's efforts were instrumental in bringing the book to completion and I could not thank him enough for all of the time and effort he put into the process.

From my son Keith, "As a result of taking on the daunting task of editing this book, I gained a newfound appreciation for my dad's side of our family. Growing up, my brother, sister, and I were surrounded by my mother's side of the family with whom we were very close, so I naturally identified more with my Italian (Bianco) half. On the other hand, visits with my father's side of the family were usually limited to very special occasions or vacations because they didn't live nearby, so it wasn't until adulthood that I truly started to value the Heron half of my lineage. Through helping with this book, I came away with a broader understanding of my Heron ancestors, developed a sense of pride in their characteristics and accomplishments, and ultimately emerged even more grateful to belong to my family.

As I listened to my dad recount many of his stories and reminisce about his life, I also learned a lot about what he was like growing up that I had never known before. What I found most striking was that my dad and I have more in common than I had previously realized. I felt a strong personal connection to my dad when I discovered interesting parallels between our lives which helped me start to understand him, and how he became the man he is today, on a deeper level. On a lighter note, I found some of the foolish things my dad and his friends did growing up to be not only comical but also eerily similar to some of the stunts I pulled in my younger days. Either way, I guess the old adages 'like father, like son' and 'the apple doesn't fall far from the tree' really do hold true! And I hope that those adages continue to hold true as I discover even more similarities between my dad and throughout the rest of my lifetime. Having now learned many of my dad's life lessons more clearly, I hope that I too can apply that wisdom to raise a successful, intelligent, and happy family just like my dad did, when the time is right for me.

As with any worthwhile venture in life, there were ups and downs throughout the process of bringing this book to fruition, but in the end, it was worth the effort and a it was a joyful experience to have helped make this book come alive! All of the time and effort I spent working on this project couldn't possibly repay my dad for all of the time and effort he has given to our family, and to myself, over the course of our lives."

Thank you to everyone who helped make this incredible story come to life. I hope that our efforts resulted in a story that you enjoyed reading. I couldn't have done it without each and every one of you!

Made in the USA
Monee, IL
18 August 2024

ce451a2a-72b1-4f54-b311-28c16740337dR01